THIRD EDITION

THE ENGAGED SOCIOLOGIST

This book is dedicated to the memory of Aiden Tomkins Odell and to all the families working to find a cure for spinal muscular atrophy (SMA). You can learn about SMA and how to help find a cure by going to www.fsma.org.

To read Aiden's story, go to www.fsma.org/FSMACommunity/ Photos/memorialphotos/index.cfm?SR=51&LS=2378/ and click on Odell, Aiden Tomkins.

THIRD EDITION

THE ENGAGED SOCIOLOGIST

Connecting the Classroom to the Community

Kathleen Odell Korgen ■ Jonathan M. White

William Paterson University *Bridgewater State College*

Los Angeles | London | New Delhi
Singapore | Washington DC

For information:

Pine Forge Press
A Sage Publications Company
2455 Teller Road
Thousand Oaks,
    California 91320
E-mail: order@sagepub.com

Sage Publications India Pvt. Ltd.
B 1/I 1 Mohan Cooperative
    Industrial Area
Mathura Road,
    New Delhi 110 044
India

Sage Publications Ltd.
1 Oliver's Yard
55 City Road
London EC1Y 1SP
United Kingdom

Sage Publications Asia-Pacific Pte. Ltd.
33 Pekin Street #02-01
Far East Square
Singapore 048763

Printed in the United States of America

Library of Congress Cataloging-in-Publication Data

Korgen, Kathleen Odell
The engaged sociologist: connecting the classroom to the community/Kathleen Odell Korgen, Jonathan M. White.
    p. cm.
Includes bibliographical references and index.
ISBN 978-1-4129-7949-8 (pbk.)
    1. Service learning—United States. 2. Sociology—Study and teaching (Higher)—United States. I. White, Jonathan M. (Jonathan Michael) II. Title.

LC221.K68 2011
301.071′173—dc22   2009043868

This book is printed on acid-free paper.

10 11 12 13 14 10 9 8 7 6 5 4 3 2

Acquisitions Editor:	David Repetto
Editorial Assistant:	Nancy Scrofano
Production Editor:	Karen Wiley
Copy Editor:	Teresa Herlinger
Proofreader:	Andrea Martin
Typesetter:	C&M Digitals (P) Ltd.
Indexer:	Jeanne Busemeyer
Cover Designer:	Arup Giri
Marketing Manager:	Carmel Withers

Contents

Preface

A Note From the Authors to the Students Reading This Book

Sociology is the coolest academic discipline. Seriously, what other area of study is better at helping you figure out how society operates and how you can use that knowledge to create social change? Both of us were drawn to sociology because we wanted to figure out how to fight injustice and promote democracy more effectively. It has also guided us with everyday life tasks, such as figuring out how to get policies passed on campus, deciding whom to vote for, and learning why it's vital to earn a college degree in a service-based economy. This book is part of our efforts to get students hooked on sociology and, in the process, help them to become engaged and effective citizens who can strengthen our democratic society.

This book is also part of a larger, national effort to "educate citizens" by encouraging students to participate in civic engagement exercises that connect the classroom to the community. Organizations like The Democracy Imperative, Campus Compact, and the American Democracy Project are establishing movements to make civic engagement a part of the college experience for all undergraduates. College leaders all across the country realize that we are obligated to give students the tools they will require to be effective citizens as well as the skills they will need in the workforce. Leaders in *all* sectors of society understand that higher education, when connected to the larger society, benefits everyone, on *and* off campus.

We believe, as leaders of the American Sociological Association have noted when promoting public sociology, that sociology is particularly suited to teaching students what they need to become effective and full members of our society. As prominent sociologist Randall Collins has pointed out, the two core commitments of sociology are (a) to understand how society works and (b) to use that knowledge to make society better. We believe that helping students learn how to think sociologically and use sociological tools is, in effect, enabling them to become better citizens. No doubt, the professors who assigned this book to you also share this belief. They will gladly tell you why *they* think sociology is an incredibly useful and practical academic discipline.

We also know that sociology is fun to learn and to teach. That's why we created a book that we hope will be enjoyable to use for both students and teachers. The exercises throughout the chapters allow students to connect the sociological knowledge they are learning to their campus and the larger community. So, as soon as you develop your sociological eye, you will make use of it! *Please note that you will need to make sure you follow the rules for research on human subjects and get approval from the Internal Review Board (IRB) on your campus before carrying out some of these exercises.* (Your professor will tell you how to do so.) This book will also help you to connect your own life to the larger society, as you learn about the "sociological imagination" and the power it has to positively affect your community. The Sociologist in Action sections in each chapter will show you powerful examples of how sociology students and professional sociologists (both professors and applied sociologists) use sociology in myriad ways in efforts to improve society. By the end of the book, you can create your own Sociologist in Action section, in which you'll show how you used sociological tools in efforts to influence society.

We look forward to seeing your Sociology in Action pieces and featuring many of them in future editions of this book and on the Web site for *The Engaged Sociologist.* In the meantime, we hope you enjoy the book and use the knowledge and skills you gain from it to make yourself a more effective citizen, strengthen our democracy, and work for a more just and civil society. We think that you will discover what we discovered when we began our journey as sociologists—that sociology is a cool and powerful tool. And, of course, we hope that you have a lot of fun in the process!

Acknowledgments

This third edition would not have been possible without the very able assistance of many people. We would first like to thank David Repetto, who brings a commitment to connecting the classroom to the community, wonderful insight, and a wealth of good judgment to this project. We are delighted to be working with him. We would also like to thank Ben Penner, our original editor, for his excellent work and for believing in the vision of this book. His enthusiasm for *The Engaged Sociologist* and public sociology, in general, inspired us as we conceptualized and wrote this book. We remain indebted to him for his good humor and his passion and insight regarding the powerful connections between sociology and student engagement. We also are indebted to Karen Wiley, our Production Editor, and to Nancy Scrofano, our Editorial Assistant, for their strong support and ability to guide us throughout the course of this project. We would particularly like to thank Teresa Herlinger for her exceptionally astute and thoughtful work copyediting the book. We owe a special debt of gratitude to our colleague, Howard Lune, for his contributions to this book.

Finally, we would both like to thank the following reviewers whose thoughtful and excellent suggestions helped us make this book so much better than it otherwise would be: Beverly L. Stiles, Midwestern State University; Stephen Light, SUNY Plattsburgh; Ronda Copher, University of Minnesota; Kooros M. Mahmoudi, Northern Arizona University; Amy Holzgang, Cerritos College; Peter J. Stein, William Paterson University; Eric K. Leung, Los Angeles Valley College; and John Lynxwiler, The University of Central Florida.

The following reviewers helped us make the second edition of this book even better than the first: Jack Estes, Borough of Manhattan Community College, City University of New York; Werner Lange, Edinboro University of Pennsylvania; Rachel Bandy, Simpson College; Beverly L. Rogers, Collin County Community College District; Chiquita D. Howard-Bolstic, Virginia Polytechnic Institute and State University; and Janice K. Purk, Mansfield University.

Kathleen would like to thank her encouraging, accommodating, and over-all wonderful husband, Jeff; daughters Julie and Jessica; and mother, Patricia Odell, for putting up with the many late nights, early mornings, and week-ends this project consumed. Jeff and Patricia also read innumerable early drafts with good cheer and made many helpful suggestions. This book would never have been completed on time if we didn't live together, Mom. Thank you! Thanks also to Judy and Ben Korgen, Ann Odell, Mike Odell, John Odell, Nancy Baffa, and Conor Odell.

Jonathan would like to thank his wife and best friend, Shelley, for her incredible friendship, love, and support. Our amazing partnership continues to energize me to be able to continue moving forward as a public sociologist and scholar-activist. I also want to thank the many students who have inspired me with their energy, intellect, and unwavering belief that social change is indeed possible. A huge thanks also goes to my family, who pro-vide me with unwavering support, love, and happiness and who inspire me to continuously work toward creating a stronger civil society. And a very special group of people, my 13 nephews and nieces, deserve a special debt of gratitude because they are particularly inspirational in so many ways!

The Engaged Sociologist

The Sociological Perspective and the Connections Among Sociology, Democracy, and Civic Engagement

Have you ever wanted to change society? Do you want to have a voice in how things work throughout your life? If so, you've come to the right discipline. Sociology helps you to understand how society operates and, in turn, how to make society better.

As sociologists, we see how individuals both shape and are shaped by larger social forces. By developing what is called a *sociological eye* (Collins 1998; Hughes 1971), we are able to look beneath the surface of society and see how it really works. For example, with a sociological eye, we can recognize the tremendous influence of culture on individuals. Imagine how different you might be if you had grown up in Sweden, Ethiopia, Bangladesh, or another country with a culture very different from our own.[1] You would still look about the same (though you'd have different mannerisms, speak a different language, and have a different haircut and clothes), but your values, norms, and beliefs would be different. Your view of the proper roles of men and women, your religious or secular values, career goals, education, and so forth are shaped by the society in which you grew up.

Look at the differences between your immediate family and some of your relatives who may have much more or much less money. Does social class cause the differences, or do the differences help to determine the social class to which we will belong?[2] Consider the varying perspectives that your male relatives and your female relatives bring to the same questions. They all live in the same world, in close proximity perhaps, but they have had such different experiences of it that some people even joke that men and women come from different planets (Gray 1992). By using the sociological eye, we can look at the world from a unique angle, notice what is often unobserved, and make connections among the patterns in everyday events that the average person might not notice. In doing so, we can understand how different organizations, institutions, and societies function; how social forces shape individual lives and ideas; and, in turn, how individuals shape organizations and institutions.

By viewing society through the perspective of a *social world model,* we can study different levels of social units, from small- to large-scale parts of the world, that interact with one another. For example, we could study participation in the democratic process through examining *interpersonal and local organizations* (e.g., political activism among students on your campus and your school's College Democrats and College Republicans clubs); *larger organizations and institutions* (e.g., national Democratic and Republican Parties and state boards of elections); and *nations or global communities* (e.g., the U.S. presidential electoral process and the UN Millennium Declaration implementation). Depending on the social unit we are interested in studying, we would utilize different levels of analysis. We would use *micro* for interpersonal and local organizations, *meso* for larger organizations and institutions, and *macro* for nations and the global community. At all times, however, we would notice the connections between the varying social groups. For example, using the social world model would help us to see that individuals are impacted by and can influence their classmates, their political party, their nation, and their global community.

The social world model also enables us to recognize persistent patterns that work to create disadvantages for certain groups in society, resulting in institutional discrimination (intentional or unintentional structural biases). For example, U.S. society functioned in such a way for over 200 years that there were no female Supreme Court justices before President Ronald Reagan appointed Sandra Day O'Connor in 1981. Sociologists, using the sociological eye, recognize that the long-standing all-male makeup of the Supreme Court was part of a larger pattern of sex discrimination. Some of the discrimination was deliberate and based on people's ideas about gender. Some of it was political, based on a calculation of how the public would respond to the nomination of a woman to such a post. Some of it even had to do with the fact that our culture tends to use similar language and ideas to describe both *leadership qualities* and *masculinity*. Thus, when people think of leadership, they tend to associate it with the qualities that men often bring to the table (Schein 2001).[3] Social science research on the connections among gender roles, socialization, and sex discrimination, such as Betty Friedan's book *The Feminine Mystique* (1963), which shattered the myth that women could only find fulfillment as wives and homemakers, became part of public knowledge and was used to make the case for the women's movement in the 1960s and 1970s. Ultimately, this movement paved the way for a political environment conducive to the appointment of Sandra Day O'Connor and, eventually, Ruth Bader Ginsberg and Sonia Sotomayor.

Use of the sociological eye also helps efforts to persuade government office holders to initiate social policies addressing social inequities. By looking beneath the surface of government operations, we can answer the following questions: To whom do office holders tend to respond the most? Why? How can we use this information to make sure that they respond to us? What social forces compelled Ronald Reagan, one of our most conservative presidents and not known as a women's rights advocate, to choose a female Supreme Court justice?

According to Randall Collins (1998), using the sociological eye is one of two "core commitments" of sociology. The second is *social activism*. Once we understand how society operates, we are obligated to participate actively in efforts to improve it. The sociological eye and social activism go hand-in-hand. The sociological eye helps us to become effective, engaged citizens. It is something we gain with training—much as muscles are gained with weight lifting and working out. The more you train yourself as a sociologist, the stronger your sociological eye and ability to practice effective and constructive social activism will become. This book is filled with examples of *sociologists in action,* those who have honed their sociological eye and successfully used their skills to create social change.

The Sociological Imagination

To understand how we might influence society, we must first understand how we are affected by it. C. Wright Mills (1967) described this ability as the "sociological imagination." When we begin to relate personal troubles to public issues, connecting our individual lives to what's happening in our society, we are using the sociological imagination.

For instance, both of the authors of this book experienced their parents divorcing. As individuals, this was a personal trouble for each of us. Using the sociological imagination, we see that we were a part of a cohort of American children who lived through the great rise in the divorce rate in the 1970s. If we had been children during the 1870s, our parents would most likely have remained married. However, the changes that our society went through in the 1960s and 1970s (legal rights and protections for women that enabled more women to exit relationships, the decline of religiosity, cost of living increases that required more women to join the workforce, etc.) resulted in an increase in the divorce rate and, in turn, our own parents' divorces. Our personal troubles (the divorces of our parents) were directly related to a public issue (the societywide rise in the divorce rate).

Today, one of us is having a difficult time finding clothes for her young daughters that do not resemble those in Paris Hilton's closet. As a mother, she's horrified that anyone would expect little girls to wear such skimpy outfits (particularly *her* little girls!). As a sociologist, she can look at a sample of clothing stores and advertisements in the United States and quickly realize that her experience is part of a societywide pattern of sexualizing girls—even very young girls. She can then start to research why a society like ours, with such a long history of public activism around "standards of moral decency," is so consistent—almost aggressive—in the sexualizing of girls. One hypothesis she might test is that this social behavior is related to the relative absence of mothers in the highest positions of fashion design and marketing. If she were to discover this to be true, she could use her findings to work for social change, trying to make these workplaces more open and inviting for fashion designers and marketers who are mothers.

One of the functions of sociology, as C. Wright Mills (1959/2000) defined it, should be to "translate personal troubles into public issues" (p. 187). Once you start using your sociological imagination and looking at the world through the sociological eye and the social world model, it's impossible not to notice the connections between ourselves as individuals and larger societal patterns. Consider the kind of job you hope to get after leaving college. Will you make an annual salary or an hourly wage? Will you have full health care coverage, or will you live without insurance and hope for the best? And if you get a "good" job, will your good fortune depend somehow on the fact that others do not have what you seek? Are the private troubles of sweatshop workers around the world connected to a global public problem?

Sweatshops are production sites where workers face near-slavery conditions with few or no protections from unsafe work environments or arbitrary punishments, and where they work at pay rates that are less than what one needs for basic survival. Sweatshop jobs do not come with insurance, sick days, retirement plans, or protection against arbitrary termination. On the surface, colleges and sweatshops seem to have nothing to do with one another. However, if you look underneath the surface (or, perhaps, at what you or your classmates are wearing), you may see a connection. The students at Duke University did: When they learned of the horrible sweatshop conditions in which most of their Duke-labeled clothes were being manufactured, they mobilized and established a United Students Against Sweatshops group on campus. Their efforts, and those of several administrators at Duke (particularly the director of Duke Store Operations), sparked a campuswide discussion about sweatshops and the university's responsibility to ensure that clothing with a Duke label is "sweat-free." In 1997, Duke was the first institution of higher education in the United States to adopt a code of conduct mandating that the apparel companies with which they do business must submit to independent monitoring of the conditions in their factories. The following year, Duke established an independent Worker Rights Consortium (WRC) to assist in the enforcement of the codes of conduct established between colleges and universities and those who manufacture clothes for them.[4] As of 2009, a total of 186 institutions of higher education have joined the movement sparked by Duke students and have become WRC affiliates.[5]

Sociology and the Critical Consumption of Information

In addition to having a trained sociological eye and making use of the sociological imagination, sociologists are informed and critical consumers of the barrage of information coming at us from all directions. Sociological research methods guide how we conduct research and how we interpret information relayed by others. By understanding how good research is done, we can evaluate the information disseminated throughout society and know what news sources are trustworthy. These skills help us in our efforts to both understand and change society. In Chapter 3, we outline in greater detail how sociological research methods can be used in this way.

Sociology and Democracy

Through reading this book and carrying out the exercises within it, you will learn how to look beneath the surface of social events, connect personal troubles to public issues, and know what information sources are trustworthy. You can then use these sociological tools to strengthen our society, make our nation more democratic, and work toward ensuring the rights and well-being of people all around the world. Although democracy is defined in different ways by a multitude of scholars, all point out that it is a system of governance that instills state power in citizenship rather than in government. This book shows how sociology can enable citizens (like you!) to become knowledgeable, active, and effective participants in our democratic society.

Exercise 1.1	How Is Higher Education Related to Democracy?

If you live in a democracy, then you have inherited certain social obligations. What do you think they are? Is voting one of them? How about going to college? Think about the connection between democracy and higher education and answer the following questions:

1. What do you think is the purpose of higher education?

2. Why did you decide to go to college?

3. Do you think your college education will help you become a better citizen? Why or why not?

4. Now go to the Campus Compact Web page at www.compact.org/resources-for-presidents/presidents-declaration-on-the-civic-responsibility-of-higher-education and read the "Presidents' Declaration on the Civic Responsibility of Higher Education."

5. Did your answer to Question 1 relate to the presidents' description of the purpose of public higher education? Why do you think it did or did not?

6. Why is an educated public necessary for a strong democratic society?

7. Is a public higher education attainable for all Americans? Why or why not? If not, what are the ramifications of this situation for our democracy? How can you, using what your sociological eye has uncovered, work to make public higher education more attainable and realizable for more people?

Exercise 1.2	Walking Billboards

You occupy many *social roles* in your life: You are a student; somebody's friend; somebody's child; and maybe you are a parent, sibling, employee, teammate, boss, neighbor, girlfriend/boyfriend, or mentor. To many thousands of companies out there, your main role is that of *consumer*. How do apparel companies market themselves, specifically, to men, women, and different racial/ethnic groups? How do members of each of these groups act as "walking billboards" for the apparel companies that make the clothing they wear?

Next time you are in one of your other classes, note the following:

1. How many students are there? How many are male and how many are female?

2. How many of each sex are wearing visible product or company logos on their clothing, including footwear, baseball caps, etc.? (Include yourself in your answers.)

3. Are there any logos that occur more than once throughout the class?

4. Are there any logos or brands that are considered "in" on your campus?

5. Using your newly trained "sociological eye," analyze the results you have gathered. What institutional and societal forces might be at work? Do you notice any specific trends along race or gender lines? Do people from certain sex or racial/ethnic groups, teams, or cliques exhibit trends in their dress? How about the faculty? Do you detect any trends among your teachers? What does all of this tell you about consumerism, values, norms, and the culture of your campus?

Exercise 1.3   What's the Connection Between College Students and Sweatshops?

1. Watch clips of the online video *Behind the Labels* from the Human Rights Video Project at www.humanrightsproject.org/vid_detail.php?film_id=1&asset=clip.

2. Determine if your campus belongs to the Fair Labor Association (FLA). You can find this out at www.fairlabor.org/fla_affiliates_d1.html or the Worker Rights Consortium (WRC) at www.workersrights.org/about/as.asp.

3. If your campus does not belong to FLA or WRC, find out what vendors your campus bookstore uses to obtain the clothes it sells.

4. Ask the campus bookstore manager if he or she is aware of the conditions under which the vendors' employees work.

5. Do some research to find information about the vendors. The United Students Against Sweatshops' Sweatfree Campus Campaign Web site that

(Continued)

(Continued)

you can access through www.studentsagainstsweatshops.org is one useful site. You should also check out the Web sites for the Business & Human Rights Resource Centre at www.business-humanrights.org/Categories/Individualcompanies and Green America's Responsible Shopper at www.greenamericatoday.org/programs/responsibleshopper.

6. Listen to the following stories on NPR: "Student Protests" at www.npr.org/templates/story/story.php?storyId=1127377 and "Made in a Sweatshop? Clues for Consumers" at www.npr.org/templates/story/story.php?storyId=17358785.

7. What did you learn from these stories that can help you determine actions you and your college might take regarding the use of sweatshop labor?

8. Write a four-page report on the results of your research. Be sure to make clear the connection between campus consumerism and the workers who make the apparel sold in the campus bookstore.

Extra Credit: Find out where your school's sports teams get their jerseys, and repeat the exercises above, or find out where your Community Service Office gets its jerseys and repeat the exercises above.

Exercise 1.4	**Worried About the Increasingly High Cost of Tuition?**

You are not alone. According to the College Board (2007, 2009), *after adjusting for inflation,* from 1997–1998 to 2007–2008, tuition and fees increased by 54% at 4-year state colleges and universities, 17% at 2-year colleges, and 33% at 4-year private institutions. In 2008–2009, the average cost for tuition and fees was $25,143 (up 5.9% from 2007–2008) at private 4-year colleges, $6,585 (up 6.4% from 2007–2008) at 4-year public institutions, and $2,402 (up 4.7% from 2007–2008) at public 2-year institutions.

1. How would strategies to deal with the increase in tuition vary depending on whether it is viewed as (a) a personal trouble or (b) a public issue?

2. What are some of the actions you could take to convince state legislators to increase funding for public higher education in your state?

3. Choose one of the actions you've listed in Question 2 that is a manageable action for you to take. Now, carry out the plan you devised and write a report that describes (a) what you did and (b) the outcome of your actions. Note that you might have to wait a while to complete (b), so you should start (a) right away.

SOCIOLOGIST IN ACTION: JOE BANDY

In recent decades, changes in the global economy have presented momentous possibilities and problems for everyone in the developing and developed world. On the one hand, greater transnational flows of capital and technology have opened some opportunities for economic development. On the other, the global economy faces persistent inequalities, economic instability, and environmental crisis, bringing great suffering and protest. Joe Bandy's research has addressed these complexities and has sought to engage with working people and their social movements to arrive at effective solutions to the worst of these impacts. This work has taken place in two very different settings. One is northern Mexico's export processing zones where he has studied workers' movements to ensure labor rights. The other is the rapidly changing economy of the communities surrounding Maine's North Woods, which reveal many class-based conflicts around development and natural resource use. In both settings, he has used participatory action methods to help guarantee his research is relevant to both scholarly sociology and the efforts of working people as they attempt to address social problems. His work has been published widely in journals and books, and he has edited a book with Jackie Smith, *Coalitions Across Borders* (Bandy and Smith 2004).

In his teaching at Bowdoin College, he has encouraged students to be publicly engaged in important social issues through community-based research projects. To date, Bandy has led 50 different community research projects in a variety of courses on environmental injustice, class inequality, and poverty, in addition to independent studies and honors projects. Through these projects, students have had the opportunity to conduct original research designed in a collaborative process with faculty, students, and a community organization. The projects typically have studied some dimension of a social problem or policy, yielding information that will assist the organization to better understand and respond to the community's needs.

For example, two groups of students in two successive offerings of his course "Class, Labor, and Power" worked with Tedford Housing in Brunswick, Maine, to conduct a local public opinion survey regarding homelessness, which assisted Tedford in orienting itself more effectively to public concerns regarding housing policy. One overarching finding was that the local public, while sympathetic to

(Continued)

(Continued)

the problems faced by the homeless, often did not have a very clear understanding of the causes of or solutions to homelessness, particularly the problems of affordable housing. The information gleaned from the survey allowed Tedford Housing to focus its public outreach and education on the problem of inadequate affordable housing in the region. This, in turn, helped Tedford to build the support necessary from the public and policy makers to successfully pursue its project of developing affordable housing, among its many other projects.

Another example is a group of students from his course "Environmental Sociology," who worked with Cultivating Community in Portland, Maine, an organization that operates community gardens and provides environmental education for disadvantaged youth. In its early stages of development, Cultivating Community needed assistance in locating financial resources to continue its work. In response, the students developed an extensive binder of philanthropic and governmental funding opportunities that helped the organization seek funding to maintain its current efforts and to develop its educational programs in local schools. Also addressing an issue of environmental education, another group of students in "Environmental Sociology" recorded short films on renewable energy technologies that the Maine Energy Investment Corporation posted on its Web site to help educate the public about sustainable energy alternatives in the state.

The results of these projects have been inspiring. At their conclusion, students often express great appreciation for the chance to put the sociological tools they have gained in the classroom into action. They appreciate the opportunity to enhance their critical thinking skills through problem solving on projects that are publicly relevant. They also enjoy carrying out original sociological research that enables them to gain a more intimate and personal understanding of inequality from their community partners. Likewise, community partners express appreciation, not only for the positive impact of the students' research in the community, but also for the opportunity to teach and collaborate with students on important issues. These projects have done much to reduce the distance that too often exists between "town and gown." These positive outcomes have prompted Joe Bandy to work as an advocate for community-based teaching and research. He has modeled best practices in community-based teaching with Campus Compact, the national organization dedicated to enhancing civic engagement in higher education, and helped Bowdoin College to become more publicly engaged through the McKeen Center for the Common Good. The latter fosters a mutually supportive relationship between the ideals of liberal arts education and community engagement, assisting Bowdoin to further fulfill the goal of its first president, Joseph McKeen (1802), who declared, "literary institutions are founded and endowed for the common good, and not for the private advantage of those who resort to them for education" (n.p.).

SOCIOLOGIST IN ACTION: THE SOCIAL JUSTICE LEAGUE AT BRIDGEWATER STATE COLLEGE

Joshua Warren, Bria Wilbur, Curtis Holland, and Jillian Micelli are four sociology majors at Bridgewater State College (BSC) who used their sociological eyes to make the connection between their campus and community. Wanting to use the knowledge they learned in their courses to help affect positive social change, they created a student group called the Social Justice League. This group organized many events to educate the campus community about social justice issues, raise funds, and move the college toward more just practices.

One of the Social Justice League's big events in 2007 was the creation of a "Tent City"—students, faculty, and staff slept outside in tents during a cold week in November. Each day, Tent City speakers from area shelters and organizations spoke to the campus community, and faculty from all across the campus brought their classes to these lectures. Students sleeping in Tent City were not allowed to use computers or cell phones, ate their meals in a "mock soup kitchen" set up in the cafeteria, and could bathe only by using public showers during set hours. In addition to creating the educational and symbolic components of Tent City, the students also raised several thousand dollars in cash and supplies to support a local homeless shelter.

In 2008, the Social Justice League launched another strategic and powerful education and awareness campaign on campus when members organized a series of educational events and demonstrations about sweatshop labor and the clothes sold at their college bookstore. They showed videos on the topic of sweatshops to the campus, gave talks to classes, and staged a "mock sweatshop." Through these efforts, the students created a high level of campus awareness about sweatshops.

The Social Justice League also brought the issue of sweatshops to the direct attention of Dr. Dana Mohler-Faria, the president of Bridgewater State College, who worked with the group to form a campus council to research the suppliers of clothing sold at the student bookstore. After carefully examining the issue, the president agreed that BSC should join the Worker Rights Consortium. Bria summed up the campaign by saying, "We worked extremely hard and I never felt more proud of myself than when I got the phone call that our campaign was successful and that BSC was going to join the Worker Rights Consortium! It was through sociology that I learned about these issues." Thanks to the efforts of the skilled and passionate members of the Social Justice League, BSC joined the growing ranks of colleges committed to ensuring that their campuses are sweat-free.

(Continued)

(Continued)

Jillian described the connection between her sociological training and her actions to work for the betterment of society like this: "Within one year, my life changed dramatically. [By changing] my major to sociology the night before classes started, not only did I gain a degree in sociology, I also gained knowledge I would have never gained otherwise. The training and skills I learned from courses on genocide to courses on social inequality truly motivated me to strive for social change not only in the Social Justice League, but beyond. It taught me the connection I have with the global market and how if one pushes for something they believe in, social change will follow."

Speaking of his work as president of the Social Justice League, Josh says, "By combining what I've learned in my studies with my passion for social justice and civic engagement, I am able to not only serve those immediately in need, but also think about the reasons for why there is a need. It enables me to do more than just put a 'band-aid' on a problem. I can act proactively to find the source of the issue, and uproot it!"

Curtis made his awareness of the two core commitments of sociology clear when he said, "As I began to realize that I was becoming a burgeoning sociologist, I realized simultaneously that the knowledge I was gaining from sociological inquiry came with a great responsibility."

As you read the rest of this book, please think about what these sociology students have accomplished, and think about how you, too, can use what you learn from this course to become a *sociologist in action!*

Discussion Questions

1. Before reading this chapter, had you ever recognized a connection between your own life and the lives of people working in sweatshops? Why or why not? Do you now see a connection? Now that you have thought about this, how will you proceed?

2. Are you worried about being able to obtain adequate health care coverage? Why or why not? What are some steps that you can take to work toward ensuring that you and others will have a better chance at adequate health care coverage in your lives?

3. Do you know what the president of the United States, your state senators, and your representative are doing about (a) sweatshops and (b) ensuring adequate health care? If you don't know, why do you think you are unaware of their positions on

these issues? Would (or have) their positions on these issues influence whether or not you would vote for them? Why or why not?

4. Do you think you could use your sociological eye to do something similar to what the members of the Social Justice League did at Bridgewater State College? Why or why not? What are some of the ideas you have?

Suggestions for Specific Actions

1. Join an already established campus group working against sweatshops. (You may substitute a different issue or campaign if you are already involved or interested in one, with permission of your instructor.)

2. Establish your own campus group to fight sweatshops. Go to http://we.freethe children.com/get-involved and www.studentsagainstsweatshops.org (click on "Get Your School to Join the WRC") to learn how to form a local group to combat sweatshops.

3. Go to your representative's and senators' Web sites (you can find them at www.house.gov and www.senate.gov). Send them an email or letter that conveys your thoughts and feelings about the health care coverage crisis.

4. Investigate the kind of health care coverage and the safety of the work/living environment provided for students, faculty, professional staff, and support staff on your campus. If there are clear deficiencies or inequities, organize a group of students, faculty, and professional and support staff to advocate for improved conditions for all campus workers. For the past few years, sociology students at the University of California, Berkeley, have carried out just this type of research and activism. You can find "Berkeley's Betrayal: Wages and Working Conditions at CAL" at www.upte-cwa.org/UCLA/BKbetrayal.pdf.

Please go to our Web site at www.pineforge.com/korgen3e to find further civic engagement opportunities, resources, peer-reviewed articles, and updated Web links related to this chapter.

Endnotes

1. If you did grow up in Sweden, Ethiopia, or Bangladesh, then imagine you grew up in New Jersey.

2. It works both ways, of course. And bonus points to you for looking at the endnote.

3. We should note that this view is less prevalent today than it was at the time of Sandra Day O'Connor's appointment to the Supreme Court.

4. To learn more about the history of the sweat-free campus movement at Duke, go to Paul Baerman's article at www.dukemagazine.duke.edu/alumni/dm18/sweat shop.html.

5. See the Worker Rights Consortium Web site at www.workersrights.org.

References

Bandy, Joe and Jackie Smith, eds. 2004. *Coalitions Across Borders.* Lanham, MD: Rowman & Littlefield.

College Board. 2007. "A Thirty-Year Look at College Pricing Reveals That Rapidly Rising Prices Are Not a New Development." *2007 Trends in Higher Education Series: Tuition and Fees Over Time.* Retrieved January 7, 2008 (http://www.college board.com/prod_downloads/about/news_info/trends/tuition_fees.pdf).

College Board. 2009. "2008–09 College Prices: Keep Increases in Perspective." Retrieved May 20, 2009 (http://www.collegeboard.com/student/pay/add-it-up/4494.html).

Collins, Randall. 1998. "The Sociological Eye and Its Blinders." *Contemporary Sociology* 27(1):2–7.

Friedan, Betty. 1963. *The Feminine Mystique.* New York: Norton.

Gray, John. 1992. *Men Are From Mars, Women Are From Venus: A Practical Guide for Improving Communication and Getting What You Want in Your Relationships.* New York: HarperCollins.

Hughes, Everett C. 1971. *The Sociological Eye: Selected Papers.* Chicago: Aldine-Atherton.

McKeen, Joseph. 1802. "Joseph McKeen's Inaugural Address." Retrieved September 16, 2009 (http://www.bowdoincollege.edu/mckeen-center/mission/inaugural-address.shtml).

Mills, C. Wright. [1959] 2000. *The Sociological Imagination.* New York: Oxford University Press.

Schein, Virginia. E. 2001. "A Global Look at Psychological Barriers to Women's Progress in Management." *Journal of Social Issues* 57:675–88.

2

Founders and Foundations of Sociology

Theory

Sociology was founded by social scientists eager to (a) understand the major social changes of the late 19th and early 20th centuries and (b) make society better. In this chapter, you will learn how five of the founders of sociology—Karl Marx, Max Weber, Émile Durkheim, George Herbert Mead, and Jane Addams—carried out the two core commitments of sociology. Each of the theorists, in his or her own way, looked underneath the surface of society to understand how it operates and used this knowledge to improve society.

Although all of these founders responded to aspects of the social forces related to industrialization, their works are myriad and focus on a variety of subjects. Marx and Weber are considered conflict theorists,[1] Durkheim was a functionalist, and Mead and Addams were symbolic interactionists. However, to one degree or another, all of them looked at the roots of inequality in society and the possible solutions to this social problem. They used theories to explain how society works and how it might be improved. Like all explanations, some theories are more convincing than others. As you read through the chapter, think about which theories are most helpful to you as you try to understand how society operates and how you might work to make it better.

Karl Marx

According to Marx (1818–1883), class conflict over the control of the production of goods leads to inequality in society. He maintained that in every economic age, there is a dominant class (the owners) that owns and controls the means of production and exploits the other class (the workers).

For example, in the feudal era, there were landowners and serfs, and in the industrial era, there were factory owners and factory workers. Marx believed that the workers would eventually overthrow the owners when

1. The economic means of production was sufficiently technologically advanced that it could easily support everyone in society, and

2. The workers united, realizing that they, as a class, were being exploited by the owners.

Marx believed that the workers (*proletariat*) were under a "false consciousness" regarding their social class arrangements. That is, although they were conscious that there were class differences, they didn't understand why these differences existed, how those in power had manipulated the system to create these differences, or even the extent of these differences. Thus, their *consciousness* of the class differences was *false*.

Marx believed that the owners (*bourgeoisie*) owned not only the means of production for market goods, but also the means for the production of *ideas* in society. In Marx's words,

> The ideas of the ruling class are in every epoch the ruling ideas, i.e., the class which is the ruling material force of society is at the same time its ruling intellectual force. The class which has the means of material production at its disposal has control at the same time over the means of mental production, so that thereby, generally speaking, the ideas of those who lack the means of mental production are subject to it. (Marx and Engels 1970:64)

This false consciousness prevented the workers from realizing that the capitalist system was designed to exploit them, rather than benefit them.

To counteract this false consciousness, Marx spent much of his life trying to unite the proletariat, encouraging them to establish a "class consciousness," overthrow the ownership society, and transform the economic system from capitalism to communism. Consciousness was key to Marx's approach. As long as millions of individual workers saw themselves as struggling alone or in competition with other workers, nothing would change. Marx wanted to impart a larger, societal view of the system to the working class, in which they would understand the role of the class system in their personal lives and act collectively against the system itself. His most famous attempt was *The Communist Manifesto* (Marx and Engels 1848/2002), which concludes, "Let the ruling classes tremble at a Communist revolution. The proletarians have nothing to lose but their chains. They have a world to win. Workingmen of all countries, unite!" (p. 258).

Conflict theory is a modern extension of Marx's insights, although many conflict theorists support democracy, not communism. In its general form, *conflict theory* begins with the assumption that at any point in time, in any society, there will be different interest groups, different strata of society who have conflicting needs, and that much of what happens politically, socially, or economically is a manifestation of this conflict. Conflict theorists maintain that at the core of society lies the struggle for power among these competing groups.

Max Weber

Whereas Marx focused on class conflict and economic systems, Max Weber (1864–1920) looked more at the combination of economic and political power. Weber expanded Marx's idea of class into three dimensions of stratification: *class* (based on possession of economic resources—most important in industrial capitalist societies), *status* (prestige—most important in traditional societies), and *party* (organization formed to achieve a goal in a planned manner, like political parties, unions, and professional associations—most important in advanced industrial, highly rational societies). In most eras, there would be a great deal of overlap among the three dimensions. For example, someone high in class would also tend to be high in status and political power.

Unlike Marx, Weber was very pessimistic about attempts to eliminate inequality from society. He believed that even if one aspect of conflict and inequality could be eliminated, others would remain and perhaps become an even more important basis for inequality (e.g., the rise of the importance of difference in party position in the Soviet Union after status inequality had largely been eliminated). Weber's definition of power—"the chance of a man or a number of men to realize their own will in a communal action even against the resistance of others who are participating in the action" (1946, quoted in Gerth and Mills 1958:180)—remains the starting point for most modern sociological explorations of power relations.

Weber's work on bureaucratic institutions helps us understand how power is won and held within advanced industrial societies of all types (whether capitalist, communist, or anything in between). Thanks to Weber, we now comprehend how powerful bureaucratic structures can be and how much of the structure remains intact, even when the individuals in charge are replaced. For example, whoever controls the government bureaucracy in a highly developed nation can exert tremendous power over all aspects of that society. Controlling the government bureaucracy enables one to control key institutions in society (including the military) and to define the standards by which other bureaucracies will be created, evaluated, and carried forth.

The crucial element of a power structure is its perceived *legitimacy*. Because the power of lower-level functionaries depends on the same system that empowers those in higher positions, it becomes difficult and dangerous, and therefore unlikely, for someone in a lower stratum to really challenge the upper strata. The bureaucracy protects itself.

When properly managed, bureaucratic structures are extremely efficient, whether they are being used well or poorly. One infamous example of this is that the same highly efficient train system that existed in Germany before Hitler came to power (to transport workers and travelers) was used to transport men, women, and children to the death camps of the Third Reich. In fact, Hitler and the Nazis used many of the mechanisms of Germany's bureaucracy to carry out one of the most efficient (albeit horrible—nearly incomprehensible) acts in human history.

Although Weber cautioned against the establishment of sociology as a science that should direct society, he did not shy away from using his knowledge to try to guide his country (Germany) in turbulent times. He may have been pessimistic about anyone's potential to eradicate inequality, but he nonetheless felt obliged to do what he could to promote democracy in his society. Weber was deeply involved in the political realm throughout his life. His greatest impact on German society, as an engaged citizen, came toward the end of his life, during and right after World War I. He wrote many newspaper articles, memos to public officials, and papers against the annexationist policies of the German government during the war, and he advocated for a strong, democratically elected parliament and against the extreme ideologies of both the right and the left (Coser 1977:242).

Émile Durkheim

Whereas Karl Marx and Max Weber were conflict theorists, Émile Durkheim (1858–1917) adopted a functionalist perspective. According to this perspective, society is like a biological organism, with each organ dependent on the others for survival. Functionalists believe that society is made up of interdependent parts, each working for the good of the whole, rather than being composed of competing interests (as conflict theorists maintain). Durkheim believed that humans are selfish by nature and must be channeled and controlled through proper socialization by institutions in society. According to Durkheim, properly functioning institutions, such as the education system, family, occupational associations, and religion, will ensure that people work for the good of society, rather than just for themselves as individuals.

Durkheim (1933) maintained that society is held together by a sense of connectedness, or *solidarity,* that its members feel. This type of bond changes as society moves from simple (e.g., agrarian) to more complex (e.g., industrial and postindustrial). The simpler societies, in which almost everyone shares a common way of life, are based on what Durkheim called *mechanical solidarity.* In this type of society, there is little room for individualism. People are bound to one another through tradition and a common way of life.

The more complex societies, in which people perform different and often highly selective tasks, are founded on *organic solidarity.* In this type of society, people come together to exchange services with one another. It is the many exchanges, and the interactions during those exchanges, that bind the members of the group to one another. They rely upon one another for needed goods and services and understand (to some degree) each other's different perspectives through communicating during their exchanges. In these societies, there is more room for individualism. However, while the members are dependent on one another to survive and prosper, the ties holding the community together are weaker.

Seeing the political and social upheaval that plagued his home country of France during his lifetime, Durkheim studied how society operates and sought ways to make improvements. According to Durkheim, at the core of a smooth society lies solidarity. Societies with increased divisions of labor can achieve stability only if its members are socialized through its institutions to believe that they are obligated to one another, as members of a common community.

Durkheim argued that the existence of *external inequality* in an industrial society indicates that its institutions are not functioning properly. He divided inequalities into *internal* (based on people's natural abilities) and *external* (those forced upon people). Because an organic society needs all its members doing what they do best in order for it to function most effectively, external inequality that prevents some people from fulfilling their innate talents damages all of society and should be eradicated. For example, if someone with the potential to find a cure for cancer—or just to be a good physician—never gets to fulfill this potential because she was raised in a poor neighborhood and attended a terrible school with teachers who never encouraged her to go to college, all of society suffers.

Among Durkheim's concerns were the problems of how to reduce external inequalities and increase social consensus (solidarity). He maintained that it was up to the various institutions in society to create opportunities and incentives for all its members to become engaged citizens and share their gifts. Durkheim used his various positions in the educational system to mold France's public schools around these ideas.

George Herbert Mead

George Herbert Mead (1863–1931), the founder of symbolic interactionism, was the first sociologist to focus on how the mind and the self are created through social processes. Instead of looking at the individual as either distinct from or controlled by society, Mead saw that people are both shaped by and shapers of society. He was particularly interested in how the human self develops through communicating with others via language and other symbolic behavior (symbolic interaction).

According to Mead, humans are not truly human unless they interact with one another. In turn, the nature of our interactions with others determines how we see ourselves and our role in society. *Symbolic interactionists maintain that society is a social construction, continually created and recreated by humans.* We may not realize it, but society is maintained by our implicit agreement to interact with one another in certain ways. As we "practice" certain patterns of interaction, we reinforce the belief system that society "just works that way." Therefore, by changing how we interact with one another, we can change society.

Mead used his sociological expertise about the influence of the social environment to contribute to several social programs and movements in Chicago. For example, he served as treasurer of Hull House (the social service "settlement house" cofounded by Jane Addams and Helen Gates Starr; see below), was a member of the progressive City Club, participated in a variety of local movements and social programs in the city, and edited the journal *Elementary School Teacher*. Mead also spoke publicly and often on behalf of the immigrant population of Chicago, encouraging school reform to aid immigrants in the assimilation process.[2]

Jane Addams

Jane Addams (1860–1935) was both a sociologist and the cofounder of Hull House, the settlement house and activist organization that advocated for women, racial and ethnic minorities, immigrants, the poor, and world peace. Well-known locally, nationally, and internationally, Addams had risen to prominence in an era when few women were perceived as capable of public leadership. Recognition of Addams as a leader in the reform and peace movements culminated in 1931 when she became the first woman to receive the Nobel Peace Prize.

Addams worked closely with George Herbert Mead on social issues concerning women and immigrant workers. Her sociological research in Chicago focused on issues related to the need for social reform, reducing inequality, and bridging the divide between the rich and poor. Addams (with her friend Ellen Gates Starr) founded Hull House in a poor, inner-city, immigrant neighborhood in Chicago in 1889, and it quickly became "an underground university for women activists focusing on questions of housing, sanitation, and public health" (Berger 1997).

One of the more colorful Hull House studies involved researching garbage collection in Chicago. Lack of proper collection was allowing disease to spread, particularly in poor, immigrant communities. In response, the Hull House Women's Club stepped out of the roles expected of them as ladies in late 19th-century Chicago and began to personally collect the garbage that was polluting the poor neighborhoods! Before doing that, however, they used their sociological eyes and research skills to carry out

> a major investigation into the city's garbage collection system. Then Addams submitted to the city government her own bid to collect garbage. The resulting public uproar forced the mayor to appoint Addams as garbage inspector for her ward. The Hull House women formed a garbage patrol, getting up at 6 a.m. to follow the garbage trucks, mapping routes and dump sites, and making citizens arrests of landlords whose properties were a health hazard. Their vigilance moved garbage reform to the top of Chicago's civic agenda, forcing industry to take responsibility for its trash. (Berger 1997:n.p.)

Addams and the other Hull House residents were also responsible (to varying degrees) for the establishment of the juvenile justice system and myriad other social reforms in the areas of women's suffrage, workers' rights, and child labor laws.[3]

The founders of sociology were deeply interested in using their knowledge for the good of society. One wonders how they might make sense of society today and what changes they would recommend to curb current systems of inequality. As we can see, their respective views of the world influenced how they perceived the social issues of the day and their proposed solutions for them.

| Exercise 2.1 | What Would the Founders of Sociology Say About . . . ? |

1. Consider some public issue of inequality today (e.g., the movement to privatize the world's water, the relaxation of U.S. environmental laws, the reduction of federal and state aid for state colleges and universities, the high cost of running for public office, the decrease in funding for housing for poor people, etc.).

2. Describe how each of the five founders of sociology discussed above might respond when told about this issue. Be sure that your answer also briefly summarizes what the issue is about.

3. Which of the responses makes the most sense to you? Why?

4. Is there anything you feel is missing from the founders' perspectives that you might want to add? If so, explain what you would like to add and why. If not, explain why you think their perspective does not need to be expanded or revised.

Theory and Society

Sociologists use theory to elucidate and make sense of social patterns. Without theories, we would have little or no understanding of why society operates the way it does and how we might improve it. Looking at the world through a theoretical perspective can also help us detect patterns that we might otherwise overlook and help us to figure out where we should concentrate our focus. For instance, conflict theorists are more likely to notice discrimination, class inequality, and struggles for power in society than are those who do not view society through a similar lens. Similarly, symbolic interactionists tend to be more aware of the impact of small-group interactions and symbols. For example, such theorists are quick to observe that seemingly minor behaviors (e.g., sitting with legs crossed or uncrossed) can have serious diplomatic repercussions.[4]

The level of analysis also varies among the theoretical perspectives. Some portray the world through a wide-angle lens, looking at larger (macro and meso) social patterns (like functionalism and conflict theory), whereas others (such as symbolic interactionism) view society close-up, from a more detailed (micro) angle. Sometimes, as the "Sociologist in Action" section below illustrates, theories help us to achieve important practical goals. It is important to remember that whenever people use a particular theoretical lens (or any point of view), they will be more attuned to some social patterns than others.

SOCIOLOGIST IN ACTION: TIM WOODS

Dr. Tim Woods grew up in a small farming community in Oklahoma. As an undergraduate majoring in sociology at Southwestern Oklahoma State University, he joined a group of two sociology professors and a handful of students who volunteered at a local prison. In the prison, the faculty and students served as associates and advisers to the Lifers' Club, an organization of prisoners who were serving a life sentence. While the prison volunteer program had no formal ties to the sociology curriculum, this experience left a lasting impression on Woods's work and teaching.

Interacting with the inmates forced Woods to question some fundamental ideas he held, especially those concerning the roles of individual responsibility and self-efficacy. A key event concerned a very religious inmate Woods had befriended. While many inmates joked that no one in the prison was guilty, this particular inmate vociferously and continually proclaimed his innocence, explaining that God had sent him to prison to help other inmates. Wary of the inmate's stories, Woods understood these proclamations to be psychological dissonance, either a denial of individual responsibility or mental illness. However, some 2 years after he left the prison for graduate school, Woods received word that new evidence had been discovered establishing the inmate's innocence. He was released from prison. This became an important example to Woods of the real-world connections among social structure, power, and the lived experiences of individuals.

Dr. Woods is now the chair of the Department of Political Science and Sociology at Manchester Community College in Manchester, Connecticut. Wishing for his students to have the same type of opportunity to learn and contribute to their community that he had had at the prison, Woods began embedding community engagement into the formal coursework in sociology. He wanted students to develop a sociological imagination through their interaction with the community. As they served in and reflected upon life in their community, students began to connect first their own and then others' personal troubles to social issues in their community and the larger world. This experience also advanced students' understanding of broader sociological concepts and theories by visibly connecting those concepts to their own lived experiences and those of others in the community.

(Continued)

(Continued)

Initially, Woods's students simply volunteered at a variety of community nonprofit organizations and related their experiences there to the course material. Over time, Woods and his students' roles grew from merely volunteering to publicly advocating for structural community change. Their sociological imagination enabled them to recognize the need for and potential of collective action to address social needs in the community. Joining forces with the local homeless shelter, religious organizations, and town officials, they helped to establish the Manchester Initiative for Supportive Housing and have taken a leading role in advocating for supportive housing as a long-term solution to homelessness. Their strategy for community awareness has become a topic of discussion among supportive housing advocates as far from Connecticut as California.

Woods believes that community colleges provide a unique opportunity for sociologists interested in teaching about and engaging in public sociology and community change. Unlike most students in 4-year colleges and universities, community college students are more strongly embedded in their communities, where they live, work, worship, and go to college, and, as a result, they have long-term stakes in the community. While it is certainly possible for professors and students at 4-year schools to make a positive impact on the communities surrounding their campus, they must often make extra efforts to know and be accepted by members of the local community. Tim Woods's students, similar to Jane Addams and the other Hull House researchers and activists, live in the community they are trying to improve. Also, community college students are usually more representative of the diversity (in terms of race/ethnicity, class, age, religion, etc.) that one finds in the community. These factors increase the legitimacy and success of student projects in the community and make the connection between classroom and community more authentic and enduring.

Exercise 2.2   Going Deeper

As noted above, the founding theorists we discuss in this chapter were deeply influenced by the social problems that existed in their societies. Choose one of the theorists and obtain more information about that person's society. How did the social issues prevalent at that time influence his or her sociological perspective (theory) and research topics?

SOCIOLOGIST IN ACTION: BRIAN J. REED

Social network theory helped the U.S. Army to capture Saddam Hussein. Major Brian J. Reed, a doctoral candidate in the Department of Sociology at the University of Maryland, College Park, used his sociological training in social network analysis when he was stationed in Iraq and assigned the task of devising a strategy to capture the former Iraqi dictator. He described his use of social network theory in locating Hussein in the following way:

> The intelligence background and link diagrams that we built [to capture Hussein] were rooted in the concepts of network analysis. We constructed an elaborate product that traced the tribal and family linkages of Saddam Hussein, thereby allowing us to focus on certain individuals who may have had (or presently had) close ties to [him]. (Hougham 2005:3)

Reed's expertise in network analysis allowed him and soldiers under his command to recreate and study a detailed picture of Hussein's social network, thereby determining where he would be most likely to hide.

Reed also maintains that his sociological training helped him to comprehend the Iraqi culture and, because of this understanding, more effectively carry out military operations in that country. Recognizing the practical applications of sociological research and theory, the Army Research Institute gave $1.1 million in 2005 to the University of Maryland's Center for Research on Military Organization (CRMO), of which Reed is a member, to conduct research on social structure, social systems, and social networks.

Exercise 2.3	Different Perspectives Lead to Different News

This assignment will require you to watch the news for at least 1.5 hours a day for 1 week. It will also require you to have access to a wide range of stations. Watch CNN, BBC World News (now available in the United States on most cable networks and accessible online), and Fox News, each for half an hour a day for 1 week.

As you are doing so, keep notes on (a) what stories they show on the news, (b) how they portray the news events (positively or negatively, for example),

(Continued)

(Continued)

and (c) how they compare with one another. Pay attention to which stories are addressed by all three and which stories are only covered on one of the news outlets.

As you do so, complete the questions below.

Pick one news story that all of the networks carry and answer the following questions.

1. How much time do CNN, BBC World News, and Fox News each give the story?

2. Are the events at the center of the story portrayed positively or negatively (or both) by each of the three networks? How do the positive and negative portrayals differ from one another?

3. How would your knowledge of the news story be different if you watched just one of the news networks?

4. How would your perception of the news story (whether the story was important, negative or positive, etc.) be different if you watched just one of the news networks?

5. After the week is over, compare the different news stations' perspectives on the world. Were you able to clearly perceive three different perspectives? If so, how did they differ? Research and analyze, in detail, why it is that those differences exist. What does this tell you about the objectivity of news and news stories?

Extra Credit: Go to the Web site for the organization Fairness & Accuracy In Reporting (FAIR, at www.fair.org/index.php). Look through the articles and identify stories you think are important but were not covered by the news stations you analyzed in Questions 1–4. What is your analysis of why these stories were not included, and what does this tell you about mainstream news coverage?

Exercise 2.4   Analysis of the Print News Media

Visit the Web sites of two national newspapers and one local paper. Some of the national papers you can use are the *New York Times* (www.nytimes .com), *The Washington Post* (www.washingtonpost.com), and *USA Today* (www.usatoday.com). A good place to search for your local paper is the Web site Hometown News (www.hometownnews.com).

1. What are the two or three lead stories in each paper? (Make sure that you are looking at all of them at approximately the same time on the same day.)

2. How similar are they in their editorial approaches? That is, to what extent do the different papers make similar decisions about which stories are most important? If they are similar, why do you think this is so? If they differ, why do you think they do so?

3. Look at a couple of "inside" sections of all three papers, such as sports or entertainment. Repeat the comparison above by comparing the lead stories in each of those sections or the films or books chosen for review that day. How similar are these sections of each paper?

4. Listen to these two stories from National Public Radio: "Big Media Unbound," at www.onpointradio.org/shows/2003/06/20030602_b_ main.asp and "Covering the Coverage of the 2008 Campaign" at www .npr.org/templates/story/story.php?storyId=89472118. Also read "Behind TV Analysts, Pentagon's Hidden Hand" at www.nytimes.com/2008/04/ 20/washington/20generals.html?ex=1209614400&en=9c12097f381226 fa&ei=5070&emc=eta1.

5. What did you learn from these stories that helped you to further your analysis? How, if at all, does a corporatized media monopoly potentially affect (a) the layout of a newspaper, (b) the amount of coverage given to stories, (c) the "spin" that a story might have, and (d) the range of potentially important stories that could be included but are not?

6. How do bloggers influence news coverage? What are the pros and cons of this "democratization" of the media?

Extra Credit: Repeat the same observations for 5 consecutive days. Then,

a. Describe any patterns you have noticed.

b. Repeat the same exercise using one conservative media source (such as WorldNetDaily at www.worldnetdaily.com or Intellectual Conservative at www.intellectualconservative.com or Free Republic at http://www .freerepublic.com/tag/*/index) and one liberal source (such as Salon at

(Continued)

(Continued)

www.salon.com or *The Nation* online at www.thenation.com or ZNet at www.zmag.org/weluser.htm or *Mother Jones* at http://www.mother-jones.com).

c. Try the same exercise using one online news magazine targeted toward women (such as iVillage at www.ivillage.com or Women's eNews at www.womensenews.org/index.cfm) and one geared toward the general public (such as *Newsweek* online at www.msnbc.msn.com/id/3032542/site/newsweek or *Time* online at www.time.com/time).

Exercise 2.5   Learning How Theory Is Applied

Go to this book's Web site at www.pineforge.com/korgen3e to find articles that use the three main theoretical perspectives discussed in this chapter (functionalism, conflict theory, and symbolic interactionism).

Find one article for each of the respective theories and describe (a) the theoretical perspective that is used, (b) how the author(s) use it, and (c) whether either of the other two theories might also be helpful in making sense of the findings (and why or why not).

Discussion Questions

1. Sociology has always been viewed a bit warily by leaders in most societies. Why do you think this might be? What is it about a sociological perspective that might feel threatening to those in power and those benefiting from the current system?

2. Imagine you are a sociological theorist. What social issue would you choose to study first? Why? Which of the three primary sociological perspectives (functionalism, conflict theory, or symbolic interactionism) do you think you would use to explain your findings? Why?

3. If, as symbolic interactionists maintain, society is merely a social construction (that is created and recreated anew through our interactions with one another),

why is it so hard to address social issues effectively? How might a symbolic interactionist respond to this question?

4. Which sociological perspective (conflict theory, functionalism, or symbolic interactionism) do you think is best able to explain inequality in the United States today? Why do you think so?

5. Which of the theorists described in this chapter do you think best fulfilled the two core commitments of sociology? Why?

Suggestions for Specific Actions

1. Many sociologists note that sociological studies have pointed out good solutions to social issues but have been largely ignored by government leaders and the media. Go to the American Sociological Association Web site at www.asanet.org or the Society for the Study of Social Problems Web site at www.sssp1.org. Look around each site and find a study that provides a good basis for the use of sociological research in public policy.

2. Write a letter to your school newspaper or another local paper describing the study and what you think would be a good public policy based on it. The following link from the Free the Children Web site will help you carry out this assignment: www.freethechildren.com/index.php.

Please go to our Web site at www.pineforge.com/korgen3e to find further civic engagement opportunities, resources, peer-reviewed articles, and updated Web links related to this chapter.

Endnotes

1. Some consider Weber a functionalist.

2. See the University of Chicago Centennial Catalogue's faculty Web page on Mead at www.lib.uchicago.edu/e/spcl/centcat/fac/facch12_01.html.

3. See the article on the Hull House Museum's Web site, "About Jane Addams," available at www.uic.edu/jaddams/hull/newdesign/ja.html.

4. In Arab nations, it is regarded as impolite to cross one's legs. In India, it is impolite to show the bottom of your shoe, as you would by crossing one foot over your knee instead of crossing your ankles.

References

Berger, Rose Marie. 1997, July/August. "The Good Housekeeping Award: Women Heroes of Environmental Activism." *Sojourners*. Retrieved September 16, 2009 (http://www.sojo.net/index.cfm?action=magazine.article&issue=soj9707&article =970722).

Coser, Lewis A. 1977. *Masters of Sociological Thought: Ideas in Historical and Social Context*. 2nd ed. New York: Harcourt Brace Jovanovich.

Durkheim, Émile. 1933. *The Division of Labor in Society*. Translated by George Simpson. New York: The Free Press.

Gerth, H., and C. Wright Mills. 1958. *From Max Weber: Essays in Sociology*. New York: Oxford University Press.

Hougham, Victoria. 2005, July/August. "Sociological Skills Used in the Capture of Saddam Hussein." *Footnotes,* p. 3.

Marx, Karl and Friedrich Engels. [1848] 2002. *The Communist Manifesto*. Edited by G. S. Jones. New York: Penguin Classics.

Marx, Karl and Friedrich Engels. 1970. *The German Ideology*. London: Lawrence and Wishart.

3

How Do We Know
What We Think We Know?

Sociological Methods

In one memorable scene in the iconic 1975 comedy film *Monty Python and the Holy Grail,* a group of peasants drags a woman to the center of town to be burned at the stake. Sir Bedevere, the local lord, intervenes to be sure that justice is carried out.

Sir Bedevere: What makes you think she's a witch?

Peasant 3: Well, she turned me into a newt.

Sir Bedevere: A newt?

Peasant 3: [pause] . . . I got better.

Crowd: [shouts] Burn her anyway![1]

How much is revealed in this simple scene!

First, this is the Early Middle Ages, sometime around the mid-600s. This was a time of superstition, uncertainty, and fear for many people. It was a time before science, when religious spirituality contested with other spiritualities and forms of magic in explaining the world. Both Christians and pagans believed that witches walked the earth and that one must be on guard against them. Certainly, there were no widely held assumptions about the nature of cause and effect or the logic of demonstrating that one thing caused another. Evidence did not need to be seen or examined; "proof" could come from the fact that a lot of people agreed on something. "Burn her anyway" is a strong argument when shouted by a large crowd of people.

The scene is carried by the self-reflective totality of its logic. We start with a belief system common during the Middle Ages that includes the existence of witches, and humans being transformed by witches. We add an event: A man thinks he was turned into a newt, and those around him accuse someone of being a witch. Challenged to support the claim (*she* is a witch), they resort to the original definition of the event (there is a witch). Any evidence that worked in her favor could, of course, be interpreted to prove just how tricky those witches are. There is no space in the argument to consider counterclaims that she is not a witch or that there are no witches. You might as well light the fire. There is no way out of this logic.

Of course, things have changed a little in 14 centuries. Fewer people believe in witches,[2] most serious accusations are dealt with in the courtroom, and science has considerably more support than magic does, and it rests alongside religion as a widely accepted method of explaining the world. But scientific explanations rely on the logic of cause and effect, on the careful definition of our terms and assumptions, and on the idea that evidence can be tested. Even a casual observation of United States society suggests that these concepts are not as widely understood or applied as we might hope. One means of finding out if the research we read about is trustworthy is to check and see if the researchers followed the basic steps of the scientific process.

The basic steps of all social science research are these:

1. Choose a research topic.

2. Find out what other researchers have discovered about that topic.

3. Choose a methodology (how you will collect your data).

4. Collect and analyze your data.

5. Relate your findings to those of other researchers.

6. Present findings for public review and critique.

The Three Questions

In addition to following the basic steps of scientific research, social scientists must establish the answers to three basic questions about their work before they publicize their findings: (1) How do you know? (2) So what? (Why is it important we know this?) and (3) Now what? (What do we do with this new information?) Let us consider each of these questions, from the last to the first.

The "Now What?" Question

Research is the path toward answering questions. Before we can discover new findings, we first have to raise a question. Further, we like to assume that both the question and the answer are important and can influence society in some way. When we find the answer to our question, we should do something with that knowledge.

It has been popular to picture Newton "discovering" gravity as an apple fell on his head. It would be absurd to suggest that up to that point (mid-1600s, about 1,000 years past the time in which the Monty Python skit was set), no one had noticed that things fall. But it is interesting to wonder how the observation (that things fall) became a question (How and why do things fall?).

Something in the social, political, or scientific world had changed so that it became useful to answer these questions. Did things fall any differently after Newton had named the process? No. However, he discovered new information that powerfully influenced his and future societies when he answered the questions about why and how objects fall. His general theory of gravity changed the world (Eves 1976).

Your work does not have to change the way people view reality and the cosmos to have meaning. In the late 1950s, Harold Garfinkel (1967) attempted to explain the personal situation of a woman who had been born with male primary sexual characteristics (a penis), who in puberty had developed female secondary sexual characteristics (breasts), and who had to make a choice—accompanied by surgery—to define her sexual identity. Such cases are extremely rare and mostly unseen by the majority of our society (see Sax 2002). One might think that sociologists would not be concerned with a lone case. Yet to appreciate and explain the case of "Agnes," Garfinkel had to address sexual norms, the power of "belonging," sanctions against deviance, and the strategies by which those with "abnormal" conditions may try to "cover" them. Agnes's biophysical condition combined with a vast and complex social world of meaning to create a problem that she had to solve. It was not, strictly speaking, the ambiguity of whether she was "really" male or female that defined the problem, but the social need for her to be unambiguous about it. This research raises questions about (a) the social categories within which personal identities and sexual identities are constructed, (b) how norms become normal and what happens when you violate them, and (c) how we define and use notions of what is or is not "natural." Of course, once we have raised those questions, we have to start looking at everything that is considered natural and everything that is feared or hated because it is seen as unnatural.

Very few people in this country are burned at the stake anymore, but hate crimes and vigilante assaults still occur frequently. The usefulness of Garfinkel's research was not about Agnes. It was about what the rest of us *think* of Agnes and many other people and things that frighten or confuse us or don't fit into the norms we have constructed for our society. Answers to the "Now what?" question often challenge us, both as individuals and as a society, to rethink our most comfortable and unquestioned assumptions (norms and values) about the world.

The "So What?" Question

When we prepare our research, we have to have some idea of what new knowledge we are after and why it may be useful. The "So what?" question is like the "Now what?" question. But where the "Now what (do we do with these findings)?" question asks how we might make use of what we learned from our research, the "So what?" question asks why sociologists need to research something in the first place.

To answer the "So what?" question, we do not need to show that lives hang in the balance. We simply need to show that there is something to be learned about our society or culture (or a different society or culture) that is worth knowing. Even abstract knowledge "for its own sake" is valuable in the quest to understand our lives, our world, and how they interact, since even seemingly inconsequential behavior adds up, collectively, to create the totality of human behavior.

Suppose we were to analyze every scene and underlying theme in *Monty Python and the Holy Grail*. (Both fans and academics have done so, though neither of the authors of this work has weighed in—yet.) How would we justify all of that effort on a 34-year-old movie by a defunct British comedy group? Shouldn't we be putting our time to better use, like examining political regimes, industrial shifts, or responses to natural disasters? Perhaps. However, there is still a lot to learn from and about popular culture. If, for example, we concluded that the Monty Python group was a pretty funny bunch of guys, we would not be doing much. If, on the other hand, we concluded that the Monty Python players were popular and widely accepted when they were making fun of the British monarchy in general but less so when they were making fun of living members of the government, then we would be using popular culture to learn something about political culture.

The "How Do You Know?" Question

This is the big one, and most of the rest of the chapter will address it. To put it simply, we know that our findings are valid if we design scientific studies that are theoretically sound and driven by data. We ask questions, determine the kinds of data needed to answer them, figure out a plan for getting the data, and define a set of clear and consistent criteria for finding the answers in the data. Only then do we actually start collecting any data. We will explain each of these steps in further detail below.

All of us can do research, but it takes special skills to conduct *social scientific* studies. Research done by social scientists (and physical scientists) seeks to answer questions for which answers are not already known. Going to AccuWeather.com on the Internet to check the forecast for tomorrow is not the same thing as conducting research on the weather. Similarly, if I am wondering whether there are any good movies on television tonight, and I look at the listing of scheduled programs and find that there aren't, then I have answered my question. But I have not done social scientific research.[3] I might not know from day to day what is being broadcast, but that does not mean this information is not known. Social scientific research is a tool used to discover *new* findings.

Social scientific research is not carried out exactly like studies conducted in the natural or physical sciences.[4] We study things that are always changing and always dependent on the time and place in which we are looking. A physicist can ask, "What is the boiling point of water (at a given atmospheric pressure)?" A sociologist cannot ask, "What is the boiling-over point of social unrest?" There isn't any such thing that can be nailed down. Instead, we have to ask, "How does the occurrence of a single event of great injustice contribute to the likelihood that social unrest will lead to collective social action?" The answer is not a yes or a no or a number. It is a description of a social process in which some events lead to the possibility of other events. It's a probability estimate, but it is not a guess. We can show that our answers are reliable (consistent) and valid (accurate). Our questions are about how things work, and why they work as they do. And the most interesting part is that no answer is ever final. There are always new circumstances, such as differences in history, culture, politics, economy, and geography, to take into account.

Once we have our questions, we have to figure out what data will answer them. If, for example, we wanted to know whether people in the United States generally want lower taxes, we could conduct a national *survey* with a couple of tax questions on it. You have probably seen surveys. Most are collections of short, simple questions on a set of related topics in which you choose your answer to each question from a short list of choices. Surveys allow researchers to collect a few basic measures of something from a very large number of people, in a short amount of time, and in exactly the same way. (If you collect data from some people one way and other people a different way, it is not usually valid to treat the data as equivalent.) The answers given by any individual *respondent* (the person who responds to the questions) are not really important to us. What we really look at is the pattern of answers across hundreds, or thousands, of cases. Surveys that contain questions followed by sets of answers from which respondents are asked to choose, give us *quantitative* (or numerical) data on which we can perform statistical analyses. Statistical data give us the big picture of trends and social changes.

Perhaps we already have reason to believe that people want lower taxes. So, now we might want to know what Americans are willing to give up for lower taxes (because lower taxes mean less government income and hence, usually, less government spending, meaning fewer programs). One might think this could be done with a survey, if we make the format more complex. We could, for example, identify long lists of things that the government spends money on and ask people which ones they would be willing to do without if they could get lower taxes. But then, how do we choose the list? And if we ask, "Which items would you trade?" how do we know that we aren't leading people to just identify the programs that they dislike, regardless of what they think about taxes? So just asking questions is not always the best way to find information.

Often, as researchers, we need to know more than just whether people do or do not approve of something. We need to know *why* they do or do not approve. We need to sit down and listen to people. This process is called an *interview*. Interviews involve asking people a series of *open-ended* questions on the research topic and letting them answer in whatever way they like. *Probe questions* are also often used to encourage the respondents to dig deeper in their answers and analysis and also to keep the respondents from straying too far off topic. The data gleaned from interviews are not a pattern of "yes" or "no" opinions, but the respondents' own words. This type of data collection is *qualitative* and elicits data based on words that describe "qualities," feelings, and first-hand accounts.

Interviews allow us to listen to and question respondents at length, and investigate intangibles such as *why* they feel as they do. A survey might ask whether the respondent thinks our nation should spend more or less than we do on loans to other nations. But we can't determine, for sure, *why* the individual believes we should spend more or less by asking a survey question. An interview gives more depth and more context than a survey, but it is longer, and harder to carry out, and more expensive. Also, because time and money constraints usually mean that we can interview far fewer people than we could survey, it's difficult to make good generalizations from interview data.

Surveys and interviews rely on *self-reported data.* That means that people tell us the answers. Yet research and common sense both tell us that people do not always know why they feel or act as they do or how they will respond to certain circumstances. Few of us want to think of ourselves as people who will walk away from someone in need of help, or cause harm just because we have been so instructed. If you ask people what they would do under circumstances in which strangers need help or in which their own actions cause harm, what do you think they will tell you?[5] For this reason, sometimes you may need to observe without asking.[6]

Experiments are one technique for observing how people will react to different conditions. In experimental research, the researcher measures the relationship between two variables by manipulating one of them and observing the other. If I want to know whether people will help a stranger in need, for example, I can create a situation in which someone appears to be in need of help. That's the *cause* part of a cause-and-effect relationship (the first variable). Then I can control circumstances so that a variety of people, one at a time, encounter the situation. Some of them will help, and others will not. That's the *effect* (the second variable). As much as possible, I would create a controlled environment in which almost nothing else can affect the outcome. For example, to control whether the *subjects* (the people being observed) were in a hurry or not, I might set up conditions in which they think they are either late or early for a meeting with me.

The classic model of an experiment, which you have probably seen acted out in movies, involves researchers (in white coats) in a lab, looking through a one-way mirror while subjects respond to different *stimuli* (the "cause" part of cause and effect). *Fieldwork* provides another way of measuring how people respond to stimuli. Fieldwork is, in some respects, the opposite of experimental research. It requires the researcher to go out into the real world, where things are happening that he or she does not manipulate at all.

The place where you choose to do your experimental work is called your *field site*. Field sites might include a park on a nice day, a campaign office during the course of a political election, spring training with a baseball team, an office, a courtroom, a classroom, or any other place where the kinds of activities in which you are interested happen. As researchers, we cannot control, or really change at all, any of the many things that affect what people do. We can't create the stimulus. But, unlike in a laboratory setting, we can observe things as they actually occur in people's lives.

There are other techniques for data gathering and analysis, including the *content analysis* of the products of popular culture, such as the Monty Python movies, and combinations of the techniques described here. For example, *focus groups*, or interviews conducted with a group of people, are a modification of interview techniques that incorporates some of the advantages of doing fieldwork.

SOCIOLOGIST IN ACTION: JOHANNA E. FOSTER

Informed by sociological data that consistently show that access to higher education has the single greatest impact on reducing rates of recidivism of convicted criminals, Johanna Foster, along with her colleague Gina Shea, decided to apply her academic training in feminist sociology to cofound College Connections, a college-in-prison project for incarcerated women in the greater New York City metropolitan area.

Prior to 1994, federal and state money supported higher education programs for incarcerated people. College-in-prison programs were numerous and accounted for a well-documented decrease in the rates of reincarceration. Today, higher education as a road to rehabilitation is almost entirely closed off for most of the millions of people currently incarcerated in the United States. For women prisoners, whose rate of incarceration has increased by more than 800% in the past three decades (Institute on Women & Criminal Justice 2009), the number of on-site college programs is dangerously small despite their proven effectiveness in reducing crime.

To help fill this gap in rehabilitation services, Foster obtained permission from administrators at a state prison in her community to conduct a needs assessment survey of the population so as to identify women inmates' interest in, eligibility for, and level of preparedness for a nondegree, non-credit, college-bound educational program at that particular facility. Foster and her colleagues then used the findings from the needs assessment survey to persuade area educational institutions to matriculate students from the prison into what would eventually become a credit-bearing college program serving more than 400 women in that prison with the support of Mercy College, Nyack College, and Vassar College.

In another kind of applied sociology, Foster also teaches sociology and women's studies in the prison program she has established, passing on C. Wright Mills's concept of the "sociological imagination" to students inside so that they can connect their "personal troubles" of incarceration to the "public issues" of race, class, and gender inequality. In doing so, Foster hopes to inspire student-inmates to use sociology themselves to understand their present circumstances and to improve their life chances once released.

Foster continues to conduct policy research on the state of higher education programming for women in prison nationwide, research that she most recently used to establish the NO GOING BACK Coalition for Incarcerated Women (NGBC), based in New Jersey. The NGBC regularly uses applied social research to educate a range of stakeholders about the importance of higher education and viable job-training programs for incarcerated women and men alike. For more information, you can contact Johanna Foster via email at johanna .e.foster@gmail.com.

As you have just seen, we can use numbers to make connections between politics and the day-to-day realities of people who suffer from the effects of bad decisions. But it is ethnographic fieldwork that really embraces the lived experiences of those whose lives and circumstances we study. *Ethnography refers to the study of cultural information, such as values and meanings, as opposed to data about structures, politics, and economics.* Elliot Liebow's classic 1967 study of an American ghetto, *Tally's Corner,* for example, was praised when it was first published, for the author's ability "to grasp the native's point of view" while emphasizing that "these 'natives' are other Americans; that their society is his society" (Rainwater 1968). More recently, feminist sociologists have turned to ethnography[7] as a way of overcoming the cultural biases of research itself while conducting research on cultural biases (Ribbons and Edwards 1997).

Exercise 3.1	Ethnography

1. Choose a public setting in which you can sit and take notes for at least an hour. The setting should be open to anyone and have lively social interaction. It must also be very unfamiliar to you so that you can experience it as an "outsider." Begin your observations by writing out a general description of your setting. Who is there and what are they doing? What sorts of activities go on in this place?

2. Describe how you fit into the setting. Are people noticing that you are observing them? How do you think these people view you?

3. For a 15-minute period, write down *everything* that you see happening. Try not to read anything into what you are observing. Observation notes might include things like "two adults (1WM, 1WF)[8] walk in pushing a stroller with a very young child in it. They talk. The man goes to the counter while the woman takes a table. The man orders and purchases two drinks and brings them to the table." Notes should not incorporate a lot of interpretation, the way this example does: "A couple with a child comes in. The husband asks his wife what she wants and then goes to get the drinks." You don't really know those things. You know the two people are adults, but you don't know their relationship or the details of their conversation. Don't write down assumptions about what you see—just what you actually observe.

(Continued)

(Continued)

4. After your notes are complete, try to make sense of them.

   a. What patterns of interactions did you see?

   b. What do you think they reveal?

   c. Why do you think that?

   d. What other explanations can you come up with?

   e. What would you need to observe or learn in order to know which explanation is the most likely?

5. What are the advantages and disadvantages of this type of data collection?

6. Would this be your preferred mode of data collection to understand what you observed? Why or why not?

The Theory Problem

The authors of this book recently saw a political survey sent out by a senator to all of her constituents. Most of the questions asked respondents to rate certain proposals on a 5-point scale that consisted of 1. "strongly disagree," 2. "disagree," 3. "neutral," 4. "agree," and 5. "strongly agree." (This is called a *Likert scale,* which is a common way to solicit political opinions.) But it was the questions that were remarkable. Many were of the form, *"How do you feel about the federal government running up huge debts in order to . . . ?"*[9] The problem should be obvious: The question is so leading that the only acceptable answer is to disapprove. Yet the senator will be completely within her rights to later state that some overwhelming percentage of her constituents disapproves of whatever the issue is. Although it is an all-too-common tactic in political and marketing research, creating the answers you want is not at all scientific or valid.

As social scientists, we need to guard against this sort of data abuse in many ways, but two particularly apply. The first is that we have to be open about our methods. We have to describe, in detail, where and how we got our data, including making our questions public. The second significant protection against misleading data interpretations is to define and describe clear and consistent criteria for data evaluation before we even collect our data. These criteria have to follow from our research questions.

As social scientists, we also have to demonstrate the reliability and validity of our findings. We need to let our readers know, through a clear discussion of how we collected our data, just how sure we can be that our data accurately represent the population studied (validity) and whether or not we can expect that other researchers, using the same methods, would find similar results (reliability). And we have to be honest, analytical, and trustworthy in doing so! Although not every study has to be high in both reliability and validity (depending on the methodology used, sometimes that is impossible), we must clearly indicate just how valid and reliable our findings are. Unless we do so, those who read and rely on what we present will not be able to accurately judge the veracity of our findings.

Returning to the example of political policies, suppose we want to determine how popular or unpopular a group of policies is with voters. We would start by designing a set of procedures for measuring people's opinions. This might be in the form of a survey with a number of Likert-scale questions on it (though not the questions from the survey we have just seen). Recall that we had defined a 5-point scale, in which answers 1 and 2 indicated disapproval, 3 was neutral, and ratings 4 and 5 indicated approval. In this case, the analysis is easy. When all of the respondents' answers to the same question are averaged, the number can be interpreted on the same scale: More than 3 indicates approval. Of course, real studies often require much more complex criteria involving the interactions of many variables under different conditions. But the process always involves first laying out the criteria by which the data will be used to answer the question, then collecting the data, and only then drawing conclusions.

Where do clear and consistent criteria come from? How can we say that it is reasonable to expect a particular outcome or pattern of behavior and that it would be odd to find something else? The answer, of course, is that our research is driven by theory. Sociological theories offer explanations for group behavior. *Theories*—tested notions of how and why people do things—lead to testable propositions about how and why specific sets of people would do particular things. Conflict theory, for example, tells us that dominant groups will usually act in a great many consistent and predictable ways to maintain their dominance, including making claims about others' inherent inferiorities. Theories of gender and social roles in the United States tell us that men expect to have dominance in public roles, particularly those that involve the greatest amount of decision making and moneymaking—areas that preserve and reproduce this advantage. A gender-role theorist might predict that men in leadership positions will routinely suggest that women are less capable of exercising leadership. *Do* they suggest that? That's a research question.

Exercise 3.2   Gender and Leadership

1. Write a 10-question survey about the differences between men and women. Three of the questions should deal with issues of leadership and decision making. For each question, offer respondents the same three answers to choose from: Yes, No, or Not Sure.

2. Survey 10 people, and summarize the results. Describe what these results reveal.

3. Interview three people. Ask them the same questions about leadership, but for each answer they give, ask them why they think so. Do not lead them to answer in any particular way. Just ask them to explain themselves, and let them say whatever they want. Write down their answers in as much detail as you can.

4. For each of your interviews, analyze the reasons people give for their beliefs.

   a. How often do they express their answers in terms of personal beliefs or personal experiences?

   b. How often do they express their answers in terms of anecdotes—stories that they might have heard about people they do or do not know?

   c. How often do they refer to information they learned in one of their classes (if your respondents are students) or news reports from reliable sources?

   d. How else do people explain their beliefs?

5. What do the answers to these four questions tell you about how most people in your sample form their beliefs about (a) gender and (b) how gender is related to leadership?

6. Compare your findings from your interviews and surveys. What kind of information did you get from each methodology? What benefits can be obtained by using both qualitative and quantitative data collection when you research a topic?

Exercise 3.3   Hate Speech and Freedom of Access

Hate speech raises an interesting intersection between our dual constitutional rights of freedom of speech and *freedom of access*—people's ability to access their constitutional rights, free of threat and discrimination. What happens when one of these rights is exercised by an individual or group and, in so doing, the rights of another individual or group are violated? Hate crimes have a special place in the American legal structure because they are considered both illegal acts (the crimes themselves) and acts that interfere with another group's freedom of access.

For this exercise,

1. Listen to the following three stories from National Public Radio: "Latino Hate Crimes on the Rise" at www.npr.org/templates/story/story.php?storyId=17563862, "Baltimore Beating Sparks Hate Crime Debate" at www.npr.org/templates/story/story.php?storyId=17395257, and "Crimes Against Race: Hate or Ignorance?" at www.npr.org/templates/story/story.php?storyId=14522720.

2. Research your college's policy on hate crimes. (This information will likely be in your Student Handbook or may be accessed by using the search engine on your college's Web site and typing in the keywords "hate crime policy.")

3. Interview five students to find out (a) what they know about hate crimes and, specifically, if they know the definition of a hate crime, and (b) what their opinion is about hate crimes occupying a separate legal category from other crimes.

   Your research will likely yield the most interesting results if some, but not all, of those you interview come from historical out-groups that have often been targeted by hate crimes (e.g., African American, Jewish, gay or lesbian, immigrant, Latino).

4. Write a two-page paper analyzing your interviews in the context of the NPR stories.

Exercise 3.4   The Pros and Cons of Different Methodologies

In this chapter, we've described a variety of *methodologies* (means of collecting data), including classic experiments, fieldwork, interviews, and surveys. Each has its own set of strengths and weaknesses.

(Continued)

(Continued)

In a one- to two-page paper, briefly describe the following:

a. What you see as the strengths and weaknesses of each methodology discussed in the chapter (classic experiments, fieldwork, interviews, and surveys), and

b. How you might use each methodology to examine unemployment in your state. What would be the advantages and disadvantages of each of these means of studying this issue?

Discussion Questions

1. Political polls often ask potential voters whether they support or oppose something, but rarely ask them whether they know much (or anything) about the topic. How do you think people with little or no knowledge of the topic come up with their answers to those questions?

2. Based on what you've read in this chapter, how will you determine if a politician is providing you with trustworthy or misleading information?

3. Think of something that you and members of your family have long believed to be true. How would you test this belief? If your research led you to change your mind, how could you convince others in your family to reconsider their own assumptions on the issue?

4. Which methodology covered in this chapter would you use to determine your classmates' attitudes toward the war in Afghanistan? Why?

5. Which methodologies covered in this chapter would typically be most useful for someone researching a topic from the perspective of (a) a conflict theorist, (b) a functionalist, and (c) a symbolic interactionist?

Suggestions for Specific Actions

1. Find a Web site for an organization that advocates for or protests against something. Most such organizations have Web sites these days, so you can start by choosing an issue about which people fight (e.g., legalized abortion, a flat tax, the death penalty), and then search out the groups that have positions on the issue.

Select a Web site used by one of the groups. Identify two or three major claims that they offer on the Web site, in support of their position. Do they present real evidence to back up these claims? How well do they document their sources? Try to verify the data on your own. Also try to find contradictory information. Do you think they are being honest? What makes you think so? Create your own Web site (or alternate form of presentation such as a fact sheet or PowerPoint presentation) that describes the same issue in a more balanced way.

2. Research a policy decision recently made by your college or university. Ascertain how the policy was designed. In particular, determine what research was undertaken to decide if the new policy was necessary. Was the research done in a social scientific manner? Based on the research undertaken, do you think the university policy was clearly needed and well-formulated? Write a letter to the editor of your school paper that describes your examination of the policy and the research that culminated in it. Be sure to include your evaluation of the research in your letter.

Please go to the book's Web site at www.pineforge.com/korgen3e to find further civic engagement opportunities, resources, peer-reviewed articles, and updated Web links related to this chapter.

Endnotes

1. Dialogue found in The Internet Movie Database (www.imdb.com).

2. However, it's important to remember that the passage of time does not always result in more rational thought among populations. Just three centuries ago, "witches" were being put to death in Salem, Massachusetts!

3. Similarly, "researching" what is the best car to buy by reading consumer guides like *Consumer Reports* is not conducting true social scientific research.

4. Sociology, like psychology, anthropology, and political science, is a social science. Physics, chemistry, and biology are natural sciences in that they study the physical world, or nature.

5. If you think you have an answer to that question, it's likely you are incorrect. Some people will exaggerate one way; others will exaggerate the other way. Many will guess, and almost none will really know. But there will always be a lot of different answers if you ask a lot of different people!

6. Please note that observational research, like all research dealing with human subjects, must be approved by your school's Internal Review Board. In almost all cases, you will need to obtain written approval from the people you plan to observe and provide assurances that no psychological or physical harm will come to them as a result of your research. See the book's Web site for more information about the ethics of social scientific research.

7. Many feminist researchers view traditional, social scientific, quantitative research methods as constructed by men and influenced by a male-dominated view of society. Ethnography and other types of qualitative research, in contrast to quantitative work, tend to provide a more complete picture of, and a greater voice for, the individuals being observed.

8. Shorthand for "one white male, one white female."

9. This was not an actual question. We're exaggerating just a little to make the point.

References

Eves, Howard. 1976. *An Introduction to the History of Mathematics.* 4th ed. New York: Holt, Rinehart & Winston.

Garfinkel, Harold. 1967. *Studies in Ethnomethodology.* Englewood Cliffs, NJ: Prentice Hall.

Institute on Women & Criminal Justice. 2009. "Quick Facts: Women & Criminal Justice—2009." Retrieved September 18, 2009 (http://www.wpaonline.org/pdf/Quick%20Facts%20Women%20and%20CJ%202009.pdf).

Liebow, Elliot. 1967. *Tally's Corner.* Boston: Little, Brown.

Rainwater, Lee. 1968. Review of *Tally's Corner: A Study of Negro Street-Corner Men* by Elliot Liebow. *Social Forces* 46(3):431–32.

Ribbons, Jane and Rosalind Edwards. 1997. *Feminist Dilemmas in Qualitative Research: Public Knowledge and Private Lives.* Thousand Oaks, CA: Sage.

Sax, Leonard. 2002. "How Common Is Intersex? A Response to Anne Fausto-Sterling." *Journal of Sex Research* 39:174–79.

4

Creating Civic Engagement Versus Creating Apathy

Culture

Have you seen the *SpongeBob SquarePants* episode where SpongeBob goes to Sandy's house for the first time? If you have seen the show, you know that SpongeBob is an underwater creature (a sponge), and Sandy is a squirrel (from Texas) who lives in an air-filled, underwater structure. SpongeBob did not appreciate the fact that he relied on water to survive until he stepped into Sandy's air-filled home, couldn't breathe, became brittle, and started to disintegrate. Similarly, most people do not recognize how much they rely on their culture until they find themselves immersed in somebody else's.

Whether we are aware of it or not, we rely on culture for almost everything we do. All our decisions—what clothes to wear, what to eat (and how to eat it), with whom to live, and what to do with our lives—are made based on our culture. Similarly, the languages we speak, the religion we follow, the sports team we root for, and our goals for what will make our lives "successful" are all heavily influenced by our culture.

Generally, sociologists divide the study of culture into the following three categories: (1) values—what members of society deem important, (2) norms—the rules and expectations for behavior that guide people as to how to act in society, and (3) artifacts (material culture)—the tangible objects that people from a particular culture create and use. If values are what we believe in, what we want, and how we think our lives should be, norms are the set of rules we have established that govern how we can achieve those things we value. The values and norms that a society establishes will then influence which artifacts members of that society will develop and how they will make and use them.

Values and norms are social constructions, constantly created and recreated through interaction. That is, values and norms are produced and reproduced by social processes, often without plan, discussion, or decision. We just get used to doing things in a certain way that has been taught to us and modeled through our culture. Values are often debated, but there is no forum in which to "vote" on society's values. These values change over time, and they differ from society to society. Although there are some values that are shared by many societies (e.g., most capitalistic societies value hard work, money, and material possessions), values are not universal. For example, when a very trim and physically fit person we know spent a year in a poor South Asian nation as a member of the Peace Corps, the villagers with whom she lived were constantly encouraging her to eat and gain some weight. The people there associated her thin figure with poverty, a condition to be pitied. Meanwhile, back in the United States, she often experienced just the opposite reaction from people around her. Many people envied her physique and wished they could have a similar one! When one of the authors traveled to Lesotho, a small country in southern Africa, he was using a cane due to an injury. In Lesotho, he discovered that people who walk with canes are the most respected members of the society, those who have earned the cane through their wisdom. There is only a limited number of canes (and other supplies) in these communities, so they are given first to the elderly, those viewed to be the wisest members of the community. On his return to the United States, the author was quickly reminded that having a cane in our country is a sign of injury and weakness—a stark contrast to the admiration and respect it brought him while in Lesotho.

Like values, social norms vary over time and from society to society. For example, in the contemporary United States, expected behaviors for men and women continue to change as new forms of interaction arise. Only a decade ago, it was commonly suggested that only desperate people might use the Internet to find a date, but "singles bars" were popular. Today, arranging dates through Internet services is much more socially acceptable or "normal." According to a recent poll, almost one-third of American adults know someone who has made use of an online dating service, and 15% of American adults say that they know someone who met their spouse/long-term partner online (Madden and Lenhart 2006). A brother of one of the authors met his wife online! Where people go on their dates also varies from culture to culture. One of the authors remembers being rather startled as she took a stroll at dusk through a park in Cuernavaca, Mexico, to find *every* park bench filled with young couples. Most young people there lacked the money to gain access to the private (or at least indoor) places people typically go on dates in the United States. The other author was surprised to find in his travels to the Maasai Mara region of Kenya that in some of the villages, uncles often arranged marriages between two young people who never even had the opportunity to meet prior to their wedding ceremony.

Girls and boys are also socialized differently in different cultures. For example, girls from one culture may be trained to hide their bodies, whereas those from another are taught to flaunt their physiques. While writing these words, one of us looked out the window of her New Jersey home and saw several women get out of their car to look at the house that was for sale next door. It was a hot August day, but the women were completely covered by dark robes. The driver wore black leather gloves that extended far up her arms and only her eyes were uncovered. Although many other people had stopped to look at the house without drawing much attention from the author, her focus was (momentarily) diverted to this group of prospective buyers because of the clothing the women wore. Their manner of dress indicated that they were members of a subculture, meaning that they are a part of the larger U.S. society but also part of a smaller group within it that has its own norms, values, and artifacts.

Exercise 4.1   Student Survival Guide

Pretend one of your classmates is new to the United States (and from a very different culture).

1. Make a list of what he or she will need to know about the dominant culture in the United States. Make sure to include explanations about clothing, food, music, television, and everything that a non-American might need to know in order to "make it" in the United States.

2. Once your list is complete, make a list of the norms and values that the items on your list represent.

3. Look at the list of norms and values and write a one-page essay analyzing what they tell us about American society.

4. Now, repeat this same exercise but pretend that you are writing it for a transfer student or an incoming first-year student to your campus who was born in the United States but who will need to adjust to the subculture on your campus.

Subcultures

To varying degrees, subcultures exist within dominant cultures (the culture upheld by the group that has the most power in a society). A subculture is a group of people with cultural patterns (values, norms, and artifacts) that distinguish them from the dominant culture. College students, firefighters, stay-at-home parents, first-generation Jamaican Americans, environmental activists, Mormon Americans, paraplegic athletes, white anti-racism activists, and working-class Americans are some of the many examples of subcultures in the United States. Chances are that *you* belong to one or more subcultures as well! Subcultures often arise around shared backgrounds. Italian Americans in an Italian enclave of a big city may form a subculture, whereas more "integrated" Italian Americans may not be a part of that group or may teeter between the subculture and the dominant culture. Subcultures also grow around shared activities. Surfers form one subculture, bikers another, and jugglers, perhaps, a third.

Yet sharing an activity is not enough to ensure the emergence of a subculture. There must also be times, places, activities, or habits that are shared by members of the group, and not by those in the dominant culture. There must be enough interaction for a common base of knowledge, habit, ritual, meaning, and values to develop. For example, college students, as a group, tend to share certain values, norms, and artifacts that are different from those of people who are not enrolled in college. They may value high grades instead of big paychecks (perhaps as a means to get big paychecks in the future), tend not to sleep during the same times of day (or for the same number of hours) as most Americans, and research and write papers instead of handling or crafting material goods for purchase. They may also share patterns of leisure activity and home furnishings that are not seen elsewhere.

Although they have some noticeably different ways of thinking and behaving, members of subcultures share the same *guiding* values, norms, and artifacts of the dominant culture. The things they do and think that distinguish them do not threaten or work against the dominant values, norms, and artifacts of their society. For example, your classmates on the football team and your classmates who are members of the College Republicans may learn to think and behave in some different ways. Through doing so, each group creates its own subculture. However, the majority of both college football players and College Republicans follow the dominant norms and share the dominant values of the school and the larger society. Likewise, first-generation immigrant Jamaican Americans may enjoy different types of food from the majority of Americans and may tend to be more family-oriented than Americans socialized only under the dominant American culture. However, both groups (albeit to varying extents) share and follow most of the primary values of U.S. culture (e.g., material success, progress, freedom, and hard work).

Members of subcultures both influence and are influenced by the dominant culture. For example, second-generation Jamaican Americans will tend to hold and follow dominant American values and norms more than their parents did. At the same time, the larger culture changes somewhat as immigrant groups interact with other members of society. The increasing variety of ethnic foods becoming common fare for many Americans is a good example of how norms (in this case, what most Americans eat) change as the demographic makeup of the United States changes.

Countercultures

Groups of people who have cultural attributes that *oppose* those of the dominant culture are known as members of a counterculture. Such groups can be peace-loving, like the "flower children" of the 1960s, or willing to use violence, such as the Ku Klux Klan (KKK) and neo-Nazis. Members of countercultures often find it difficult to avoid violent confrontations (and some incite them), simply because they stand in direct opposition to some of the core values, norms, and artifacts of the dominant culture. The violence that erupted during the American Indian movement (led by the group called AIM) of the early 1970s provides a good example of how the opposition of dominant and countercultural values and norms can lead to violent clashes. AIM is a countercultural group with views that directly challenge many of the dominant U.S. values and norms, such as individual ownership of property and faith in the integrity of the U.S. justice and political systems. AIM's goals include a review of more than 300 treaties signed between Indian nations and the U.S. government (that the AIM leaders argued were broken by the U.S. government), autonomy for tribal governments, and a return to the traditional culture of the Native American nations.

Those who challenge dominant cultural rules, beliefs, and values can face dramatic and harsh reactions by those who adhere to the dominant culture. For example, when many of the dominant U.S. values and norms (individual ownership of property, faith in the U.S. justice and political systems) were directly challenged by AIM, the U.S. government responded to this threat with powerful efforts to stop AIM by jailing leaders and surrounding protest enclaves with heavy weaponry, which resulted in several shootouts. One member of AIM, Native American political activist Leonard Peltier, was convicted and imprisoned for murder 30 years ago. However, he is widely believed to be innocent of the crime for which he was convicted and thus is thought to be a political prisoner.[1]

Other countercultures include extreme religious organizations, cults, or other groups whose beliefs or goals place them in opposition to national laws. Such counterculture groups range from fundamentalist Mormons[2] who believe in polygamy, to radical Islamic groups such as Al Qaeda and extreme right-wing Christian fundamentalists[3] who use terrorism to promote their beliefs. All countercultural groups reject the dominant values, norms, and artifacts, and seek out different ways of living. In some cases, they also try to impose their own culture against the will of the other members of society.

Recognizing Cultural Patterns

Now that we know what comprises a culture, we can begin to look for the patterns that help us to recognize the dominant norms, values, and artifacts of different cultures, subcultures, and countercultures. Members of almost any group of people who gather together on a regular basis create their own subculture. Think of your own groups of friends. You probably have ways of speaking to one another, in-jokes, and perhaps even modes of dress that set you apart, somewhat, from the rest of society or at least the immediate dominant culture in which you live. The same is true for the group of people who comprise your school's student body. Every campus has its own subculture(s). You have probably heard people talking about the "campus culture." What they are referring to are the values, norms, and artifacts most people on your campus share, which are often different from those found on other campuses or in the town where your campus is located.

Every college or university has a reputation that is, in part, derived from the campus culture. For example, one of the authors received her undergraduate degree at a school known for its strong liberal arts education, Catholicism, heavy drinking among the student body, commitment to social justice, and the ability to bring wealthy Catholics together to improve society and network effectively. As you can see, although we often speak of "the culture" of a community, it is clear that contradictory norms and values can exist within one culture or subculture.

The campus culture at this author's alma mater included valuing sports, competition, academic achievement, friendship, practicing the Catholic faith, working for social justice, and partying (not necessarily in that order). Some of the dominant norms were studying, playing sports, volunteering to help those in need, attending Mass, hanging out with friends, hooking up (rather than dating), drinking lots of beer, and wearing J. Crew clothing (not necessarily in that order). The artifacts of the campus included finely manicured lawns (award-winning, in fact); a well-financed and popular Campus Ministry office; beautifully maintained old buildings (including chapels) in which to study, learn, and pray; cramped on-campus housing; run-down off-campus apartments to party in nearby; and J. Crew clothing on almost every student on campus. These artifacts are more than just objects; they are manifestations of the values (some contradictory) of the college and the collective membership of the college community. The finely manicured lawns reflected a value of spending money on campus aesthetics rather than, for example, using some of that money to offer more scholarships to students from poor families. The Campus Ministry office, on the other hand, is indicative of the school's emphasis on Catholic social teaching and work for social justice.

Exercise 4.2   Campus Culture: Seeing What's Around Us

In an approximately three-page paper, answer the following questions:

1. Think about your own campus. List five of the dominant values on your campus. Now list five dominant norms and five artifacts that reflect those values or contradict them.

2. Do you think your campus culture is different from or typical of most college campus cultures? How do you know this, or why don't you know enough to answer this question?

3. Identify some of the visible subcultures on campus. What makes each a subculture, rather than just a bunch of people who have something in common?

4. Do you feel as though you are part of the dominant culture on campus? A subculture? A counterculture? Some of these? All of these? Explain.

5. Why is a campus culture important? How does it influence how you spend your time and energy in college?

6. Do you think the campus culture has encouraged you to become a more active citizen? Are you engaged with activities on campus? Off campus? Why or why not? If not, is there something in your campus culture that has *discouraged* your active citizenship? If there is, what is it and what do you think might help to change this type of culture?

Exercise 4.3   A Consumer Culture?

1. Write down an extensive list of what material goals you hope to achieve by the age of 30 (car or cars, house, wardrobe, lifestyle, etc.). Or, if you are an older student, what do you hope to achieve by the next relevant decade?

2. Listen to these two stories from National Public Radio: "Overspent," at www.npr.org/templates/story/story.php?storyId=1007060 and "Activist Asks, 'What Would Jesus Buy?'" at www.npr.org/templates/story/story.php?storyId=11272527.

3. Outline the major points made by the experts interviewed for the NPR stories.

4. Now, analyze your own consumeristic goals in light of the arguments made on the NPR shows. Why do you think you have the consumeristic goals that you have? What in American culture drives you in your quest for material success? Are there any downsides to having these consumeristic goals? What do cultures that emphasize consumerism less than ours have that you find to be enviable, if anything?

5. How, if at all, has the economic recession that began in 2008 impacted your material goals? Elaborate.

Extra Credit: If you have concluded that Americans are too steeped in a consumeristic culture, create a campaign to educate your campus about the issue. Produce a fact sheet to help argue your case with information you can find at www.newdream.org/consumer/index.php and www.adbusters.org or from other readily available sources on the Internet.

Exercise 4.4   A Consumer Culture During a Recession

Go to www.npr.org/templates/player/mediaPlayer.html?action=1&t=1&islist=false&id=101951259&m=101951254 and listen to "Op-Ed: 'Frugal Chic' Shouldn't Be for Everyone." Then answer the following questions:

1. What are the main points made in this story?

2. How do your own experiences relate to what you heard in the story?

3. Do you think the recession has impacted your level of materialism? Why or why not?

4. Do you think the recession has impacted/will impact the overall culture of U.S. society? Why or why not? If yes, do you think the impact will persist even once we are out of the recession? Why or why not?

5. How do you think your own social class influences your answers to questions 2–4?

Campus Culture and Civic Engagement

Studies examining the political culture in the United States reveal that most people are not politically engaged (Pew Research Center 2007; Skocpol 2003). Far less than half of the eligible electorate vote in most elections (McDonald 2007). Few know the issues for which candidates stand. Many do not even know the names of their elected officials. In a recent survey at the university where one of the authors works, fewer than half of the students could name the vice president of the United States. Only a handful of the hundreds surveyed could name one of their senators. Less than a handful knew the name of their representative. Political knowledge appears not to be valued, and political participation is not the norm on that campus.

Nina Eliasoph, a sociologist and the author of *Avoiding Politics: How Americans Produce Apathy in Everyday Life* (1998), provides some clues as to why so many Americans avoid civic engagement and why even those who volunteer their time to do good work avoid political conversation. Intensive participant observation of several volunteer and activist organizations led her to determine that our culture *teaches us* that political discussions and activism are divisive, fruitless, negative exercises that should be skirted, if at all possible. In her research, she looked for patterns in the behavior and conversations of members of several volunteer civic and recreational organizations to determine the dominant values and norms of the groups. However "civic" the groups might have been, they did not foster a culture in which members would discuss and debate issues of political significance. The few members of the groups who did bring up political topics of conversation in a "public" setting (in the group, rather than in private conversation) or who did suggest taking political action (other than the "normal" actions on the issues that the activist groups pursued) were discouraged from doing so. It appears to be a norm in American culture to make displays of consensus rather than broach important topics over which people might disagree.

The good news is that civic engagement does seem to be on the rise on college campuses. The Obama campaign drew more young people into politics during the 2008 presidential election and led to a 4–5% increase in voters under the age of 30 (CIRCLE 2009). Today, student activism for social and environmental justice causes can also be found on campuses all over the United States. For example, on April 1, 2009, at colleges such as University of North Carolina, Asheville, and University of Kentucky, students participated in Fossil Fools Day, an environmental demonstration day in which citizens in the United States, Canada, United Kingdom, and South Africa carry out protest actions to encourage the use of energy alternatives to fossil fuel (National Student News Service 2009; also see www.fossilfoolsdayofaction.org/2009/category/front-page). In February 2008, colleges and high schools across the United States participated in the National Campus Energy Challenge to create sustainable energy policies on campuses.[4] Every March, tens of thousands of students take a 24-hour "Vow of Silence" to raise consciousness and funds for youth around the world whose voices are silenced due to their lack of human rights (see Free the Children at http://we.freethechildren.com/campaign/vow-of-silence).

By 2005, the "Boot the Bell" campaign, which demanded that Taco Bell and its parent company, Yum, stop the practice of indentured servitude and increase the wages of tomato pickers, had spread to more than 300 college and university campuses when it ended in victory. As of 2009, there were 250 high schools, colleges, and universities affiliated with the Students Against Sweatshops–sponsored Worker Rights Consortium (WRC), an organization that monitors the enforcement of the Codes of Conduct signed by colleges and universities to ensure that clothing with their schools' logos is made in sweat-free factories. As discussed in Chapter 1, students at many schools (e.g., Wayne State University, Florida State University, the University of Pennsylvania, the State Universities of New York, the University of Arizona, Boston College, Duke University, and Georgetown) have convinced their university administrators to stop buying apparel made in sweatshops and to have the WRC monitor the operation of the apparel factories they use (to prevent abuses of workers). Many students across the country have also made their campuses *divest* (withdraw all investments) from any corporations that are doing business with the genocidal regime in Darfur, Sudan. As of early 2009, there were over 800 high school and college chapters of the STAND organization, which organizes students to stand up against genocide in Darfur, Burma, the Democratic Republic of Congo, and throughout the world.

University administrative leaders also now realize the importance of teaching students how to effectively fulfill their obligations as citizens. Today, 231 state colleges and universities participate in the American Democracy Project, which focuses on providing service learning opportunities for students. In addition, more than 565 college and university presidents have signed the Campus Compact pledge to "educate citizens." Over 600 U.S. institutions of higher education have signed on to the American College and University Presidents' Climate Commitment to reduce global warming and "green" their campuses. Sociology students can use the tools of the discipline to be at the forefront of these efforts and make sure they are carried out in effective and just ways.

SOCIOLOGIST IN ACTION: DOUG McADAMS

Doug McAdams (1988), a professor of sociology at Stanford University, used sociological research to figure out what compelled so many (predominantly white and middle-class) Northern college students to go to Mississippi to help register black voters during the famous "Freedom Summer" of 1964. Of the 961 who applied to work as part of the Student Nonviolent Coordinating Committee's drive to register black voters, McAdams found that the 720 who actually followed through and went to Mississippi (as compared to the 241 who did not) were much more likely to have had previous experience in civil rights activities and social activist organizations (many church-related) as well as connections to other Freedom Summer participants. These results indicate that those who were willing to risk their lives, at that time, to register black voters were part of a subculture with norms that supported social activism and efforts to promote civil rights.

| Exercise 4.5 | Political Culture Data Collection for Dorm Dwellers |

Use participant observation to examine the political culture in your dorm.

1. Look at your dorm's list of organized events (social events, lectures, etc.) as well as unorganized, spontaneous events, and attend as many of them over the course of 1 month as possible.

2. Try to participate in as many informal discussions as possible with your dorm mates during the same month.

3. At each gathering, carefully note the following: (a) what type of gathering it is (friends studying together, watching a movie, gossiping about relationships, or, if it's a dorm event, the topic of the event, etc.), (b) how many times political topics were raised (if at all), (c) how many times political issues could have fit into the conversation but were not raised,

(Continued)

(Continued)

(d) the reactions of others if and when political topics were raised (Did the person who raised them receive positive or negative feedback/sanctions?), and (if political topics were raised) (e) whether someone mentioned participating in a political action to address the topic, and (f) the reaction to that suggestion.

4. What do your findings indicate about the political culture in your dorm?

Extra Credit: Devise a plan to make your dorm a place that is more welcoming and even encouraging for political discussion. Be thoughtful, strategic, and specific.

Exercise 4.6	Participant Observation of a Political Protest or Other Political Event

Conduct a participant observation of a political event on campus.

1. Find out what student activist groups (officially recognized or ad hoc) exist on campus by talking to other students, professors, people in the campus activities office, and so forth.

2. Choose an organization whose goals you feel comfortable supporting. Do not "infiltrate" a group by misrepresenting your own views.

3. Participate in organizing and carrying out at least one campus event (protests count).

4. Throughout your time with the group, take note of how political issues are discussed. Do they represent dominant culture, subculture, or counterculture values and norms? Elaborate.

5. Which conversational topics are encouraged and which are discouraged (result in sanctions) in the group?

6. What are the reactions to the efforts of the group from fellow students, professors, professional staff, and administrators?

7. What do your answers to the questions above tell you about the norms and values of (a) the culture of the group in which you participated and (b) your campus culture?

Exercise 4.7	**Environmental Values and United States Policy**

Do dominant U.S. *values* about the environment match U.S. *policy* on the environment?

1. Go to the Web site www.publicagenda.org and click on "Issue Guides" and then on "Environment."

2. Pick an issue under the Environment Issue Guides that you believe relates to a dominant value in U.S. culture.

3. Peruse the information available and write a paper that answers the following questions:

   a. What was the issue you chose to study and how does it relate to a dominant U.S. value?

   b. What were your own views on the issue before reading the information on the site, and how did you form your viewpoint on the issue (what aspects of your culture influenced your point of view)?

   c. Did your view on the issue change after reading the information on the site? Why or why not?

   d. Recommend several practical suggestions for working for change on the issue. Include a discussion of what can be done on your campus to work for change and what you can personally do.

Extra Credit: Based on your suggestions in 3(d), organize a student group to begin working for these changes.

Exercise 4.8	**Globalization: The Great Cultural Divider?**

Go to David Brooks' column "All Cultures Are Not Equal" at http://query .nytimes.com/gst/fullpage.html?res=990CE2DA143EF932A2575BC0A9639C8 B63 and answer the following questions:

1. Do you agree with Brooks that U.S. citizens are increasingly separating into distinct and isolated subcultures? Do you think that

(Continued)

(Continued)

this trend could lead (or has led) to more countercultures in the United States?

2. Write a one-page outline of how you would carry out research to test one (or more) of David Brooks' statements in the above article.

Discussion Questions

1. Can you recall a time when you gave discouraging feedback to someone who wanted you to engage in a conversation about political issues? If not, why not? If so, why do you think you discouraged the person?

2. Can you recall a time when someone gave you discouraging feedback when you attempted to engage in a conversation about political issues? If so, why do you think the person discouraged you? How did it make you feel? How do you think you could have approached that conversation in a way that would have been better able to engage that person in a discussion about political issues?

3. Do you think it's important to talk about political issues? Why or why not? If so, with whom?

4. How often do you talk to others about political issues? When you do, with whom do you usually discuss them? Why? With whom do you usually *avoid* discussing them and why? Are you willing and able to discuss politics in a public setting, or does it make you uncomfortable? Explain your answer.

5. Do you think political knowledge is valued on your campus? Provide examples to back up your answer.

6. Think about the dominant culture in the United States. What are some of the dominant norms, values, and artifacts that (a) encourage and (b) discourage political participation by Americans?

7. How do you know what your obligations are as a citizen? What are they? Who taught you what they are? How were you taught? When?

8. Do you think recycling is a norm on your campus? What makes you think so? If it is a norm, what do you think brought about the addition of recycling to the campus culture norms? If recycling is not now a norm on your campus, why do you think that is? What could you do to help promote recycling on campus?

9. What methodology would you use if you wanted to determine the norms, values, and artifacts that represent your campus's subculture? Why? What theoretical perspective would you use to guide your research and make sense of your findings? Why?

Suggestions for Specific Actions

1. Brainstorm with two or three of your classmates as to how you might promote civic engagement within the existing campus subculture. If you do not think it is possible to do this within the existing subculture, how might you change the subculture to promote civic engagement on campus? Act upon these ideas.

2. Organize a campus debate about a civic issue that affects the life chances (the chances one has to improve his or her social class position and quality of life) of students on campus. Analyze the campus culture to figure out how to most effectively promote and advertise the event (and do so!).

3. Conduct three focus groups (after obtaining proper Internal Review Board approval) that explore (a) how your fellow students define the ideal campus culture and (b) the actual dominant norms and values of the campus culture. Recruit interested members of the focus groups to come up with an action plan to disseminate and act on your findings.

Please go to this book's Web site at www.pineforge.com/korgen3e to find further civic engagement opportunities, resources, peer-reviewed articles, and updated Web links related to this chapter.

Endnotes

1. Two of the most well-known books that supply information about the Peltier case are Jim Messerschmidt's *The Trial of Leonard Peltier* (1983) and Peter Matthiessen's *In the Spirit of Crazy Horse* (1983/1992).

2. The Church of Jesus Christ of Latter-Day Saints banned polygamy in 1890.

3. For example, Eric Robert Rudolph, member of the white supremacist Christian Identity movement, carried out the 1996 Centennial Olympic Park bombing and other bombings that targeted gay and lesbian Americans and abortion clinics.

4. For more information on the National Campus Energy Challenge, go to www.climatechallenge.org/ncec.

References

Brooks, David. 2005, August 11. "All Cultures Are Not Equal." *New York Times.* Retrieved May 19, 2009 (http://query.nytimes.com/gst/fullpage.html?res=990 CE2DA143EF932A2575BC0A9639C8B63).

CIRCLE. 2009. "Youth Voting." Retrieved February 13, 2009 (http://www.civic youth.org/?page_id=241).

Eliasoph, Nina. 1998. *Avoiding Politics: How Americans Produce Apathy in Everyday Life.* Cambridge, UK: Cambridge University Press.

Madden, Mary and Amanda Lenhart. 2006, March 5. "Online Dating." Pew Internet and American Life Project. Retrieved May 14, 2009 (http://www.pewinternet.org/Reports/2006/Online-Dating.aspx).

Matthiessen, Peter. [1983] 1992. *In the Spirit of Crazy Horse.* New York: Viking Press.

McAdams, Doug. 1988. *Freedom Summer.* New York: Oxford University Press.

McDonald, Moira. 2007, March. "Getting Out the Vote." *State Legislatures* 33(3):5.

Messerschmidt, Jim. 1983. *The Trial of Leonard Peltier.* Boston: South End Press.

National Student News Service. 2009. "Campuses Take on International Fossil Fools Day." Retrieved May 14, 2009 (http://www.nsns.org/news/campuses-take-on-international-fossil-fools-day).

Pew Research Center. 2007, April 15. "Public Knowledge of Current Affairs Little Changed by News and Information Revolutions—What Americans Know: 1989–2007." Retrieved April 29, 2008 (http://people-press.org/reports/display.php3?ReportID=319).

Skocpol, Theda. 2003. *Diminished Democracy: From Membership to Management in American Civic Life.* Norman: University of Oklahoma Press.

5

Learning How to Act in Society

Socialization

Would you like to make someone smile? Smile at the person! It's almost impossible not to smile back when someone is smiling at you. A smile is one of the first symbols we learn to use to communicate with others.

Babies learn to smile by interacting with their caregivers who (often) smile at them as they play with, change, and feed them (see Messinger 2005; Venezia et al. 2004). They quickly learn that smiling can make their parents happy (and, in particular, happy with them). The second daughter of one of the authors learned this trick, to great effect, when she was an infant. She could even get her exhausted parents to smile while changing her at 3:00 AM. After fumbling their way to the changing table, they would look down to see her beaming at them with a big grin. Even those *very* sleep-deprived people couldn't resist the urge to smile back at the baby who had just awakened them from their slumber. How could they not? She looked so happy to see them!

On a more somber note about learned behavior, have you heard the tragic story of Isabelle, a girl who was kept locked in a closet until she was 6 years old (Davis 1947)? When she was finally released, her behavior was like that of an untrained animal. She didn't know how to speak, eat with utensils, use a toilet, or even smile. Her lack of interaction with other humans had prevented her from going through a process of *socialization,* the way in which we learn how to interact effectively in society. Isabelle's experience (and that of other children deprived of social interaction) indicates that human contact and social interaction are crucial for proper human development.

The Looking-Glass Self

Everyone around us influences our self-perception and our behavior in some way. The early symbolic interactionist Charles Horton Cooley (1902) described how others affect our self-image with the term *looking-glass self*. By this, he meant that we perceive ourselves based on how we *think* others see us. For instance, the authors of this book often find ourselves experiencing the looking-glass self when teaching a class. It is part of the job of a professor to continuously discern whether or not students understand a lecture and are engaged with the subject matter. Often, when we look out at our classes and see blank expressions, we assume this means the class does not understand what we are saying. We may react to this by re-explaining the concept or trying to find a new way to present it. But what if the students are exhibiting the blank expressions because the concept was simple and the professor had already spent too much time on it? (Or what if they look that way because it's how they look when they are watching television, and they have blurred the difference between a recorded broadcast and a live interaction?) What Cooley's looking-glass self demonstrates is that our actions and behaviors are reactions to our *interpretations* of the people, objects, and situations we encounter.

What matters in the above scenario is *not* what the students are actually thinking, but what the professors *think* they are thinking. This interpretation leads to subsequent behaviors, in this case reiterating a concept that the students already understood! Cooley's theory can best be summed up this way: "I am not what I think I am and I am not what you think I am. I am what I think you think I am."

The Generalized Other

George Herbert Mead established a theory of social behavior to show how individuals' personalities are developed through social experience. According to Mead (1913), we develop a *self* (the part of our personality that is a combination of self-image and self-awareness) by (a) interacting with others through the use of symbols and (b) being able to see ourselves through the perspective of others. "It is out of this conduct and this consciousness that human society grows" (Mead 1918:578).

Eventually, through social interaction, we complete our creation of the social self by developing a sense of how we might be seen through the eyes of any person (the *generalized other*) who espouses the prevailing norms and values of the society in which we live. We find ourselves watching and judging our own actions through the eyes of this generalized other, even when no other is present. Ultimately, we internalize the awareness of how our behaviors *seem* socially. Our personal identities, therefore, contain our sense of who we are in society. No self can develop without social interaction.

The Id, the Superego, and the Ego

Sigmund Freud developed a theory of personality in the early 1900s that has influenced almost all studies of human personality since then. A crucial part of his work was to explore the role of the *unconscious* in human identity and behavior. He broke down the unconscious into three sections: the id, the superego, and the ego. According to Freud (Freud and Strachey 1949/1989), the *id* consists of people's innate desires and urges (which are primarily centered on instant gratification, especially through sex and violence). The *superego* is the part of our unconscious that has internalized the dominant norms and mores of society (particularly what comprises "right" and "wrong" behavior). It represents our awareness of others, especially their reactions to ourselves. The *ego* works to balance the desires of the id with the moral impulses of the superego. The ego is the part of the self with which we choose to act or not act on our desires. For Freud, the ego is constantly testing our sense of what we want against our sense of what is expected of us. Freud (2005) believed that "it is impossible to overlook the extent to which civilization is built up upon a renunciation of instinct" (p. 85). We learn about the dominant norms of society and how to balance them with our innate desires through socialization with other human beings.

Primary Socializing Agents

Of course, some people make more of an impact on us than others. These people tend to comprise or come from one or more of the primary socialization agents in our society. Today in the United States, there are five primary socializing agents: family, peers, education, the media, and religion.

Family

We cannot choose our parents, but they do have a tremendous influence over who we become. For most of us, from the moment we are born, our family members—particularly our parents—are those with whom we interact first and for the greatest amount of time. Whether a parent constantly tells us that we are mean and stupid or repeatedly praises us for being so caring and brilliant (or anything in between) can largely determine how we view ourselves (as dumb or smart) and how we behave (meanly or kindly). Similarly, being encouraged to be persistent and to keep working at difficult things until we succeed, or being scoffed at for failing to do things quickly, impacts how we will deal with challenging situations in the future. These lessons of socialization can influence what we become. For example, we are much more likely to put time and energy into our work if we believe we are smart and capable and that persistence pays off than if we think we are neither bright nor professionally competent if we don't get it "right" the first time.

Socialization also teaches us what we want (values) and helps to give us a roadmap to achieve these things (norms). We are not *born* as authors or Muslims or leaders or Republicans or _____ (fill in the blank). We *become* these things because our families and other socializing agents have socialized us into becoming them. Parents from different societies (with different values and norms) socialize their children in different ways. For example, parents in the United States are likely to teach their children to desire different things from what parents in other societies, such as those in Afghanistan, El Salvador, or even Canada, would teach.

Families also influence how we behave as public citizens. For example, young adults are more likely to vote if they have parents who discuss political issues with them (McIntosh, Hart, and Youniss 2007). Engaged parents often shape engaged young Americans. Youth activists and Free the Children founders Craig and Marc Kielburger discuss the ways their parents encouraged them to be global citizens from a young age, and offer great insight into how to raise civically engaged young people in their new book, *The World Needs Your Kid: How to Raise Children Who Care and Contribute* (Kielburger, Kielburger, and Page 2009).

Exercise 5.1	Family Influence and Civic Engagement

Think about how your family has influenced your level of civic engagement.

1. Did your parents and other family members discuss political issues with each other when they were around you (at the dinner table, over coffee, etc.)?

2. Did your parents and other family members discuss political issues with you when you were growing up? Do you discuss political issues with them now? Why or why not?

3. If yes to the above question, have they asked you to participate in political activities with them? Have you? If so, in what ways? How did those experiences influence your own view of the importance of civic engagement?

4. If your parents and other family members are not active citizens, why do you think they are not? What do you think might encourage them to become active?

5. Overall, how do you think your parents' and other family members' level of civic engagement affected your own level of civic engagement?

6. After taking a moment to really evaluate the implications of this, describe how you feel about your own level of civic engagement.

7. How will you influence your own children's political participation (when or if you have kids)?

Peers

Our peers also have a great effect on how we view ourselves, how we interact with others, and what we become. Who hasn't wanted to impress their friends, and who hasn't at some point or other taken on some of the values and norms of their peer group, even if sometimes they have contradicted the values of their families? As soon as we are able to interact with people outside of our family, we begin to be influenced by peers (those similar to us in terms of age, social class, etc.).

The children you played with in your neighborhood, school, sports teams, and so forth comprised your peer group as you were growing up. To varying degrees, our peers influence our self-perception and behavior in the same way our family does. It is through our associations with others who are "like us," our *peer reference group,* that we learn what people like us are like.

One Web site for a summer camp included a quote from a camper saying, "At school I'm a nerd, but here I'm cool." You have probably heard other stories of people growing up with two different peer groups (for instance, one that consists of classmates during the school year and campmates or children in the area where one vacations during the summer). The authors of this book are aware of one young man who remembers being perceived (and thinking of himself) as a cool kid and a jock when around summer friends and as a lonely loser when among school peers. As a result, he found himself acting out the roles attributed to him by the different groups. He kept to himself and was rather shy and aloof with his classmates but found himself leading his summer friends on wild adventures he never would have dreamed of pursuing during the school year. His self-perception actually became a self-fulfilling prophecy. He changed his behavior from one environment to the other to become the person he thought his peers saw. This young man's story is a great illustration of the looking-glass self. Both his self-perception and his behavior were strongly influenced by how he imagined his peers viewed him.

When one of the authors interviewed people who have both a black and a white parent for an earlier book project, she found that even people's racial identity could be influenced by how they think others view them. Phillip, a biracial young man whose physical features did not clearly indicate his racial background, adapted his racial identity to avoid getting beaten up in some of the rough neighborhoods in which he grew up. He described how his experience in a Puerto Rican and black inner-city neighborhood influenced his racial identity in the following way:

> I got beat up by [some] black kids for being half-white. I started saying, "No, no, no. I'm Puerto Rican. I'm Puerto Rican. I'm Puerto Rican." And then, next thing I know, it's all cool because of the fact that my uncle married a Puerto Rican woman. Another uncle of mine married a Puerto Rican. So that's two different sets of interbreeding and families, Puerto Rican, blacks, till it's all Puerto Rican. . . . I'm Puerto Rican.

Not only did Phillip change his declaration of racial identity, he actually began to believe that he was Puerto Rican instead of black and white. Supported by his Puerto Rican relatives and his ambiguous racial features, Phillip became Puerto Rican (Korgen 1999:73).

Exercise 5.2   Your Many Selves

Everyone acts (at least somewhat) differently among different groups of people. Write a one-page essay describing different situations in your life in which you act almost as though you are different people. Why do you act differently in these different situations? What role do you think the generalized other (Mead) and the looking-glass self (Cooley) play in socializing you into these different roles? Be specific and dig beneath the surface in your analysis.

Exercise 5.3   Peers and Civic Engagement

Think about how your peers have influenced your level of civic engagement.

  1. Do your peers discuss political issues with each other when they are around you?

2. Did your peers discuss political issues with you when you were growing up? Do you discuss political issues with your peers now? Why or why not?

3. Do your peers vote? Have you ever gone to the polls with a peer? If so, what was that like?

4. Are your peers civically active? If yes, in what ways? Have they asked you to participate with them? Have you? If so, in what ways? How did those experiences influence your own view of the importance of civic engagement? If they asked you to participate with them and you didn't, why didn't you? What do you think you might have lost out on by not participating? If your peers are not active citizens, why do you think they are not? What do you think might encourage them to become active?

5. Overall, how do you think your peers' level of civic engagement has affected your own activism?

Extra Credit: Read "The Youth Vote: Young and Powerful" from Rock the Vote, at www.rockthevote.com/act-out/field-kit/young-voter-facts.pdf. Having read this, does it change your perceptions about (a) the importance of voting, (b) whether you might vote in upcoming elections, or (c) the ways you and your peers talk (or don't talk) about politics?

Education

Institutions have multiple roles. Our educational experiences play a major, though often somewhat hidden, role in our socialization process. Schools serve the primary purposes of giving us the tools we will need to operate in society and socializing us to adapt to and follow the values that society has deemed most important. One of the goals of schools is to teach Americans a "hidden curriculum": to respect the rules of how our society operates, to not challenge the status quo, and to act in nondisruptive ways (ways that will not disrupt the dominant norms of society). For example, among the first things you learn in school are how to raise your hand, wait your turn, sit quietly, and follow directions. Many of these habits are useful skills that kids need to learn to interact with other people. Yet these same practices also reveal the school's need for children to be disciplined so that they can be managed in large numbers.

School also teaches the basic values and beliefs of our dominant culture (as outlined in Chapter 4). What we learn about different racial, ethnic, gender, and social class groups through our schools and textbooks (or what we *don't* learn because the information in school curricula and texts is limited and carefully selected) influences how we perceive and judge these groups throughout our lives. It also helps us understand our own social status and role in society.

Dominant (or popular) values and beliefs determine, to a great extent, what is taught in our schools at any given time. It is important to remember that history is taught through the perspective of the dominant groups in our society. An examination of how the portrayal of U.S. history has changed over the years (as different racial/ethnic groups have gained power in the United States) reveals this fact.

Exercise 5.4	**The Hidden Curriculum: History, Values, and Socialization**

Find a U.S. history book currently used at a local public grammar, middle, or high school.

1. Note the title of the book. What image does the title convey? Is there a photograph or illustration on the cover of the book? If so, what message does it convey?

2. Look at the table of contents. What topics are covered? Think of five additional chapters you think could or should have been included in the book. Why do you think they could or should have been included? Why do you think they were not included? What does your study of this textbook tell you, sociologically, about the values that the school's curriculum indicates are most important? Besides the need to keep textbooks a certain length, why else do you think that certain topics are not included?

3. Compare how different racial, ethnic, gender, and social class groups are covered (or not covered) in the book.

4. Compare the Civil War chapter in the history book you obtained with Howard Zinn's chapter on the Civil War in his book, *A People's History of the United States, 1492–Present* (2003)—your school library should have a copy, and you can find it online at http://libcom.org/a-peoples-history-of-the-united-states-howard-zinn/10-the-other-civil-war. What are the similarities? What are the differences? How do you think the differences relate to the "hidden curriculum" of the public school system in the United States?

5. How do you think members of different races and ethnicities, genders, and social classes would view their respective status positions and roles in society after reading each of the two chapters? What might they say is missing? What might they want to add?

Exercise 5.5   College and (Re)Socialization

Think back to when you were first accepted to college. As soon as you learned which college you would be attending, you most likely embarked on *anticipatory socialization*, during which you began to rehearse the new roles you would carry out as a college student. College is often a time for *resocialization*, when students learn to adapt to a different subculture and establish a new social identity. As noted in Chapter 4, college life in general, and each individual institution of higher learning in particular, has its own subculture. Each college has its unique set of norms, values, and artifacts, which students must become familiar with and adjust to in order to interact effectively on campus.

College, especially for students who attend a school with few, if any, people from their hometown, provides an opportunity to establish a new sense of self. For example, a shy, aloof high school student can become an outgoing, popular college student (or a popular high school student can become a shy college student) in the new setting of the college campus. Students have the chance to establish a new "self" when they are surrounded by people who have no preconceived view of them. Often, college can be like the summer camp experience of the boy described above who acted almost like a different person depending on whether he was with his school classmates or his summer friends.

Different environments impact the degree of resocialization needed. For example, a commuter student attending college for the first time will undergo less resocialization than a residential student because he or she will only be involved in *some* aspects of the culture of the campus. Also, a young adult who is active in a civic organization 2 days a week, like volunteering at a local nursing home or becoming an officer in a student group with a mission to create social change, will learn some new norms and values and become familiar with some new artifacts. This activity, though, will not necessarily completely change his or her sense of self. However, those who enter a *total institution*

(Continued)

(Continued)

(a setting in which all parts of one's life are directed by the institution), like the military or a prison, will undergo a more complete process of resocialization as they learn to adapt to a very different, all-encompassing environment. Their sense of who they are and how they are perceived by others changes radically as they adapt to this new environment.

1. Describe how you became resocialized when you began college. In doing so, be sure to answer the questions that follow.

2. What were some of the norms, values, and artifacts with which you had to become acquainted when you started college?

3. How do you think your status as a residential or commuter student impacted your degree of resocialization?

4. How do you think your race, social class, and gender impacted your degree of resocialization?

5. How did the college resocialization process influence your sense of self?

Media

The *media* refers to any instrument or "medium" that disseminates information on a wide scale. Among the various media outlets, television is arguably the most important socializing agent today. The average household in the United States has a television turned on for 8 hours and 14 minutes per day (Holmes 2007). During those hours, children are exposed to shows created by corporations to draw viewers to the advertisements they use to market their products before, during, and after the programs. Children's perspective of the world, therefore, is influenced to a considerable extent by a carefully selected set of images (in both the television shows and the advertisements) used to promote business for advertisers. Accurate or not, television shows are one of the major windows many Americans have on the world around them.

In a nation increasingly segregated by race, ethnicity, and social class, TV shows are also often the only way that some Americans are exposed to other groups of Americans. Our perceptions of different age, gender, racial, ethnic, and other groups, and our images of ourselves (remember the looking-glass self), are influenced by the way these groups are portrayed in the media.

Exercise 5.6	**Coverage of Social Activism on Television News Programs**

For this assignment, you will be conducting a content analysis of 10 news programs. Your focus will be on how these news programs cover social activism. Make 10 copies of the Content Coding Sheet (Figure 5.1, top). You will fill these charts in as you view your news programs. As you fill out these charts, there are a few rules:

1. You must view news programs during the same time slots (e.g., early morning, midmorning, afternoon, prime time, late night) on one particular channel (ABC, NBC, Fox News, CBS, PBS, BBC).

2. All 10 programs should be either local *or* national and international.

3. After having filled out your Content Coding Sheets, you will then fill out your Data Summary Sheet (Figure 5.1, bottom). This will give you overall numbers and percentages.

4. Once you have completed the data collection, join with three other members of your class to analyze your collective data (making sure that not all the members of your groups analyzed the same news programs). What do your results tell you about how social activism is portrayed on the news programs you examined? What does this tell you about how we are socialized to view social activists and social activism?

Religion

Americans are, overall, much more religious than citizens of other wealthy nations. Americans are twice as likely as Canadians and more than twice as likely as Japanese and Western Europeans to say that religion is "very important" to them (Pew Research Center 2002). According to a 2009 Gallup poll, 42% of Americans say they "attend religious services every week or nearly every week" (Newport 2009). Meanwhile, less than 10% of residents of France and Germany and between 10 and 15% of residents of Belgium, the Netherlands, Luxembourg, and the United Kingdom are weekly churchgoers (Manchin 2004).

Those who attend religious services and read religious writings are exposed to teachings about certain ways to view and act in the world that influence how they view themselves and interact with others. For example, many of the student activists who participated in the "Freedom Summer"

Figure 5.1   Content Coding and Data Summary Sheet

Content Coding Sheet

Type of social activism: _____

Name of news program: _____

Station viewed on (provide channel and network): _____

Local or national/international: _____

Time of day (AM or PM): _____

Note the number of examples of social activism covered and note the type—for example, (a) violent or peaceful, (b) disruptive or nondisruptive—and how it is portrayed (positively or negatively) by checking under the appropriate columns.

Examples of Activism	Violent	Peaceful	Disruptive	Nondisruptive	Positively	Negatively
1						
2						
3						
4						
5						

Data Summary Sheet

News program: _____

Station/network: _____

Local or national/international: _____

Time of day: _____

Type of Activism	Number Portrayed	
	Positively	Negatively
Violent		
Peaceful		
Disruptive		
Nondisruptive		
Total		

during the civil rights era did so because they were motivated by the Christian ethic of brotherly love they learned from attending religious services and participating in religious organizations (McAdam 1988). Similarly, Andrew Goodman and Michael Schwermer, both of whom were murdered in the violence of the Freedom Summer, were driven toward creating social justice by the values they learned through their Jewish upbringing.

In terms of civic activism, what may be as important as the message people receive from their religious leaders is their interactions with others in their religious community. Belonging to a religious group increases the number of friends people have and their opportunities and inducements to join in civic activities. There is a unique moral pressure to join the efforts of those in your faith community. As Robert Putnam puts it, "being asked to do something by a member of your congregation is different from being asked to do something by a member of your bowling league" (quoted in Burke 2009).

However, the number of Americans unaffiliated with a religious group has climbed rather dramatically over the past few years. Today, 16% of Americans are religiously unaffiliated. This does not mean that they are necessarily against religion, however. Approximately one-third of the unaffiliated who were raised as Catholic or Protestant maintain that they have just not found the "right" religious organization (Pew Forum on Religion & Public Life 2009). Not being affiliated with a religious organization, as Putnam points out, also means that they are not exposed to the types of organized civic engagement opportunities that often come with being a member of an organized religious group (quoted in Burke 2009).

Exercise 5.7   Young Voters Matter

Listen to "Young Voters Learn They Matter" at www.npr.org/templates/story/story.php?storyId=17931655 and then answer the following questions:

1. If you were old enough at the time, did you vote in the 2008 U.S. presidential (a) primary and (b) general election? Why or why not?

2. In general, how much attention did you pay to the election? Why? How aware were you of where each of the candidates stood on the major issues (e.g., the war in Iraq, health care, global warming, the economy)? Why? Where did you get your information?

3. Would you consider traveling to meet a presidential candidate in person? Why or why not?

(Continued)

(Continued)

4. Have you ever worked or would you consider working for a political candidate running for office? Why or why not?

5. Would you consider running for political office yourself? Why or why not? If yes, which one? Why?

6. Based on both your own experiences and what you learned in this NPR story, if you were to advise a presidential candidate on how to turn out the youth vote, what would you suggest that he or she do?

SOCIOLOGIST IN ACTION: SCOTT MYERS-LIPTON

In the following paragraphs, sociologist Scott Myers-Lipton describes how he and students in his courses sparked a social movement to address the poverty and suffering in Louisiana.

Social Change Through Policy-Driven Service-Learning

In November of 2006, a group of 40 San José State University students and faculty held a campus "Poverty Under the Stars" sleep-out in solidarity with the over 7,600 homeless people in Silicon Valley, one of the wealthiest communities in the world. What bound these students together was their concern for the poor and their commitment to social action.

Many of these students were either enrolled, or had been in enrolled, in my Sociology Social Action course, which is an action-oriented, solutions-based, course on community activism. Instead of just reading about how others changed social policy, students actually choose a social policy and then try to implement it. Importantly, they integrate the knowledge gained from this action with sociological concepts such as stratification, institutionalized racism, internal colonialism, and the feminization of poverty.

As part of "Poverty Under the Stars," students gathered in the center of campus to watch Spike Lee's movie *When the Levees Broke: A Requiem in Four Acts*. After each act of the movie, the students talked about the social suffering they witnessed as a result of Hurricane Katrina and the poorly designed levee system. These conversations about the racial and social class dimensions of Katrina continued late into the night.

The following morning during my Wealth, Poverty, and Privilege course, the topic was on New Deal public works projects during the Great Depression. We were moved by the suffering of the Katrina victims and inspired by the efforts of the Civil Works Administration during the Great Depression. During that class, the students and faculty decided to launch the Gulf Coast Civic Works Project (GCCWP) and call for federal legislation based on it to address the poverty and suffering in Louisiana.

Since that class three years ago, students from over 50 colleges have participated in GCCWP events, such as: (a) "Louisiana Winter," which was inspired by Mississippi Freedom Summer, and brought almost 100 students from 15 colleges together to listen to residents throughout the region about what they would like in a federal bill, (b) a national Post-Katrina Summit involving 43 campuses, (c) a national campus sleep-out engaging 6 campuses, and most recently, (d) an Advocacy Day on Capitol Hill. These activities, which have been supported by service-learning courses across the nation, led to the introduction into Congress of the Gulf Coast Civic Works (GCCW) Act of 2009.

If enacted, the GCCW Act will create and provide (a) a minimum of 100,000 good jobs and training opportunities for local and displaced workers to rebuild hospitals, roads, schools, parks, police and fire stations, water and sewer systems, and workforce housing, (b) a civic conservation corps for youth aged seventeen to twenty-four to focus on wetland restoration, forestation, and urban greenery, (c) summer and after-school employment or training opportunities for youth aged twelve to nineteen, (d) oversight and transparency through Local Advisory Boards, and (e) grants for artistic projects to highlight Gulf Coast culture and history and to chronicle the stories from the hurricanes. The program has been conceptualized from the very beginning as a pilot project. The hope is that if it works in the Gulf Coast, the GCCW Act could be used as a model to help solve the economic crisis by creating jobs and rebuilding the nation's dilapidated infrastructure.

The GCCW campaign has now gained support from more than 130 Gulf Coast and national organizations. It has also demonstrated that a service-learning project, in collaboration with community organizations, can bring about major social change. At the same time, the students involved in the project have deepened their sociological imagination in understanding, as C. Wright Mills did, that "personal troubles cannot be solved merely as troubles, but must be understood in terms of public issues." This type of transformation—on both the individual and societal level—is what the founders of the service-learning movement had in mind.

Reprinted with permission from Paradigm Publishers. This excerpt previously appeared in Scott Myers-Lipton, *Rebuild America: Solving the Economic Crisis Through Civic Works* (2009, Boulder, CO: Paradigm Publishers).

Discussion Questions

1. How do you think we can create a society in which citizens are socialized to become knowledgeable and effective participants?

2. In what ways did your socialization through each of the five primary socializing agents (family, peers, education, media, and religion) encourage you to become an engaged member of society? In what ways did each discourage you from becoming an engaged member of society?

3. Think about Cooley's concept of the looking-glass self. Do you see yourself as someone who can make a positive impact on society? Why or why not? In what ways has your own looking-glass self experience influenced this?

4. How might the world be different if our primary socializing agents did more to foster civic engagement among citizens?

5. Which primary socializing agents could most effectively foster civic engagement across the United States? Why?

6. What worldwide socializing agents might effectively encourage civic engagement across the globe?

7. Which of the following sociological theories, conflict, functionalist, or symbolic interactionist, would you find most useful if you were to conduct a study on political participation in the United States? Why?

8. Have your values and norms about environmental issues such as recycling or global warming (or the views of someone close to you) changed over recent years? If so, what were the social forces that led to this resocialization process?

9. Do you think you will go through a resocialization process after college? Why or why not?

10. When you became resocialized after starting college, did your political activism increase, decrease, or remain the same? Why? How does the culture of your college impact your response to this question?

Suggestions for Specific Actions

1. Determine whether or not your college or university has committed itself to the Educating Citizens movement and whether it has taken steps to teach its students to become knowledgeable, effective citizens. One way to do this is to find out if your president or provost has signed the Campus Compact pledge (found at www.compact.org/resources-for-presidents/presidents-declaration-on-the-civic-responsibility-of-higher-education), joined the American Democracy Project (www.aascu.org/programs/adp), or signed on

to some other such initiative to promote civic engagement in higher education. If he or she has, then compare the goals of the initiative with the results
you see on campus. Write a letter to your provost or president and your
school newspaper that includes the results of your research. If your school
has not embarked on such a mission, write a letter to your provost or president that explains what the Educating Citizens movement is about (after having looked at the Campus Compact and American Democracy Project Web
sites) and ask what steps your school has taken to encourage well-informed
and effective citizens.

2. Explore the institutional connections your college or university has established
   with the surrounding community (e.g., service-learning courses, school-sponsored
   community centers, school-sponsored tutorial programs, research partnerships
   between professors and community members, etc.), and write a letter to your
   local paper that summarizes your key findings (to help inform the campus and
   community about these matters).

3. Participate in one of the events your university uses to connect to the local community (sponsoring a community fair, volunteering to work in a soup kitchen or
   a local school, etc.). Use your sociological eye to examine the power dynamics
   behind how the event or program is coordinated through the school and community. For example, who designed the program (the school or community or
   both)? Who coordinates the program? Who has authority over the program?
   Who funds the program? How do you think this type of coordination influences
   the overall program?

4. Set up an interview with the person who coordinates the orientation program for
   first-year students at your university. Inquire as to (a) how orientation socializes
   students into successfully learning and adopting the campus rules, norms, and values, and (b) what mechanisms are used during the orientation process to socialize
   new students into the role of educated and engaged citizens. If no such mechanisms exist (or the ones that do exist are inadequate), offer some suggestions
   about what could be put into place to the person who coordinates the first-year
   orientation program.

Please go to this book's Web site at www.pineforge.com/korgen3e to find further
civic engagement opportunities, resources, peer-reviewed articles, and updated
Web links related to this chapter.

References

Burke, Daniel. 2009, May 13. "Religious People Make Better Citizens, Study Says."
    The Pew Forum on Religion & Public Life. Retrieved May 21, 2009 (http://pew
    forum.org/news/display.php?NewsID=18088).
Cooley, Charles Horton. 1902. *Human Nature and the Social Order*. New York:
    Schocken Books.

Davis, Kingsley. 1947, March. "Final Note on a Case of Extreme Isolation." *American Journal of Sociology* 52(5):432–37.

Freud, Sigmund. 2005. *Civilization and Its Discontents.* New York: Norton.

Freud, Sigmund and James Strachey, eds. [1949] 1989. *The Ego and the Id.* Translated by Joan Riviere. New York: Norton.

Holmes, Gary. 2007, October 17. "Nielsen Reports Television Tuning Remains at Record Levels." Nielsen Media Research. Retrieved September 23, 2009 (http://en-us.nielsen.com/main/news/news_releases/2007/october/Nielsen_Reports_Television_Tuning_Remains_at_Record_Levels).

Kielburger, Craig, Marc Kielburger, and Shelley Page. 2009. *The World Needs Your Kid: How to Raise Children Who Care and Contribute.* Vancouver, B.C., Canada: Greystone Books.

Korgen, Kathleen Odell. 1999. *From Black to Biracial: Transforming Racial Identity Among Americans.* Westport, CT: Praeger.

Manchin, Robert. 2004, September 21. "Religion in Europe: Trust Not Filling the Pews." Gallup.com. Retrieved June 3, 2009 (http://www.gallup.com/poll/13117/Religion-Europe-Trust-Filling-Pews.aspx).

McAdam, Doug. 1988. *Freedom Summer.* New York: Oxford University Press.

McIntosh, Hugh, Daniel Hart, and James Youniss. 2007. "The Influence of Family Political Discussion on Youth Civic Development: Which Parent Qualities Matter?" *Political Science & Politics* 40(3):495–99.

Mead, George Herbert. 1913. "The Social Self." *Journal of Philosophy, Psychology, and Scientific Methods* 10:374–80.

Mead, George Herbert. 1918. "The Psychology of Punitive Justice." *American Journal of Sociology* 23:577–602.

Messinger, Daniel. 2005. "A Measure of Early Joy? Afterword to the Republication of 'All Smiles Are Positive, But Some Smiles Are More Positive Than Others.'" Pp. 350–53 in *What the Face Reveals: Studies of Spontaneous Facial Expression Using the Facial Action Coding System (FACS).* 2nd ed. Edited by Paul Ekman and Erika Rosenberg. New York: Oxford University Press.

Newport, Frank. 2009, March 23. "Despite Recession, No Uptick in Americans' Religiosity."Gallup.com. Retrieved June 3, 2009 (http://www.gallup.com/poll/117040/Despite-Recession-No-Uptick-Americans-Religiosity.aspx).

Pew Forum on Religion & Public Life. 2009, April 19. "Faith in Flux: Changes in Religious Affiliation in the U.S." Retrieved May 21, 2009 (http://pewforum.org/docs/?DocID=409).

Pew Research Center. 2002. "Among Wealthy Nations . . . U.S. Stands Alone in Its Embrace of Religion." Retrieved May 23, 2006 (http://people-press.org/reports/display.php3?ReportID=167).

Venezia, Meaghan, Daniel S. Messinger, Danielle Thorp, and Peter Mundy. 2004. "The Development of Anticipatory Smiling." *Infancy* 6(3):397–406.

Zinn, Howard. 2003. *A People's History of the United States, 1492–Present.* New York: HarperCollins.

6

Deviant Behavior
and Social Movements

What would be your reaction if you saw a man dressed in knee-length pants, wearing a wig, and snorting tobacco? Would you think his behavior deviant? Probably! However, sniffing tobacco and wearing a wig and breeches were once considered normal. In fact, in colonial America, engaging in such behavior demonstrated high social status. Our understanding of what is deviant behavior is socially constructed and, therefore, changes over time and from society to society.

Although behaviors such as incest and killing innocent people are considered deviant in almost all societies, much else of what is considered deviant behavior varies across cultures and time periods. Notions of what constitutes deviant behavior can also be situational. There are circumstances in which acts that would normally be considered completely beyond the bounds of acceptable behavior, including many brutal acts of violence, can come to be seen as normal and appropriate. For example, soldiers' reports and memoirs frequently include accounts of acts that may seem unjustifiable once the fighting has ended but had seemed acceptable, even necessary, in the midst of it. This chapter will discuss (a) how deviance is defined, (b) how the three major theoretical perspectives and other theories view deviance, (c) why some social groups are labeled as deviant, and (d) how some social movements have changed society by "normalizing" certain deviant behavior.

As you will recall from Chapter 4, cultural norms are socially constructed expectations for behavior. A society's norms include basic behaviors, manners and etiquette, laws and legal code, and the society's unique culture and ways of doing things. As members of a society, we learn which behaviors are appropriate through socialization. Our actions are guided by how we see others behave, what we are taught by our socializing agents, and the reactions of those with whom we interact.

Folkways are norms that are enforced through *informal rewards* and *sanctions* (such as approval or disapproval from others). For example, we follow folkways when we hold the door for someone behind us, let people we speak with finish his or her sentences without interruption, and make conversation with people we meet at parties. Violating these folkways might result in a dirty look or being considered rude, socially awkward, or strange. However, this type of deviant behavior hardly ever results in serious social consequences and never results in legal repercussions.

Mores, on the other hand, are those norms related to behaviors that reflect the values society holds most dear. Good sportsmanship, abiding by social and legal contracts, and adhering to certain sexual behaviors are all mores. Violating these norms results in much stronger reactions and, perhaps, criminal charges (many mores are supported by laws). For example, refusing to support a colleague in need, cheating on a girlfriend or boyfriend, or openly announcing you are bisexual often results in people expressing strong reactions that can have negative repercussions (e.g., being labeled as "not a team player" at work, as untrustworthy and selfish by friends, or being thought of as sexually abnormal by some).

The violation of our most powerful mores, those representing our deepest values (confining sexual relations to those not closely related, limiting our meat-eating to animals rather than other humans), are called *taboos*. Incest—sexual relations between close family members—is a taboo in almost all societies. Cannibalism—the practice of eating humans—is also widely considered to be a taboo. Those who carry out such acts are regarded as socially repugnant and face widespread, if not universal, condemnation from the other members of their society.

Laws are norms that are formalized rules of behavior enacted by legislatures and enforced by formal sanctions carried out by the criminal and civil justice systems. Laws provide guidelines as to what people should do (e.g., drivers should stop at stop signs, citizens should pay taxes, parents should send their children to school) and what they should *not* do (e.g., commit rape, robbery, or insurance fraud, or possess or use certain drugs). Those who break laws are subject to fines, imprisonment, and possibly even death.

Exercise 6.1   Nonverbal Sanctions

Next time you see someone give a nonverbal, negative sanction (a look of disgust, a shake of the head, or some other nonverbal sign of disapproval), ask yourself the following questions:

1. What norm is being broken (that is, what was the act that led the person to give a nonverbal negative sanction)?

2. What was the reaction of the norm-violator to the negative sanction?

3. What was your reaction to the interaction you witnessed between the norm violator and the person giving the negative sanction?

4. Why do you think you reacted this way? How did your own socialization process influence your reaction?

Exercise 6.2   Breaching Folkways

Often, we are so used to following the norms of society, we forget that we *could* behave differently. Harold Garfinkel (1967), a sociologist most famous for his "breaching" experiments in which people would break folkways in order to expose them, had students do such things as act like boarders in their parents' home, offer to pay store clerks less or more money than the price indicated on an item, and question every statement a person made in a conversation. Through these experiments, his students challenged the norms of social interaction and, in the process, brought them to light.

Conduct your own breaching experiment on campus by carrying out the following steps:

1. The next time someone asks you how you are doing, after they say hello, tell them how you are *really* doing. In fact, take several minutes to thoroughly relate how you are feeling at that time.

2. Repeat Step 1 with four different people.

3. In a one- to two-page paper, describe (a) how the four people reacted to your experiment, (b) how you felt as you carried out the experiment, (c) how their and your reactions related to your relationship with them, and (d) what you learned about norms of interacting through carrying out this experiment.

Functionalism and Deviance

Émile Durkheim (1895/1982) established the functionalist perspective on deviance. He maintained that deviant acts and those who commit them actually serve several useful and necessary purposes, or functions, for society. Deviants can help to make the norms of society clearer to the majority population, unite the nondeviant members of society, and even promote social change.

Sometimes it is difficult to know what the norms of society are until we see someone punished for violating one. When some members of society are punished for committing deviant acts, the rules of society are clarified and reinforced for everyone. For example, seeing someone pulled over for speeding usually makes other drivers slow down. Observing a classmate punished for plagiarism helps students recognize that stealing someone else's words or ideas is unacceptable behavior and that those who do so are liable to be punished. We already knew that speeding and plagiarism are wrong, but seeing these mores violated reminds us of how important it is to abide by these rules and often (if only through fear of being punished) causes us to act as society wishes.

According to Durkheim (1895/1982), deviants can also unify members of society. When people see deviant behavior as a threat, they come together to punish and root out the deviant members of society. United, they can create social capital, a group of interconnected people who can rely on one another and work together to accomplish a goal. For example, in the mid-1990s, parishioners of St. Patrick's parish in Brockton, Massachusetts, became closely united when they organized to confront a prostitution and drug operation headquartered in abandoned buildings across the street from the church. The criminal activity centered in the abandoned buildings made the parishioners fearful when they came to the church, and they were tired of being afraid. They knew they really had to do something when the pastor was propositioned by a prostitute on the way to Mass! Working together, they compelled the city to take over the houses (in lieu of back taxes owed), raze them, and drive out those using them for deviant acts that made parishioners fear going to church. The experience of eliminating the deviants from their church neighborhood brought the parishioners closer together as they learned they could rely on one another and become a powerful force when united.

Bridging and Bonding Social Capital

The members of St. Patrick's parish were also able to make connections across the city of Brockton and join with the members of different religious organizations to address safety issues, such as crime, that all Brocktonians faced. In doing so, they showed the power of what is known as *bridging social capital*. They were able to make connections (bridges) among different religious groups in Brockton that enabled them to begin to know and work with one another effectively (social capital).

Social capital is often seen as a good thing. But when it works to bond members of a particular group to one another and isolate them from everyone else, rather than work as a bridge between groups, it can have negative effects. For example, Kraig Beyerlein and John Hipp (2005) found that crime rates in counties with greater percentages of residents affiliated with evangelical Protestant churches were consistently higher than those in counties with relatively high numbers of mainline Protestants and Catholics. Evangelical churches tended to create *bonding* social networks that unite their members but isolate them from the larger society, whereas mainline Protestants and Catholics tended to promote bridging social networks that connect them to other groups in the larger community. These bridging networks allowed members of different groups to unite and develop effective structures to combat and prevent criminal behavior.

The American people's response to the devastating effects of Hurricane Katrina in 2005 is another example of the positive function of deviant behavior and the importance of social capital. The *immediate* reaction of almost all Americans to the destruction Katrina wreaked was to contribute what they could to relief efforts. Individuals, and even whole cities (such as Houston), opened their arms to fellow Americans displaced by the hurricane and the failure of the levees. However, the relatively weak connection between the poor, predominantly black population of New Orleans and the federal government and powerful lobbying groups has contributed to the fact that, even years after Katrina, the city is still not fully repaired and remains vulnerable to future hurricanes.

Social Control and Crime

The present condition of New Orleans also provides a good example of the influence of social control on crime rates. According to *rational choice* theorists, people decide to either commit or not commit crimes based upon the perceived costs and benefits of such behavior. If the punishment for crime is fairly certain and harsh and the rewards for good behavior are reliable and enticing enough, crime rates should be relatively low. However, New Orleans' crime rate is extremely high. There are few rewards for good behavior. The school system is a wreck and jobs are scarce for the largely uneducated and unskilled population that remained in or returned to the city. Meanwhile, the police force is demoralized (many are still housed in trailers) and seemingly ineffective at stemming the spiraling crime and homicide rate in the city (Callebs and Marrapodi 2008). People they do catch committing crimes are often quickly let back out due to the under-funded "revolving door" criminal justice system. Thus, proper social controls are not in place well enough to bring down the high crime rates (Franks 2007).

Exercise 6.3	Race, Poverty, and Katrina

Listen to the story "Race, Poverty and Katrina" at www.npr.org/templates/story/story.php?storyId=4829446 and answer the following questions in a two- to three-page paper:

1. Why, in New Orleans, does water "flow away from money"?

2. Why do you think so many black residents of New Orleans lived in the areas of the city most devastated by Katrina and the failure of the levees?

3. Think about Weber's work on the connections among class, status, and party, discussed in Chapter 2. How are they reflected in (a) who was most harmed by Katrina and (b) the lack of willingness on the part of the federal government to protect and rebuild New Orleans?

Exercise 6.4	How Do You Explain Cheating?

1. Why do you, personally, think students cheat on your campus?

2. How would rational choice theory explain cheating on your campus? Do you think rational choice theory offers a good explanation? Why or why not?

3. Is there one or more important factors that rational choice theory overlooks? If so, what? Why do you think these factors are overlooked?

4. Based on your answers to questions 1 and 2, how would you propose to diminish cheating on your campus? Offer at least five practical suggestions.

Conflict Theory and Deviance

As you will recall from Chapter 2, Marxist and other conflict theorists maintain that society is made up of groups competing for power. In turn, they believe that norms and laws are largely created by and for the benefit of those who hold the most power in society. Marx argued that the members of the ruling class (the owners of the means of production) use every instrument at their disposal, including shaping norms and laws, to protect their interests. Therefore, the actions of the poor are more likely to be labeled as deviant and criminal than those of rich individuals or major corporations.

In *The Rich Get Richer and the Poor Get Prison*, Jeffrey Reiman (2003) uses the conflict perspective to argue that the criminal justice system is biased against poor people and in favor of wealthy individuals and corporations. He maintains that corporations actually do much more harm to society by committing acts that are not officially labeled "criminal" than do individuals by committing acts that are considered crimes. For example, preventable injuries and deaths resulting from or caused by unsafe workplaces (e.g., black lung disease, asbestos-based cancer, repetitive motion injuries, cave-ins in coal mines), unsafe medical practices (e.g., unnecessary surgeries, lack of proper medical care, drug interactions), environmental pollution (e.g., cigarettes, pollution from chemical and industrial factories), and lax oversight of consumer safety (e.g., defective tires, tainted meat) harm far more people than criminal acts carried out by individuals. However, they are relatively ignored by the judicial system, whereas the crimes of predominantly poor and minority citizens result in disproportionately severe punishments.

Symbolic Interactionism and Deviance

Symbolic interactionists maintain that people learn to conform to or deviate from the norms of society through their interactions with others. They stress that deviance is socially constructed and that deviant behavior is learned. Two of the most well-known theories on deviance that fall under the umbrella of the symbolic interactionist perspective are differential association theory and labeling theory.

Through his *differential association theory,* Edwin Sutherland (1947) maintains that people learn deviant behavior by associating with people who commit deviant acts. People tend to base their own behavior on the behavior of those with whom they interact. Therefore, those who are raised in families that violate social norms or spend much of their time with friends who break the norms of society will be more likely than others to act in deviant ways. For instance, one of the authors of this book is involved in a mentoring program, FAM (Friends and Mentors) for Change, for inner-city youth who are at high risk of not graduating from high school. The author's initial research results reveal that when these kids, who face negative situations at their schools or homes, are surrounded by external forces that may influence them in negative ways, they are much more likely to commit deviant acts than when they are spending time in the FAM for Change program, surrounded by more positive role models.

Labeling theory, another symbolic interactionist perspective on deviance, focuses on the categorization of people as deviant. Howard Becker (1963), the founder of labeling theory, maintains that behaviors and individuals only *become* deviant when people with some social power *label* them as deviant. Once people so labeled accept this categorization, they begin to consider themselves deviant and act accordingly. For example, when a young woman becomes known to others as a drug addict, ostracized by those who do not use illegal drugs, and given the label "druggie," she begins to socialize more and more with fellow "druggies" and to act like the "druggie" people perceive her to be. We can see the effects of this on high school campuses when kids who have been given a label that makes them outcasts (e.g., "losers," "nerds," "burnouts") begin to take on the qualities of that label, sometimes with violent results.

Labeling Some Social Groups as Deviant

As noted above, deviance is a *social construction,* which means that behaviors are not in themselves normal or deviant; they only become deviant when society defines them as such. Unfortunately, it is easy and common to define or perceive entire groups of people as deviant, rather than merely defining specific behaviors as deviant acts. For instance, *racial profiling* is a controversial practice in law enforcement that involves subjecting people to greater scrutiny, or treating some people as potentially dangerous, based on stereotypes and prejudices associated with their perceived race.

The state of New Jersey became a focal point for a national debate on racial profiling in the 1990s. Black motorists complained, and an independent review confirmed, that they were being pulled over for routine traffic stops, and even searches, far more often than members of other racial and ethnic groups, and often without cause (Lamberth 1994). A whole new term has even entered our collective lexicon to describe this unfair treatment: *Driving While Black.* A series of reviews followed, including a number of hearings in the New Jersey State Senate, resulting in the establishment of guidelines for law enforcement officers that point out that "any officer can unwittingly or subconsciously fall prey to racial or ethnic stereotypes about who is more likely to be involved in criminal activity" and mandate that officers work to counter this fact by focusing on people's conduct rather than their racial or ethnic appearance (New Jersey Division of Criminal Justice 2009).

Police and other law enforcement agencies have many forms of profiling at their disposal, most of which focus on behavior. A Rand Corporation commentary, "Racial Profiling: Lessons From the Drug War" (Riley 2002), criticizes racial profiling as ineffective. The report advocates "tactical profiling," which would focus on behaviors rather than identities. Law enforcement personnel using tactical profiling would look for reasons *not* to suspect people when making otherwise random stops and searches, rather than emphasizing reasons to target people.

Deviance and Organizing for Change

It is useful for the well-being and maintenance of society to construct norms and to recognize forms of deviance. Without these, we would need to navigate the basic rules of behavior in every situation we enter. How inefficient and chaotic that would be! However, social norms that reinforce the worldviews and interests of dominant groups (those in power) often act as repressive forces against the worldviews and interests of minority groups and all of those who would choose to deviate (even in harmless ways) from the dominant culture. Once a perspective takes on the veneer of "reality" or "truth" or "the right way," it is difficult to change. Usually, only concerted, organized effort can effectively counter such social forces. And the history of the United States is full of people doing just that—coming together to create the changes they desire for society.

In addition to noting how deviants can help bind the nondeviant members of society together, Durkheim (1895/1982) also maintained that deviants can promote social change. He believed that societies would stagnate if they did not change and that all social change begins with deviance. Laws that do more harm than good for society must be violated. Society needs people willing to break them. United States and world history is replete with examples of social deviants, such as women fighting for equal rights, American revolutionaries (before the war for independence was won), and civil rights leaders, who became heroes by protesting and helping to overturn unjust laws and governments. For example, Mildred Jeter, a black woman, and Richard Loving, a white man, were considered criminals when they married in 1958, in violation of the law in their state of Virginia that prohibited interracial marriage. However, their protest against an unjust law resulted in the 1967 Supreme Court decision *(Loving v. Virginia)* that declared such laws unconstitutional and led to a tremendous increase in the number of interracial marriages in the United States.

The U.S. civil rights movement is probably the most famous example of people performing deviant acts to organize for social change. Before that movement, segregation laws in many areas of the country prohibited black Americans from using the same facilities or drinking from the same water fountains as white Americans. Under "separate but equal" laws, blacks were relegated to inferior schools. Under "Jim Crow" laws in the South, black people were harassed when attempting to vote; some were the victims of violence, and others were simply turned away without being allowed to cast their votes. Jim Crow laws also put a large variety of other restrictions on black people that limited their rights in such areas as the workplace, schools, housing, transportation systems, parks, public swimming pools, and various business establishments. Anyone breaking these laws was considered deviant and deserving of legal punishment. It took many decades of struggle, culminating in the civil rights movement of the 1950s and 1960s, to make opposing racism a socially approved, rather than a deviant, act.

Rosa Parks, famous for her refusal to give up her bus seat to a white person, was not the only black person arrested in 1955 for violating segregation laws, but hers was the perfect "test case" to take to the Supreme Court. She was poised, respectable, and fully prepared for the negative publicity. "People always say that I didn't give up my seat because I was tired, but that isn't true," Rosa Parks (1992) wrote. "No, the only tired I was, was tired of giving in." Parks, an elected officer of the local chapter of the NAACP (National Association for the Advancement of Colored People), had been part of the group of activists strategizing the best way to challenge the segregation laws, not just in court, but in public awareness. She had not planned on getting arrested that day, but when she was told to move, she recognized the opportunity. By allowing herself to be taken off the bus by police, she provided the spark for a campaign that had already started to challenge the laws that made black Americans second-class citizens.

The activists formed the Montgomery Improvement Association, a coalition of local groups, including several church organizations, whose purpose was to demand the desegregation of buses without appearing to be too radical or threatening. A young pastor with no known enemies or personal agenda, Dr. Martin Luther King, Jr., was selected to head the campaign. Despite the hardships that poor people faced getting to work each day without public transportation, threats from motorists as they walked along the roads, and warnings that they would lose their jobs if they could not get to work each day on time, the black citizens of Montgomery organized them-selves effectively and boycotted the buses for more than a year. By the time they won their case in court, they had also fostered a national reexamina-tion of the status of black people in America. Although African Americans still face routine *de facto* (meaning in practice though not in law) segrega-tion, discrimination, and racial insults, the Montgomery bus boycott is credited with tearing down the laws that supported and "normalized" such actions.

Organizing for Environmental Change

Today, norms are being challenged in order to halt global warming. In towns and on campuses across the United States, the norms of cranking up the heat or air conditioning and throwing away trash have been replaced with efforts to conserve energy and recycle all we can. The need for more and improved public transportation has garnered attention as we have learned that our habits of driving to and from work by ourselves, rather than carpooling and driving fewer vehicles, severely damage the atmosphere.

Though we have long been dependent on coal, our growing awareness of the devastating impact of coal by-products has made the "standard" black smoke–spewing coal plant a symbol of criminal negligence by corporations and the U.S. Environmental Protection Agency (EPA), which many people now view as having failed to use its full power to protect the environment. In 2008, frustrated at the inaction of the federal government, 12 states sued the EPA for violating the Clean Air Act by not setting standards to control greenhouse gas emissions in new vehicles.[1] The Supreme Court ruled that the EPA must regulate greenhouse gases. The EPA under the Obama adminis-tration has agreed to do so, declaring that such emissions "threaten the pub-lic health and welfare of current and future generations" (Woodside 2009).

Former vice president Al Gore and the UN's Intergovernmental Panel on Climate Change won the 2007 Nobel Peace Prize for their efforts to bring the impending environmental, social, and political catastrophes of global warming to the public's attention. Through the efforts of Gore and myriad other environmental activists and scientists, more and more Americans have become aware of the growing impact of pollution from emerging nations like China and India and are demanding that the U.S. government start acting as a role model for other nations to follow. It is becoming increasingly clear to U.S. citizens and policy makers that the United States "must re-engage in the global effort and adopt strong and effective national policies" to address this growing threat to our nation and our planet (Pew Center on Global Climate Change and the Pew Center on the States 2009).

Exercise 6.5   Organizing to Curb Climate Change

If activists (for any cause) want to be the most effective, it's important to turn people on—rather than off—to their cause. This can be tricky. Listen to the opinion piece called "Green Guilt Trips Won't Inspire Personal Change" at www.npr.org/templates/player/mediaPlayer.html?action=1&t=1&islist=false& id=17319623&m=17319617.

What does it tell you about (a) how some people can be turned off from the environmental movement to stem global climate change, (b) how you might turn people "on" to this movement, and (c) how global climate change might be most effectively addressed?

Exercise 6.6   Global Climate Change and Pollution

One of the major social problems we face today is global climate change. China recently overtook the United States as the leading producer of greenhouse gases (Oster 2009). Read the article called "As China Roars, Pollution Reaches Deadly Extremes," by Joseph Kahn and Jim Yardley, at www.nytimes .com/2007/08/26/world/asia/26china.html?pagewanted=print.

Now, check out the picture of how pollution created in China spreads eastward across the globe at http://visibleearth.nasa.gov/view_rec.php?id=19687 (click on the JPEG link to the right of the photo to get an enlarged view).

After doing the above, answer the following questions:

1. According to Kahn and Yardley's article, what are some of the social forces behind the dramatic increase in pollution from China?

2. Why are some members of the Chinese leadership fearful of emphasizing environmental protection over economic growth?

3. What has the role been up to now of the United States and other Western nations in (a) global warming and (b) pollution from China?

4. If you were president of the United States, what steps would you take to address pollution from China and global warming in general?

| Exercise 6.7 | What's Your Ecological Footprint? |

Go to the Web site http://earthday.net/footprint/index.html and determine your ecological footprint and your own impact on global climate change.

1. Describe your ecological footprint.

2. Were you surprised by what you found? Why or why not?

3. Go to Earthwatch at www.earthwatch.org, click on your part of the world, and then click on "get involved." How might you work with others to use social capital to connect (a) different groups on your campus, (b) different groups in your surrounding community, and (c) your campus and surrounding community to work together to address global climate change?

| Exercise 6.8 | Lunch Counter Sit-Ins and Other Nonviolent Protests |

One of the more dramatic forms of protest during the civil rights movement was the "lunch counter sit-in." At these events, blacks took seats at lunch counters that served only whites and then refused to leave. During many of these sit-ins, white customers jeered, threw food at them, and threatened them before the police came and dragged off the protesters.

Use your library's electronic databases (such as the JSTOR or Academic Search Premier database) to find three academic articles that focus on lunch counter sit-ins during the civil rights movement. Also, watch the first segment of the *Eyes on the Prize* documentaries (your school library should have a copy), in which the sit-ins are covered. Then, write a two- to three-page paper that addresses the following questions:

1. Given the fact that the protesters knew they were not going to be served, what did they hope to gain by doing this? Were they trying to change the law? Public opinion? The policies of the lunch counter establishments?

2. Do you think their strategy was successful? What are the benefits and positives of nonviolent protest? What are the negatives and limitations?

(Continued)

(Continued)

3. Considering public opinion toward black Americans today and given what you have learned about social movements, (a) what sorts of public actions could black Americans do today to bring attention to the kinds of discrimination they face? and (b) what actions can you personally take that would help diminish racial discrimination? Hand in a complete bibliography of your sources along with your written answers.

Exercise 6.9   Studying a Social Movement

There have been numerous social movements (organized campaigns for social, cultural, or legal change) in the United States that have met with varying degrees of success over the past 50 years. The cultural period known as "the sixties" (roughly 1963–1973) saw the rise of the second wave of the women's movement[2]; the American Indian movement; the Brown Power movement (Latinos); an anti-war movement (Vietnam); and movements for poverty relief and fair housing practices, gay rights, environmental rights, animal rights, and an international student/youth movement, among others.

Pick one of these movements. Use your library's databases to search for articles using such key words and phrases as "American Indian movement," "organization, successes, failures, media portrayal," and "goals." Then answer the following questions:

1. What were/are the goals of the movement you have chosen?

2. How was/is the movement organized? How was/is it run? How was/is it viewed in the popular media? How do you think the movement was/is organized, and how has its portrayal in the media affected its ability to achieve its goals?

3. How successful or unsuccessful has the movement been in achieving its goals?

4. Imagine you were hired as a consultant to promote and advise the movement. What would you do or say to help it achieve its goals? Be specific and strategic, outlining plans to carry forth your proposal.

Exercise 6.10   Campus Activism: Then and Now

The 1960s were famous for student activism and student organizing. Who were these students and for what were they advocating? How were they portrayed in the news media at the time? How are they being portrayed by the media and history textbooks today? How successful were they? Write a three- to four-page paper that answers these questions and describes your reaction to what you've read by carrying out the following steps:

1. Go to the newspaper archive in your library.

2. Choose one regional or national paper for which there are issues available from 1963 through 1973.

3. Scan through issues published between 1963 and 1973 until you have located (and photocopied) at least 10 articles about on-campus student activism.

4. For each article, note the following: (a) Does the article tell you what the students wanted? (b) Does the article tell you why they had those goals? (c) Does the article appear to have a position in support of, neutral to, or opposed to the students? (d) For each case in which you have a clear sense of the students' goals, were they achieved? Did they change society?

5. Can you imagine sixties-style student protests happening today on your campus? If yes, would the protesters have similar or different goals from those of the 1960s protesters you read about? If no, explain why you think they would not take place today. Have other styles of protest replaced them? Have students become less likely to protest and, if so, why?

Exercise 6.11   Organizing to Address Hunger

1. Listen to the NPR story "Hunger in America" at www.npr.org/templates/story/story.php?storyId=5023829. (Make sure to listen to all three segments.)

2. Go to the End Hunger Network Web site at www.endhunger.com or WHY at www.whyhunger.org or Feeding America at http://feedingamerica.org/default.aspx?SHOW_SHOV=1. Find 5–10 facts about hunger in the United States, and create a flyer about hunger that you can pass out in the cafeteria at your school.

(Continued)

(Continued)

3. Bring the flyers to your school cafeteria at a mealtime.

4. Sit down with different groups of students you do not know, give them your flyer, and engage them in a conversation about hunger in America. Then, ask them if they would like to work with you to find a way to assist the people in your area who are hungry. Be sure to put your contact information on the flyer and to have a sign-up sheet so that those who are interested can give you their names and contact information.

5. Set a meeting time, and send an email out to announce the meeting. Then, meet with those interested and, during the meeting, formulate a plan to help the hungry in your area. For tips on how to run a meeting, you can look here on page 4: http://assets.filemobile.com/15/get-involved/resources/Campus%20in%20Action%20Toolkit.pdf.

6. Once you have formulated your plan, carry it out.

7. Report on (a) how you organized your group, (b) the results of your group's efforts, and (c) what students in general can do to help address the issue of hunger (based on what you learned on the hunger Web sites) in a letter to the editor or an article in your school's newspaper.

STUDENT SOCIOLOGISTS IN ACTION: ANTHONY MORAN AND MIKE RICHTER

Below, sociology students Anthony Moran and Mike Richter describe how they used sociological tools to form a social movement organization and make a positive impact on their college and surrounding community.

Tenants Are People Too (TAPT)

As we began our Social Movements class with Professor Robert Benford at Southern Illinois University in the fall of 2008, we were asked to come up with social injustices that we could realistically change. Ultimately, we decided that the greatest injustices facing the Carbondale, Illinois, area were poor housing conditions and the inequities facing tenants. In response, we formed Tenants Are People Too (TAPT), a social movement organization with a mission to "empower and educate tenants, while striving for improved living conditions and timely repairs."

The members of our class divided ourselves into five subgroups that included history, education, recruitment, public relations/media, and policy/complaints. The history group researched former tenants' movements within the country and more specifically in the Southern Illinois area. The education group focused on educating both the local community and the members of TAPT about the rights of tenants. This educational process included researching current laws and housing codes already established in the city of Carbondale, designing and implementing surveys of tenants, and creating pamphlets to teach the community about housing issues in Carbondale.

The recruitment subgroup's work included recruiting students to join TAPT and recruiting other registered student organizations and off-campus organizations as allies. We formed an alliance with the Students' Legal Assistance Office (SLAO) and its attorney, who has over 18 years of experience dealing with tenant/landlord disputes. The public relations/media group obtained a column in the local newspaper and multiple local radio interviews. This group also set up an electronic home base for TAPT, which allowed people to join the group and become involved in the movement's plans and progress. Finally, the policy group was in charge of finding out exactly how to go about addressing problems and issues that renters have with their landlords. We found that by splitting up our workload, we were able to efficiently conduct the preliminary steps necessary to address the injustices we were seeking to curb.

All social movements encounter challenges and difficulties, and TAPT was no exception. For example, mobilizing its current members along with the student population to accomplish certain goals was and remains our greatest challenge. For reasons we have yet to understand, motivating constituents to hold landlords responsible for their negligence is more demanding than we thought it would be when we founded our social movement. Taking into account what we perceive as the apathy of student renters, making progress toward particular strategies has proved taxing at times. It has led us to the realization that informing renters of their rights must be our first priority in our efforts to attain more members and constituents.

Although our movement faces difficulties, we have still managed to make progress in furthering our cause. During our semester-long class, TAPT officially became a registered student organization, held regular meetings, and organized an open forum, which gave the community an opportunity to voice their experiences with their less-than-accommodating landlords. Also, TAPT has collaborated with the SLAO to explain to prospective renters what they need to consider before signing a lease. TAPT has also interacted with city officials regarding recommendations and concerns for the future of housing in Carbondale. Although TAPT has only been active for less than one academic year, we have made considerable progress.

(Continued)

(Continued)

The future of TAPT is encouraging. We have managed to maintain a sustainable organization despite losing several members to graduation. Our prospects involve working more with the SLAO to educate students about the importance of understanding their lease and which landlords practice less than honest business. We also will continue working with the city to ensure that dilapidated and vacant houses are dealt with properly and that students, landlords, and the city are held responsible for healthy living conditions within Carbondale. Direct action will also become a focus, since we have spent the year becoming educated on the most prevalent issues, such as which landlords are the most problematic and negligent.

TAPT members have managed to be socially active within our community while bonding with one another and having fun. We have hosted fundraisers, attended a cooking competition, and continue to get together socially in order to maintain solidarity. Carbondale stands to benefit substantially from the continued presence and work of TAPT and, if we accomplish what we have set out to do, much change can come to this city. We feel confident that the population that suffers the most, which includes low-income individuals and people of color, will embrace this opportunity to combat systemic inequality. Establishing TAPT has also taught us that we can use sociological tools to make a positive impact on society. TAPT demonstrates that mobilizing a social movement can be a great example of putting sociology into action.

Discussion Questions

1. What was the last norm that you broke? Think of the last folkway (rather than a more) that you violated. What was the reaction of those around you? How did it make you feel? Did the reaction impact your willingness to break the folkway in the future?

2. How would a rational choice theorist explain why you broke the folkway? Would you agree? Why or why not?

3. Have you ever broken a rule or law that you considered unjust? Why did you do so? Did you organize your "deviant" behavior with other people or did you violate the norm on your own? What were the repercussions? Did your action result in any lasting social change? Why or why not?

4. What are the norms that guide your classroom behavior? What would you consider deviant classroom behavior by students? How did you learn these norms? What are the negative sanctions for those who violate classroom norms?

5. What do you think are the greatest criminal threats to U.S. society? Do you think the criminal justice system effectively addresses those threats? Why or why not?

6. Are there any laws that you find to be unfair, or legal punishments for crimes committed that you think are too strong, harsh, or outdated? If not, why not? If so, what are they? Why do you think these laws/punishments exist, even though they are unfair? What values (and *whose* values) do they reflect? What do these laws/punishments teach you about power relations in U.S. society?

7. What do you think life would be like without norms? Would it even be possible? Why or why not?

8. Think of some examples that support Durkheim's idea that deviance can serve positive functions for society. Now think of how deviance can have a negative influence on society. What are the situations in which deviance is most likely to have (a) a positive or (b) a negative effect on society?

9. Think about the social capital you have. Is it bonding or bridging—does it bond you to an isolated group in society, or does it work to connect you to other groups? What are some examples of groups on your campus that create (a) bonding or (b) bridging social capital? How do they impact the rest of the campus?

10. Do you conserve and recycle as much as you can? If so, why? If not, what would convince you to do so?

11. Remember what Cooley meant by the term *looking-glass self*. Do you think your college classmates see you as the type of person who would (a) participate in or (b) lead a protest on your college campus? Do you think your high school classmates would give the same answers? Why or why not?

Suggestions for Specific Actions

1. Read "101 Ways for a More Sustainable World," written by Ed Gillis for the Otesha Project, at www.otesha.ca/being+the+change/issues/101+ways....en.html. Then go to the Student Environmental Action Coalition Web site at http://seac.org/resources/online. Use the guides there to organize a group action on your campus. Be sure to obtain your instructor's approval before beginning your project. Actions may be local or national, educational or political. Keep a journal of your project, its outcome, feedback you get from others, and what you learned by doing it.

2. Identify a social issue that you support. (Consider movements to promote fair trade products, reduce the number of abortions, establish equal rights for gay

Americans, create universal health care, etc.) Find a campus or local organization that works on this issue.

a. Attend meetings and participate in the activities of the organization.

b. Write a letter to the campus newspaper explaining to your classmates what the issues are that the group is concerned with; how these issues affect students; how the group is trying to change people's opinions and feelings on this issue; and why they should join the organization, too!

Please go to this book's Web site at www.pineforge.com/korgen3e to find further civic engagement opportunities, resources, peer-reviewed articles, and updated Web links related to this chapter.

Endnotes

1. You can read the states' petition at www.pewclimate.org/docUploads/Mass-v-EPA-Petition.pdf.

2. The first wave of the women's movement began in 1848 and ended with the passage of the Nineteenth Amendment in 1920.

References

Becker, Howard. 1963. *Outsiders: Studies in the Sociology of Deviance.* New York: Free Press.

Beyerlein, Kraig and John R. Hipp. 2005. "Social Capital: Too Much of a Good Thing?" *Social Forces* 84, 2:993–1013.

Callebs, Sean and Eric Marrapodi. 2008, January 30. "New Orleans Cop Shot to Death With Her Own Gun." *CNN.com.* Retrieved March 26, 2009 (http://www.cnn.com/2008/CRIME/01/29/cop.shot/index.html#cnnSTCText).

Durkheim, Émile. [1895] 1982. *The Rules of the Sociological Method.* Edited by Steven Lukes; translated by W. D. Halls. New York: Free Press.

Franks, Jeff. 2007. "Crime Turning New Orleans Into Big Uneasy." *Reuters AlertNet.* Retrieved February 19, 2008 (http://www.alertnet.org/thenews/newsdesk/N19404375.htm).

Garfinkel, Harold. 1967. *Studies in Ethnomethodology.* Englewood Cliffs, NJ: Prentice Hall.

Lamberth, John. 1994. *Revised Statistical Analysis of the Incidence of Police Stops and Arrests of Black Drivers/Travelers on the New Jersey Turnpike Between Interchanges 1 and 3 From the Years 1988 Through 1991.* Unpublished manuscript. Department of Psychology, Temple University, Philadelphia. Retrieved January 11, 2006 (http://www.lamberthconsulting.com/downloads/new_jersey_study_report.pdf).

New Jersey Division of Criminal Justice. 2009. "Eradicating Racial Profiling Companion Guide." Retrieved September 23, 2009 (http://www.state.nj.us/lps/dcj/agguide/directives/racial-profiling/pdfs/ripcompanion-guide.pdf).

Oster, Shai. 2009, April 21. "Group Urges Beijing to Cut Coal Emissions." *The Wall Street Journal*. Retrieved May 27, 2009 (http://online.wsj.com/article/SB124021811385234435.html).

Parks, Rosa (with Jim Haskins). 1992. *Rosa Parks: My Story*. New York: Dial Books.

Pew Center on Global Climate Change and the Pew Center on the States. 2009. "Climate Change 101: Understanding and Responding to Global Climate Change." Retrieved March 26, 2009 (http://www.pewclimate.org/global-warming-basics/climate_change_101).

Reiman, Jeffrey. 2003. *The Rich Get Richer and the Poor Get Prison: Ideology, Class, and Criminal Justice*. 7th ed. Boston: Allyn & Bacon.

Riley, K. Jack. 2002, Summer. "Racial Profiling: Lessons From the Drug War." *Rand Review* 26(2). Retrieved January 11, 2006 (http://www.rand.org/publications/randreview/issues/rr.08.02/profiling.html).

Sutherland, Edwin H. 1947. *Principles of Criminology*. 4th ed. Philadelphia: J. B. Lippincott.

Woodside, Christine. (2009, May 19). "Was an 'Historic' EPA Ruling on GHGs Reflected by Historically Good Coverage?" The Yale Forum on Climate Change and the Media. Retrieved May 26, 2009 (http://www.yaleclimatemediaforum.org/2009/05/epa-ruling-on-ghgs).

7

Big Money Doesn't *Always* Win

Stratification and Social Class

Money, money, money. . . . It's a rich man's world.[1]

Do you agree with the lyrics to this ABBA song? Do you think, "It's a rich man's world"? In this chapter, we examine *social stratification—how societies distribute the things of value to them and rank groups of people according to their access to what is valued.* Although people may prize certain things more in some societies than others (e.g., privacy, tea or coffee, certain spices, etc.), almost everyone, everywhere, places a high value on money.

In the United States, the desire for money, combined with a lack of government oversight of some banking practices, led to the major recession that began to create a crisis in domestic and global markets in the fall of 2008. Hundreds of billions of mortgage-related investments went sour as homeowners who could not afford their mortgages had to default on their loans. Many of these so-called subprime loan holders had been pressured into taking the loans by officials who profited from the transactions and then immediately divided the mortgage loans into different pieces and sold them to other companies. Insurance companies, such as AIG, that insured loans for the mortgage-backed securities firms, like Bear Stearns and Lehman Brothers, that bought them did not have enough cash on hand to repay the highly leveraged investment companies (i.e., they gave out many more IOUs than they had cash on hand to repay) when the loans went bad. Meanwhile, credit ratings agencies like Moody's and Standard and Poor's kept giving the securities firms high credit scores (the mortgage-backed security issuers were paying them to issue credit scores) and failed to warn investors about their true likelihood to fail (Morgenson 2008). The effect was that when the financial system began to unravel, many investors were left holding relatively worthless stocks, and many financial institutions (such as Bear Stearns and Lehman Brothers) went bankrupt while others had to be saved from insolvency through huge government bailouts.

As a result of the above events, the stock market suffered the worst decline since the Great Depression. Retirees lost money they counted on for living expenses. Institutions that relied on interest and dividends from investments (e.g., state pension funds, charities, colleges, art museums, and grant funders) faced drastic cuts in their income, and many had to stop providing services and lay off employees. Lending institutions, unsure of how many bad loans they had on their books, refused to lend more money, and companies that relied on loans began to cut jobs. Between April 2008 and August 2009, the U.S. unemployment rate rose from 5 to 9.7% (Bureau of Labor Statistics [BLS] 2009b, 2009c). As jobs in the private sector were shed, tax revenues plummeted, and government services (and jobs) began to be lost as well. Unemployed homeowners who could easily pay their mortgages when working began to default on their payments. In the first quarter of 2009, an estimated 12% of homeowners were behind on their mortgage payments or in foreclosure (Associated Press 2009). This influenced the market as a whole, as consumers lost confidence and stopped or greatly decreased their purchases. As a result, manufacturers and retail outlets faced dismal sales, with the Christmas 2008 season posting the worst sales figures in 30 years ("Credit Crisis—The Essentials" 2009).

The credit crisis in the United States soon began to affect markets across the globe: Markets in Europe and Asia plunged; Iceland became bankrupt and its government was replaced; and many other nations faced issues of growing unemployment, hunger, and political unrest. The unemployment rate in Spain reached 17.4% in April of 2009 (Burnett 2009)! In that same month, the International Monetary Fund (IMF) stated that the global economy was the worst it had been since the end of World War II, in 1945 (Knowlton 2009).

As we write these words, the efforts of the Obama administration and the leaders of other nations to stimulate the global economy seem to have had some positive impact. However, most economists predict that unemployment will continue to rise for several more months and that the economic recovery will be slow. We will pay the price of this most recent episode of unbridled capitalism for many years to come, perhaps generations.

But the current recession was not an exception to the way the American system of stratification has been shaped; indeed, it was just an extension of the trends of the past several decades. Before the economic recession, the richest 1% of U.S. households owned more wealth than *all* of the bottom 90% combined! Income and wealth inequality had not been that uneven since before the Great Depression hit in 1929. The share of income going to the very rich (the top 1%) had increased dramatically, from 8% in 1980 to 22.1% in 2006. Meanwhile, the average federal tax burden on those wealthy families *decreased* from 44.4% in 1980 to 30.4% as of this writing. The end result was that the top 1% of income earners had more than double the disposable income available to them in 1980, while in real terms the poor had actually become poorer (Piketty and Saez 2007; Prante 2009). Today, the gap between the richest and poorest Americans has diminished somewhat, due to the decline in the stock market and the subsequent decline in wealth among the top earners. However, the level of inequality among the classes remains very high, as members of all classes have suffered the effects of the recession.

While the top 1% of income earners have much less money than they did before the stock market decline, almost all are still very wealthy. Most middle-class workers have faced salary freezes or cuts or fear these are impending or that they might soon be laid off. (Neighbors on either side of one of the authors have lost their jobs due to the recession, and she, herself, faces a 7-day furlough.) However, the most vulnerable workers have been hit hardest by the recession. The working poor have faced the most job cuts and the greatest number of lost work hours. As Andrew M. Sum, the director of the Center for Labor Market Studies at Northeastern University, states, "Low-income people are the big losers when the economy turns down" (quoted in Eckholm 2008). A loss of a few hours of work a week, never mind a layoff, can be devastating for workers already trying to scrape by on low-wage work.

Theories of Social Stratification

Classical Theories

Of the three main theories we discuss in this book (functionalism, conflict theory, and symbolic interactionism), the consensus among sociologists is that conflict theory is the most useful when examining social stratification. The two founders of sociology who used the conflict perspective, Karl Marx and Max Weber, provided two of the most important classical theories of stratification. All of Marx's work, and much of Weber's, focused on examining and explaining inequality in society.

As you will recall from earlier chapters, Karl Marx spent his life examining how power is unequally distributed and how we might change society to make this distribution process fair. In most of his work, he maintained that there are only two classes in society: those who own the means of production (the owners, or bourgeoisie) and those who work for them (the workers, or proletariat). Marx believed that the workers would eventually realize that their interests are in opposition to those of the owners (in the process, forming a "class consciousness" for all laborers) and ultimately overthrow the owning class.

Weber, who lived a generation or so after Marx, expanded upon Marx's ideas (see Weber 1968). Whereas Marx maintained that power in society directly relates to ownership of the means of production (those who own industries), Weber recognized that non-owners who possess useful skills can also have some power. He added a third class to Marx's two-tiered class system. He divided the non-owners into a middle class (those who had skills based on knowledge) and a working class (those who did manual labor). Weber anticipated the fact that as societies became more complicated and technologically advanced, the skills of the middle class would become more in demand than those of the working class. Those in the middle class would, therefore, be paid more and have greater access to the things that are valued in society (better schools, neighborhoods, housing, etc.) than the members of the working class. Unlike Marx, he didn't envision a class uprising that would result in the destruction of the owning class.

Contemporary Theories

Today, *power elite theories,* a modern offshoot of the classic conflict perspective, represent the dominant perspective in studies of economic and political power. These theories maintain that many people do not bother participating in the political process because they feel alienated from it. Power elite theorists, such as C. Wright Mills (1956/1970) and William Domhoff (1983, 1967/2005), note that a relatively small, organized group of people hold key positions in the major institutions of society and make continuous (and, overall, successful) efforts toward keeping themselves in power. Mills noted a connection among key players in the military, corporations (that supply the military and help to finance campaigns for those seeking office in government), and the government (that chooses which corporations will supply the military). Domhoff (1967/2005) goes further, arguing that there is a "ruling class" composed of interrelated leaders in the corporate, political, and policy-planning network worlds that "rule" America.

Exercise 7.1	The Economic Recession and Stratification in the U.S.

Go to the *New York Times'* "Credit Crisis—The Essentials" at http://topics .nytimes.com/top/reference/timestopics/subjects/c/credit_crisis/index.html? scp=1-spot&sq=credit%20crisis&st=cse.

Read three of the articles under "Latest Developments" and relate their contents to the information in this chapter. Be sure to describe how the information from the articles helped you to better understand (a) the economic recession and (b) stratification in the United States.

Social Class

What social class are you? Wait, we can guess (with at least 95% certainty) how you will answer! When asked on surveys, almost all Americans will say they are middle class. Most, however, have no social scientific understanding of what social class actually means.

According to social scientists (those who measure class professionally), people in the same social class have relatively equal access to what is valued in their society (e.g., money, power, good schools, nice neighborhoods, etc.) and have similar lifestyles. Once people realize this, they can usually recognize the many differences concealed by the almost universal "middle class" label in the United States. For example, it quickly becomes clear that, whereas both high-level managers and sales associates tend to refer to themselves as middle class, members of these respective occupations do not have similar lifestyles or access to what is valued in U.S. society. And all of this doesn't even address the fact that your answer to the question, "What social class are you?" was likely an answer about your perceived class *in the United States,* and not about your perception of your class within the global economic system. In the global economic system, the majority of Americans would be considered upper class.

Because social scientists understand that almost all Americans will simply put down "middle class" if asked their social class, most measure social class by looking at the income, education, and profession of respondents. However, this still leaves some room for error.[2] In general, most truly middle-class people in the United States have some college education, have professions with salaries (rather than jobs where they are paid by the hour), and earn within a specified range around the median income. Sometimes, social scientists break down members of the middle class into two groups: middle class (white-collar workers) and working class (blue-collar workers or pink-collar workers[3]). Blue- and pink-collar jobs, which usually do not require as much education, tend to pay less than white-collar work.[4] White-collar work tends to require at least a bachelor's degree.

The importance of attaining a college degree cannot be overstated. Those who hope to attain a class ranking of at least middle class generally need to have one or more of the following: (a) a high level of education, (b) connections to those in power, and (c) a legacy of wealth passed down to them by their family. While one has to be born lucky to have the third requirement (passed-down wealth), the second (connections to those in power) also requires a certain degree of good fortune. You need to have access to people in power in order to establish connections with them. A high degree of education, while increasingly expensive and open only to those with a certain level of aptitude, remains the most readily available path to a middle-class life for most Americans. According to the Bureau of Labor Statistics (2009c), in 2007 only 1.3% of those with college diplomas were among the working poor. However, 16.5% of workers with less than a high school diploma had jobs that did not lift them out of poverty.

Sex and race are also factors that relate to social class. In short, it helps to be male and white. Female heads of households are more than twice as likely as male heads of families to live below the poverty level (U.S. Bureau of the Census 2009a). In 2007, an estimated 12.5% of Americans were in poverty (U.S. Bureau of the Census 2009b). The poverty rate also varies dramatically according to race. In 2007, a total of 8.2% of whites, 24.5% of blacks, 10.2% of Asians, and 21.5% of Hispanics lived in poverty (U.S. Bureau of the Census 2009b). The recent subprime mortgage crisis has disproportionately impacted minorities—those most likely to have such mortgages—and broadened the wealth divide between white males and Hispanic/Latino, black, and female Americans. We'll talk more about the connections between sex and race and social class in Chapters 8 and 9.

Exercise 7.2   Who's Rich?

Answer the following questions:

1. How much money do you have to make to be rich? What makes you think so?

2. Now go to the Web page www.ctj.org/pdf/whosrich.pdf and read "Who's Rich?" Based on the information you learned from the article, have you changed your mind about how much money you need to make in order to be rich? Why or why not? Based on that article, why do you think most people tend to overestimate how many Americans are rich?

| Exercise 7.3 | Social Class and You |

At this point in the chapter, you are probably thinking about your own social class and how you became a member of it. Think about how the institutions of family, education, and occupation are related to one another and answer the following questions:

1. What is the highest level of education completed by each of your parents?

2. Were you raised by two parents? If not, who raised you?

3. When you were growing up, what was the occupation of the head(s) of your household?

4. Have you been in different social classes at different times in your life? If so, why? If not, why not?

5. How do you think your answers to questions 1–3 influenced your present social class?

Social Class and Political Representation

Voter turnout is strongly related to social class. To put it simply, poor and working-class people are much less likely to vote than middle-class and wealthier Americans. Although always a feature of U.S. elections, the class gap has now become a chasm. Those at the bottom of the income ladder are half as likely to vote as those at the top (Patterson 2004a:14). This trend continued even in the 2008 presidential election, despite the fact that a larger number of Latinos voted, and the racial voting gap between white and black Americans closed (McDonald 2009). Many poor Americans do not see the issues that they care about being addressed by politicians and, therefore, see no use in going through the hassles of registering to vote and voting. Some are also so preoccupied with finding a way to pay the rent and buy food that they have little time or energy to keep up with current political issues and to vote. Homeless Americans, without proof of residence, face even more difficulty in exercising their right to vote.

| Exercise 7.4 | Environmental Racism and Classism |

The lack of political power among poor citizens has made them inviting targets for environmental waste and pollution. Poor, often predominantly minority areas in the United States suffer much higher levels of environmental pollution than more prosperous parts of the country.

Read "Justice in the Air" at http://college.usc.edu/geography/ESPE/docu ments/justice_air_web.pdf and "Dumping in Dixie: TVA Sends Toxic Coal Ash to Poor Black Communities in Georgia and Alabama" at www.southern-studies.org/2009/05/tva-sends-spilled-coal-ash-to-impoverished-black-communities-in-georgia-and-alabama.html.

Using the information in these readings, describe in a two- to three-page paper how you might convince your fellow students that environmental racism and classism is (a) occurring, (b) something they should be concerned about, and (c) an issue that could be successfully addressed by a well-organized group of students.

Exercise 7.5   Soup Kitchens and Hunger in America

Volunteer to serve a meal at an area soup kitchen. Your Campus Activities office should be able to help you and even connect you with a group on campus that regularly volunteers at one, or you can find one by using the WHY Grassroots Resources Directory at www.whyhunger.org/resources/grassroots-resources-directory.html.

1. Set up a time when the manager can give you some background on why the guests come to the soup kitchen. (In particular, ask what makes them need the services the soup kitchen offers.)

2. When you are there, be sure to pay attention to the people eating at the soup kitchen (while still taking time to interact with them, to serve them, and to enjoy your volunteer experience) and note the following: (a) Are they mostly families or individuals? (b) What is their racial/ethnic makeup? (c) What is the age range of those who have come to eat there? (d) Do most seem hopeful? Resigned? Angry? Happy? Depressed? (e) How do they react to your being there, and what are the ways they interact with you?

3. Next, write a two- to three-page paper that describes (a) the services the soup kitchen offers, (b) the demographics and attitudes of the people eating at the soup kitchen (based on the data you have gathered in Step 2), (c) why the people who eat there need to do so, (d) how your experience at the soup kitchen made you feel, and (e) whether you could ever see yourself needing the services of a soup kitchen (and why or why not).

(Continued)

(Continued)

Extra Credit: Go to the Web site for Feeding America at http://feeding america.org, click on "Faces of Hunger," and then read the Hunger Fact Sheets under "Hunger 101." Incorporate the information from these fact sheets into the paper you just wrote.

Increasing numbers of working-class people have also become alienated from the political process. As Thomas Patterson, the author of *The Vanishing Voter* (2003), points out,

> The voting rate among those at the bottom of the income ladder is only half that of those at the top. [In the first half of the 20th century], working-class Americans were at the center of political debate and party conflict. They now occupy the periphery of a political world in which money and middle-class concerns are ascendant. (2004b:n.p.)[5,6]

This opinion is reflected in the low level of political participation among low-income Americans. For example, in the U.S. presidential election of 2004, a total of 64% of all voting-age citizens cast a vote. However, while 77% of those whose family income was greater than $50,000 voted, only 48% of those voting-age citizens whose family income was less than $20,000 cast a ballot in that election. Thus, wealthier Americans were more highly represented and poorer Americans were less represented (U.S. Bureau of the Census 2009c). This trend continued in 2008. In the presidential election of that year, 68% of voters made $50,000 dollars or more ("President: National Exit Poll" 2008), but the average per capita income of Americans was just $38,611 in 2007 (U.S. Bureau of the Census 2008). Once again, high-income Americans had more sway at the ballot box.

The decline of union power has also diminished the influence of working-class Americans on the electoral process. According to the Bureau of Labor Statistics (2006, 2009a), union membership declined from 20.1% in 1983 to 12.1% in 2007, but moved up to 12.4% in 2008 (perhaps because nonunion labor has been easier to lay off during the recession). Almost 37% of government workers are members of unions, but only 7.6% of workers in the private sector belong to a union (down from approximately 16% in 1983). In 2008, the median weekly salary of full-time union workers was $886, while the median weekly salary of full-time, nonunion workers was $691 (BLS 2009a). In addition to ensuring relatively good wages, unions have traditionally been a very powerful "get out the vote" force for (usually Democratic) candidates. However, as the power of unions has declined, so has the ability of the working class to have its economic interests addressed by politicians.

Exercise 7.6	America: Who Votes?

1. Go to "Voting and Registration in the Election of 2008" at http://www .census.gov/population/www/socdemo/voting/cps2008.html.

2. Compare voting rates by race, income, employment, and educational attainment.

3. Based on the information in this chapter, why do you think the respective groups are more or less likely to vote than other Americans? What does this tell you about the connections (at least those that are perceived) between wealth and power?

4. What steps do you think should be taken toward engaging nonvoting Americans enough so that they will register and vote?

Even Americans who do vote realize that only a very small percentage of the population has the means to run for high political office. The amount of money people must be able to raise to establish a legitimate campaign prohibits the vast majority of people from running for such positions. For example, during the 2008 congressional elections, the average candidate running for a position in the House of Representatives or the Senate spent, respectively, $682,416 and $2,491,410 (OpenSecrets.org 2009a). At the presidential level, the numbers are even more staggering: John McCain raised $368,000,000 and Barack Obama raised $745,000,000 during the presidential election of 2008 (OpenSecrets.org 2009b).

The overall result of the current electoral system[7] in the United States is that most poor and working-class Americans neither vote nor run for political office. In turn, they are largely ignored by political officeholders who must respond to constituents who do vote and contributors who help them raise the vast sums of money needed to gain and maintain their positions.

Exercise 7.7   Campaign Finance Reform

Campaign reform efforts gain momentum every few years when scandals about political corruption make the headlines. Your representatives will no doubt be voting on campaign finance reform legislation in the near future.

Check out the following three Web sites: www.publicagenda.org/citizen, www.citizen.org/congress/campaign/index.cfm, and www.OpenSecrets.org. Then answer the following questions:

1. What recent political scandals have prompted the current proposed campaign finance reform legislation?

2. Do you think campaign finance reform is necessary? Why or why not?

3. What was the result of the most recently passed campaign finance reform legislation (either federal or state)?

4. What do you think would most effectively level the electoral playing field? How might you help bring these changes about?

5. Of the different proposals that you have read, which makes the most sense to you? Can you offer even further suggestions?

The Power of Organized People

The information above may sound depressing to anyone committed to true democracy in the United States. However, it is only part of the picture. Although civic organizations may not exist in the size and number they once did (Skocpol 2003), there are many grassroots political organizations successfully representing lower-income Americans. While we usually do not hear about their efforts on the evening news, Barack Obama's experience as a community organizer has made more people aware of their existence. These organizations are accomplishing the vital task of giving voice to poor and working-class persons.

Broad-based organizing associations (organizations of organizations, including churches, synagogues, mosques, nonprofits, parents associations, and unions) are civic groups that teach people to use a "sociological eye" and a "sociological imagination" as they train them to become effective citizens. They train ordinary Americans to question the status quo, connect their personal problems to public issues, and hold politicians and business leaders accountable to the citizenry. While there are many of these organizations (the Industrial Areas Foundation, PICO National Network, Direct Action and Research Training, Organizing and Leadership Training Center, and Gamaliel are some), they all organize for power. Their ability to organize allows them to act as a kind of mediating institution for the poor, working, and middle classes and negotiate effectively with those who have political and financial power.

The following description of the Industrial Areas Foundation (IAF), located on the organization's Web site (www.industrialareasfoundation .org/iafabout/about.htm), provides insight into the efforts of these types of organizations.

> The IAF is non-ideological and strictly non-partisan, but proudly, publicly, and persistently political. The IAF builds a political base within society's rich and complex third sector—the sector of voluntary institutions that includes religious congregations, labor locals, homeowner groups, recovery groups, parents associations, settlement houses, immigrant societies, schools, seminaries, orders of men and women religious, and others. And then the leaders use that base to compete at times, to confront at times, and to cooperate at times with leaders in the public and private sectors. (n.p.)

South Bronx Churches (SBC), an IAF affiliate composed of 8 Catholic and 17 Protestant churches, also provides a good example of the power of organized people. During the 1970s and early 1980s, the South Bronx community in New York City was burning. Largely abandoned by government and business leaders, drugs were everywhere, shootings were commonplace, and arson was incessant. A turning point came when SBC members began to talk to one another about their fears, frustrations, and hopes concerning their neighborhoods. They realized that alone, none of them could do much, but together they had the power to improve their community. Part of their multifaceted plan to revitalize the area was the "Nehemiah Homes" project, the creation of 1,000 houses for poor, working-class residents.[8] SBC's effort to save the South Bronx was a long struggle that included public confrontations with powerful mayors of New York City (David Dinkins, Ed Koch, and Rudolph Giuliani) and huge efforts to raise money from business leaders. In the end, the SBC won. The organization succeeded in raising millions of dollars and convincing the city of New York to donate land for the project. Today, 1,000 low-income, working New Yorkers own their homes where there were once just burned-out and decrepit buildings.

More importantly, this accomplishment inspired those who participated in the effort, and the many more who benefited from it, to become more active citizens. In a 2004 interview (Korgen 2006), Felix Santiago, a key SBC member in the Nehemiah Homes project, described what the experience did for him.

> We own the community now! When we went around with the police in the van [identifying drug-dealing hotspots in the 1980s], we were kind of afraid. We thought that maybe the drug dealers were going to see us. But we were not afraid, together.

> Everywhere we go, from New York to Albany, from Albany back to Washington, we would carry our signatures with us and we would put them on the table and say, "These 100,000 people agree with our agenda for change." That made a big difference in our lives. We began to own more of the community. It's something you learn with South Bronx Churches. You don't fear anybody. You can stand in front of the President of the United States and you can talk to him like we are here. You have power. In 1986, I would have been afraid to sit down here and talk to you. I would say, no way, no way, you don't want to talk to me. But when you get picked to be a leader and own what you got, you have the right to represent the community.

Felix Santiago does not just have a new home and a revitalized neighborhood; he has become an empowered, knowledgeable, and effective citizen. This kind of transformation is happening all over the United States.

Today, in Ringwood, New Jersey, a group called New Jersey Together (NJT), an IAF organization, is demanding that Ford Motor Company and the EPA restart a superfund cleanup that was prematurely declared completed. The site is the homeland of the Ramapough Mountain Tribe, many of whom live in that neighborhood today.

> In the early 1990s, the EPA failed to make Ford clean up mammoth patches of toxic industrial waste it had dumped in the Upper Ringwood neighborhood, a portion of what is now Ringwood State Park and in abandoned mines. Instead, it accepted Ford's assurances of an adequate cleanup and de-listed the area as a Superfund site. (Williams 2009)

Pressed by NJT and other community leaders at a public meeting in March 2009, a director with the EPA admitted, "We blew it" (Williams 2009), and has promised to try to speed up the EPA's lengthy superfund approval process.

While Ford has managed for decades to avoid its obligation to clean up the toxic mess it made in Ringwood, the fact that the company may now really have to do so is a significant victory for organized people in the face of widespread environmental racism. Despite a 1994 Executive Order by President Clinton to agencies of the federal government to "make achieving environmental justice part of [their] mission" (Clinton 1994), today "superfund site listings in minority and poor areas are even less likely for sites discovered since the 1994 Executive Order" (O'Neil 2007). Often, it is necessary for organized people to push the government to enforce the law and make businesses clean up their toxic messes.

As of 2009, the IAF has 59 affiliates in 21 states, Canada, Germany, and the United Kingdom. They have helped to pass living-wage bills (e.g., in Texas, Arizona, and New York City), funded thousands of new homes for low-income workers (in New York City, Philadelphia, Baltimore, and Washington, D.C.), established the successful Alliance School System (in areas throughout the West and Southwest), and convinced lawmakers to enact legislation to carry out large-scale blight removal and urban revitalization (New York City).[9] As noted above, the IAF is just one of many community-based groups working to give power to organized people.

Barack Obama's experience as a community organizer in Chicago no doubt helped him during his campaign for the 2008 presidency. His ability to organize and mobilize a largely ignored group of citizens deemed notoriously unreliable in elections—young people!—helped bring about his victory in the Iowa Democratic Caucus. The participation of voters under the age of 25 in that state's 2008 caucus was 135% more than that in the 2004 election—and they responded enthusiastically to Senator Obama's calls for a "politics of hope and change." Young Iowa voters preferred Obama 4 to 1 over his competitors and gave him 20,000 of their votes. He beat Senator John Edwards by just 17,000 votes and gained the momentum needed for his later victories (Drehle 2008).

Exercise 7.8	Community Organizing

Find out what community-based organizing associations are operating in your area. You can do this by checking out the Web sites for national organizations (IAF, Gamaliel, PICO, etc.) and finding the respective affiliates in your state.

Attend a meeting of a local community organization and write a four-page paper that discusses (a) the issues upon which the organization is currently focusing, (b) how it decided upon those issues, and (c) the organization's strategy as it works on those issues. Discuss how these three items relate to (1) the sociological eye and (2) the sociological imagination, and what suggestions you can make that might help the organization to be even more successful and powerful in accomplishing its mission.

SOCIOLOGIST IN ACTION: FRANCES FOX PIVEN

Frances Fox Piven is a sociologist who never ceases to use her sociological research to influence society. When awarded the 2003 American Sociological Association's "Award for the Public Understanding of Sociology," the Distinguished Professor of Political Science and Sociology at the Graduate School and University Center of the City University of New York was described as "a scholar who is equally at home

(Continued)

(Continued)

in the university setting and the world of politics" ("ASA Award Recipients Honored" 2003). The author or coauthor of renowned sociological texts on the disenfranchisement and political power of poor Americans (e.g., *Regulating the Poor* 1972/1993; *Poor People's Movements* 1977; *The New Class War* 1982/1985; *Why Americans Don't Vote* 1988; *Why Americans Still Don't Vote* 2000), she puts her knowledge into action in the political arena. For example, in the 1960s, she used her research to expand welfare benefits. Her efforts to enfranchise the poor were instrumental in establishing the National Voter Registration Act of 1993 (popularly known as the Motor Voter Act).[10] She has fought an unrelenting battle against the "welfare reform" initiated in 1996, and has been a consistent proponent of the politics of disruption and mass protest.

In a recent article, Piven (2005) describes her advice for democratic reform movements today in the following way: "Yes, we should work on our agenda of democratic reforms, including a national right to vote, a national voter registration system, the implementation of the National Voter Registration Act, Election Day a holiday, nonpartisan election officials, and so on. But we have to do more. . . . The time when mass protest is possible will come. We should be ready and receptive, obdurate and bold. The hip-hop voter registration campaign had a slogan, 'vote or die.' They were on the right track." Piven is one of the boldest living sociologists. Importantly, she is a dedicated social scientist as well as an activist. She conducts good social scientific research that can be examined and critiqued objectively.

Although not everyone, or even all sociologists, would agree with Piven's strategies for political action, many have been inspired by her efforts to make our society a democracy in which people of all classes are represented equally.

SOCIOLOGIST IN ACTION: ADRIAN CHEVRAUX-FITZHUGH

Did you know that corporations have the legal right, under the First Amendment, to initiate and participate in political campaigns? Adrian Chevraux-Fitzhugh used sociological tools he gained as a sociology master's student at Humboldt State University to examine people's knowledge about "corporate personhood" and their attitudes toward corporate involvement in political elections. He designed a countywide telephone survey for Democracy Unlimited of Humboldt County (DUHC 2005), which revealed that "only 35% of respondents were familiar with the concept of 'corporate personhood,' which is the legal doctrine that allows corporations to claim the same constitutional rights of human beings. . . . [Moreover], a significant majority opposes allowing corporations to participate in local elections."

These results were utilized by DUHC in their ongoing efforts to educate citizens about the relationship between corporations and democracy in the United States. If you'd like to find out more about corporate personhood and determine whether you think it makes sense in a democracy, please go to www.pbs.org/now/politics/corprights.html.

Exercise 7.9   Culture and Human Rights

1. Go to the Web site for the United Nations Population Fund's "State of World Population 2008" at www.unfpa.org/swp and read the conclusion. (Feel free to read the whole report, if you would like to do so!)

2. Write a one- to two-page paper that uses the information in the report to describe the "link between cultural fluency, cultural politics and tackling the root causes of distress and denial of human rights."

Exercise 7.10   Are Fair Trade Products Worth the Extra Cash?

1. Listen to the following two stories on NPR regarding "fair trade" products: "Is Fair Trade Coffee Worth the Extra Cash?" at www.npr.org/templates/story/story.php?storyId=6380988 and "Free Trade vs. Fair Trade" at www.onpointradio.org/shows/2003/09/20030909_a_main.asp.

2. Then, read the description of fair trade on the American Friends Service Committee (AFSC) Web site at www.coopamerica.org/programs/fairtrade/whattoknow/index.cfm.

3. Write a two-page paper based on the above sources and at least two other sources that you have researched on your own, offering your analysis of the merits of the fair trade movement. Some possible resources can be found at www.fairtraderesource.org and at www.globalexchange.org/campaigns/fair-trade.

Extra Credit: Include a one-page strategy plan for working with your school cafeteria to provide fair trade coffee and other fair trade alternatives for students.

Exercise 7.11   Religion, Education, and Social Power

Listen to the NPR stories "The Revival of Public Religion in Politics" at www
.onpointradio.org/shows/2002/01/20020108_b_main.asp and "Education
Funding" at www.npr.org/templates/story/story.php?storyId=1063915. Each of
these stories discusses an issue that has been identified by some of the people
being interviewed as a social problem related to power and social stratification
in the United States that needs to be addressed. For this exercise, you should
do the following:

1. Choose either the issue of inequality in education funding or the issue
   of the increasing presence of religion in American politics.

2. Do some background research on your issue. If you have chosen
   inequality in public education, you can begin your research at www
   .civilrightsproject.ucla.edu/research/deseg/Still_Looking_to_the%20
   Future_Integration_Manual.pdf or, if you have chosen the increasing
   presence of religion in American politics, you can begin your research
   at http://pewforum.org/religion-politics.

3. Develop a three-page "Policy Proposal" that addresses the issue you
   have chosen. In doing so, you should include (a) a two-page fact
   sheet that outlines, in bulleted form, the major issues, facts, and
   arguments surrounding your issue, and (b) a one-page policy suggestion
   sheet that outlines (i) the goals you believe need to be met to
   address the issue and (ii) specific (and doable) steps you suggest to
   achieve these goals.

Discussion Questions

1. Are you a knowledgeable, active, and effective citizen? What makes you think
   you are or are not? If you are, how did you become one? If you are not, why
   not, and what do you think would make you become one?

2. What opportunities do you have *right now* to influence how your (a) school,
   (b) community, (c) nation, and (d) global community operate? How many of
   these opportunities are you now using? Why?

3. Reread the discussion of Durkheim's ideas on external and internal inequality
   in Chapter 2. How might external inequality in the United States today impact
   who might be elected to public office?

4. Think of an issue you'd like to see addressed, and conduct a power analysis of who controls the decisions about that issue and how you might influence them. For example, say you want your school to serve fair trade coffee (if it does not already). Who decides what coffee the school purchases to sell on campus? How might you convince him or her to switch to fair trade coffee?

5. Have you ever worked (or are you now working) at a relatively low-wage hourly job? Why or why not?

6. What is your immediate reaction when you think of minimum- or low-wage workers? Why?

7. Do you think unions are needed for low-wage workers? Why or why not?

8. What do you think your life would be like if you worked at a low-wage hourly job for the rest of your life? How would it affect who you may marry, what kind of family you will have, what kind of home you will live in, what you will do for entertainment, and so forth?

9. How, if at all, do you think the college degree you are planning to get will affect your social class? Why?

10. How did your social class influence your decision to (a) attend college and (b) attend the particular college in which you are enrolled?

11. Why might it make good economic sense for corporations to "go green"? If you were a CEO of a major corporation, what might prompt you to invest funds in reducing your company's "environmental footprint"? Do you think more companies will do so soon? If so, which ones (and where and why)?

Suggestions for Specific Actions

1. Find a local community organizing association in your area. (You can do this by looking for "affiliated organizations" at the Web sites of the IAF, PICO, ACORN, and so forth.) Contact the lead organizer and set up a meeting with him or her. Find out what issues the organization is working on at this time. Offer to use your skills as a college student to conduct some basic research for the group to help them learn about the issues.

2. Go to the "Rock the Vote" Web site at www.rockthevote.com/home.php and follow the directions there on how to conduct a voter registration drive on your campus.

3. Go to United for a Fair Economy's Web site at www.faireconomy.org and click on "Take Action." Look through the list of actions that they are working on

and participate in one, or organize a teach-in at your home or school on a current issue related to social class, stratification, and the economic recession.

Please go to the book's Web site at www.pineforge.com/korgen3e to find further civic engagement opportunities, resources, peer-reviewed articles, and updated Web links related to this chapter.

Endnotes

1. Lyrics to "Money, Money, Money" by ABBA retrieved September 24, 2009, from http://www.metrolyrics.com/money-money-money-lyrics-abba.html.

2. For instance, this doesn't take into account student loans, whether one has a spouse who is working outside the home, children to support, and so forth.

3. White-collar workers are office workers, including managers, professionals, and other educated and salaried workers. Blue-collar work refers to manual unskilled or semiskilled labor, like that carried out by mechanics, plumbers, and factory workers. Pink-collar work is unskilled or semiskilled work traditionally carried out by women in positions such as waitresses, clerks, secretaries, and florists.

4. In general, skilled laborers earn higher wages than unskilled blue-collar workers. Some skilled blue-collar workers even earn higher salaries than some white-collar workers. For example, in 2004, the median salary of mental health workers (white collar) was $36,630, and the median salary for electricians (blue collar) was $45,200.

5. You can read more about this online through Patterson's "Where Have All the Voters Gone?" series on the History News Network at http://hnn.us/articles/1104.html.

6. Although, as Ruy Teixeira and Joel Rogers point out in *Why the White Working Class Still Matters* (2000), the working class comprises more than half of all potential voters and can swing elections (as they seem to have done in the presidential election of 2004), they have not been able to pressure elected officials to make their class-based issues a priority while in office.

7. Actually, we do not have one unified electoral system. Elections are handled at the county and state level, with rules for registering voters, designing ballots, type of voting machine, and so forth determined by local officials rather than by the federal government.

8. Anyone who knows anything about the tremendous need for affordable housing in New York City (and across the nation) will particularly appreciate this story.

9. See the IAF Web site at www.industrialareasfoundation.org/iafabout/about.htm.

10. This act was a compromise that led to allowing those applying for a driver's license to register to vote. Poor people applying for government aid programs were also supposed to be encouraged to register. Unfortunately, although many, many Americans register to vote while acquiring their driver's license, relatively few government officials have followed through with the "Motor Voter Act's" requirement that they register poor people.

References

"ASA Award Recipients Honored in Atlanta." 2003, September/October. *Footnotes.* Retrieved December 5, 2005 (http://www.asanet.org/footnotes/septoct03/fn4.html).

Associated Press. 2009, May 28. "Mortgage Delinquencies Hit Record High in Q1." Retrieved September 23, 2009 (http://www.kolotv.com/business/headlines/46400477.html).

Bureau of Labor Statistics, U.S. Department of Labor. 2006. "Working Poor and Education in 2004." Retrieved February 1, 2008 (http://www.bls.gov/opub/ted/2006/jun/wk3/art03.htm).

Bureau of Labor Statistics, U.S. Department of Labor. 2009a. "Union Members in 2008." Retrieved September 24, 2009 (http://www.bls.gov/news.release/union2.nr0.htm).

——. 2009b, September 4. "Employment Situation Summary." *Economic News Release.* Retrieved September 24, 2009 (http://www.bls.gov/news.release/pdf/empsit.pdf).

——. 2009c, March. "A Profile of the Working Poor, 2007." Retrieved May 27, 2009 (http://www.bls.gov/cps/cpswp2007.pdf).

Burnett, Victoria. 2009, April 24. "Unemployment in Spain Hits 17.4%." *New York Times.* Retrieved May 27, 2009 (http://www.nytimes.com/2009/04/25/business/global/25euecon.html).

Clinton, William Jefferson. 1994, February 16. "Federal Actions to Address Environmental Justice in Minority Populations and Low-Income Populations: Executive Order 12898 of February 11, 1994." Federal Register Presidential Documents 59:32. Retrieved June 9, 2009 (http://www.epa.gov/fedreg/eo/eo12898.pdf).

"Credit Crisis—The Essentials." 2009, May 26. *New York Times.* Retrieved May 27, 2009 (http://topics.nytimes.com/top/reference/timestopics/subjects/c/credit_crisis/index.html?inline=nyt-classifier).

Democracy Unlimited of Humboldt County. 2005, March 30. "Survey Says: Yes to Local Democracy, No to Corporate Campaign Contributions." Retrieved March 28, 2008 (http://www.duhc.org/images/Poll%20Results%20PR.doc).

Domhoff, G. W. 1983. *Who Rules America Now?* New York: Simon & Schuster.

Domhoff, G. W. [1967] 2005. *Who Rules America? Power, Politics, and Social Change.* 5th ed. New York: McGraw-Hill.

Drehle, David Von. 2008, January 4. "Obama's Youth Vote Triumph." *Time.* Retrieved February 19, 2008 (http://www.time.com/time/politics/article/0,8599,1700525,00.html).

Eckholm, Erik. 2008. "Working Poor and Young Hit Hard in Downturn." *New York Times.* Retrieved May 27, 2009 (http://www.nytimes.com/2008/11/09/us/09young.html?scp=1&sq=working%20poor%20and%20recession&st=cse).

Knowlton, Brian. 2009, April 22. "Global Economy Worst Since 1945." *New York Times.* Retrieved June 3, 2009 (http://www.nytimes.com/2009/04/23/business/economy/23outlook.html).

Korgen, Jeffry. 2006. *My Lord and My God.* Mahwah, NJ: Paulist Press.

McDonald, Michael. 2009. "2008 Current Population Survey Voting and Registration Supplement." United States Election Project. Retrieved May 27, 2009 (http://elections.gmu.edu/CPS_2008.html).

Mills, C. Wright. [1956] 1970. *The Power Elite*. New York: Oxford University Press.

Morgenson, Gretchen. 2008, October 22. "Credit Rating Agency Heads Grilled by Lawmakers." *New York Times*. Retrieved May 29, 2009 (http://www.nytimes.com/2008/10/23/business/economy/23rating.html?_r=1).

O'Neil, Sandra George. 2007. "Superfund: Evaluating the Impact of Executive Order 12898." *Environmental Health Perspectives* 115(7):1087–93. Retrieved June 10, 2009 (http://www.ehponline.org/members/2007/9903/9903.pdf).

OpenSecrets.org. 2009a. "2008 Overview: Stats at a Glance." Retrieved May 27, 2009 (http://www.opensecrets.org/overview/index.php?cycle=2008&Type=A&Display=A).

OpenSecrets.org. 2009b. "Banking on Becoming President." Retrieved June 4, 2009 (http://www.opensecrets.org/pres08/index.php).

Patterson, Thomas E. 2003. *The Vanishing Voter: Public Involvement in an Age of Uncertainty*. New York: Vintage.

Patterson, Thomas E. 2004a, Winter. "Where Did All the Voters Go?" *Phi Kappa Phi Forum* 84(1):11–14.

Patterson, Thomas E. 2004b. "Where Have All the Voters Gone?" *History News Network*. Retrieved May 2, 2006 (http://hnn.us/articles/1104.html).

Piketty, Thomas and Emmanuel Saez. 2007. "Thomas Piketty and Emmanuel Saez Respond to Alan Reynolds." *Economist's View*. Retrieved February 1, 2008 (http://economistsview.typepad.com/economistsview/2007/01/thomas_piketty_.html).

Piven, Frances Fox. 2005, Winter. "Voting and Voters." *Logos*. Retrieved December 5, 2005 (http://www.logosjournal.com/issue_4.1/piven.htm).

Prante, Frank. 2009, July 30. "Summary of Latest Federal Individual Income Tax Data. *Fiscal Facts* No. 183." Retrieved September 24, 2009 (http://www.taxfoundation.org/news/show/250.html).

"President: National Exit Poll." 2008, November 4. *CNN.com*. Retrieved June 9, 2009 (http://www.cnn.com/ELECTION/2008/results/polls/#USP00p1).

Skocpol, Theda. 2003. *Diminished Democracy: From Membership to Management in American Civic Life*. Norman: University of Oklahoma Press.

Teixeira, Ruy and Joel Rogers. 2000. *Why the White Working Class Still Matters*. New York: Basic Books.

U.S. Bureau of the Census. 2008, March. "Personal Income Per Capita in Current Dollars, 2007." Retrieved June 9, 2009 (http://www.census.gov/statab/ranks/rank29.html).

——. 2009a. "Historical Poverty Tables." Retrieved May 27, 2009 (http://www.census.gov/hhes/www/poverty/histpov/hstpov4.html).

——. 2009b. "Poverty: 2007 Highlights." Retrieved May 27, 2009 (http://www.census.gov/hhes/www/poverty/poverty07/pov07hi.html).

——. 2009c, July 20. "Voting and Registration in the Election of 2008." Retrieved September 24, 2009 (http://www.census.gov/population/www/socdemo/voting.html).

Weber, Max. 1968. *Economy and Society*. Totowa, NJ: Bedminster Press.

Williams, Barbara. 2009, March 26. "EPA Official of Ford Superfund Site: 'We Blew It.'" Retrieved June 10, 2009 (http://www.tradingmarkets.com/.site/news/Stock%20News/2244954).

8

What Does a "Typical American" Look Like Today?

Race and Ethnicity

Does race matter? How you answer that question has a lot to do with your own experiences and your knowledge about society. Your answer also depends on your understanding of how racial groups have been treated throughout the history of the United States. In this chapter, we will examine the relationship between immigration and race/ethnicity,[1] the social construction of race, and the persistence of racism in the "color-blind" era.

Immigration and Race/Ethnicity

Emblazoned on the Statue of Liberty is a poem by Emma Lazarus (1883/2009) representing the statue as the "mother of exiles" as it proclaims "worldwide welcome" to those spurned by other nations. The mother of exiles tells the other nations to

> Give me your tired, your poor,
>
> Your huddled masses yearning to breathe free,
>
> The wretched refuse of your teeming shore.
>
> Send these, the homeless, tempest-tost to me.

Ironically, this poem was written a year after the enactment of the first law to restrict immigration in the United States, the Chinese Exclusion Act of 1882.

Whereas earlier immigrants came primarily from Northern and Western Europe, the late 1800s saw Southern and Eastern Europeans seeking economic opportunity or refuge from persecution. On the West Coast of the United States, Chinese and Japanese immigrants also began to arrive, looking for jobs. Pseudoscience that "proved" Western Europeans were from a race superior to Eastern Europeans, Southern Europeans, and all people of color spurred negative racial *prejudice* (irrational feelings about a racial group) and racial *discrimination* (actions for or against people based on their race) against the groups deemed to be inferior. This racism, coupled with periodic economic downturns that led to increased competition for work, resulted in restricted race-based immigration policies that remained in place until 1965.

After the Chinese Exclusion Act of 1882 and the Gentlemen's Agreement of 1907, which largely curtailed Japanese immigration, a series of further laws prohibited or limited immigration of non-Western Europeans. These restrictions on immigration culminated in the National Origins Acts of 1921 and 1924, which established quotas and allowed only a trickle of immigration to continue. The 1924 Immigration Act enacted 2% immigration quotas per nation, based on the 1890 U.S. Census.[2] So, for example, Italy could send only 2% of the number of Italian people residing in the United States in 1890. A provision to the 1924 act limited immigration to those eligible for citizenship. Because only those of white and African American descent could become citizens, this, in effect, prohibited all further Asian immigration.

These restrictions remained in effect until the Immigration Act of 1965 was passed at the height of the civil rights movement and amidst worldwide pressure to overturn legalized racial discrimination in the United States. It abolished national quotas (replacing them with quotas for the Eastern and Western Hemispheres) and did much to increase immigration and alter the racial makeup of the United States. The foreign-born population rose from 4.7% in 1970 (Gibson and Lennon 1999) to 13% in 2007 (U.S. Bureau of the Census 2007). Projections indicate that by 2050, an estimated 19% of those residing in the United States will be foreign born (Passel and Cohn 2008). Among those U.S. residents in 2006 who had been born outside the United States, 30.8% were from Mexico, 23.6% from South and East Asia, 9% from the Caribbean, 7.1% from Central America, 6.7% from South America, 3.4% from the Middle East, and 19.4% from other areas of the globe (Pew Hispanic Center 2008).

As you will recall from earlier chapters, the process of globalization has benefited some nations at the expense of others. Latin American nations, for instance, have suffered greatly under globalization. The status of various immigrant groups in the United States reflects the global status of their nation of origin and their levels of education. Most Latin American nations are extremely poor, with many of their citizens drawn to the United States to find work. It is important to understand that people do not generally just up and leave their homes and families unless they are desperate (due to economic, social, or political reasons). Some of today's immigrants are even desperate enough to cross the dangerous Mexican–U.S. border illegally[3] to find jobs in the United States.

Some Asian immigrants (such as war refugees from Vietnam, Cambodia, and Laos) came to the United States with little money or education. Today, some Asians are brought over illegally to work as indentured servants in sweatshops in the Chinatowns of major cities. The vast majority of Asians immigrating to the United States today, however, are educated people with some money who immigrate legally to find greater economic opportunity than exists in their nation of origin. On the other hand, Latin American immigrants are better able to enter the United States in relatively large numbers without either education or money because of their closer proximity. One result of the disparity in education levels of the various entering immigrant groups is the differences in the positions they achieve in the U.S. workforce and in their subsequent socioeconomic status. For example, the percentage of foreign-born individuals in management and professional occupations is highest among Asians (47%) and lowest among those from Latin America (12.7%), particularly from Central America (7.9%) (Larsen 2004).

The Social Construction of Race

How do you know what race you are? It depends on where and when you live. Race is a social construction, meaning that it is defined differently from society to society and sometimes, over time, even within the same society. For example, unlike the United States, Brazil has gradations from white to black within its system of racial demarcation.

In the United States, some groups have been placed in different racial categories over time. For example, in the 1930 U.S. Census, Mexican Americans were included under the category "Mexican." However, in 1940, they were placed under "White" "unless they appeared to census interviewers to be 'definitely Indian or of other Nonwhite races' (U.S. Bureau of the Census 1943:3)" (Rodriguez 2000:84). Today, they are asked to choose a racial category listed on the Census and indicate that they are ethnically Hispanic-Latino/Mexican. In many ways, Hispanics/Latinos are treated like a distinct racial group because of their appearance and language or accent (all of which vary and largely determine the extent to which they face racial discrimination [Rodriguez 2000:84]).

Many young Italian and Irish Americans may be surprised to learn that most Americans considered them to be "less than" white until decades after they arrived in the United States in large numbers.[4] Today, sociologists define a race as a group of people *perceived* to be distinct on the basis of physical appearance (not genetic makeup[5] [Rosenfeld 2007]). Ethnicity refers to cultural rather than physical differences. This all gets even more complicated when dealing with Hispanic-Latino Americans, who, as noted above, are a distinct ethnic umbrella group but can be of any race.

Exercise 8.1   Africa and the Legacy of Colonialism

At the same time the civil rights movement was underway in the United States, a global movement for black rights was taking place. One of the results of this global movement was the end of colonial rule in Africa. (All of Africa, except Liberia and Ethiopia, had been colonized by European nations.)

1. Go to the Library of Congress's Country Studies Web site at http://lcweb2 .loc.gov/frd/cs/.

2. Select an African nation (other than Liberia or Ethiopia) and write a background paper that includes information about (a) when it was colonized, (b) what nation colonized it, (c) when it became a free nation, (d) how its borders were established, (e) how the establishment of its borders affects the nation today, and (f) the overall legacy of colonialism in the nation.

Extra Credit: Analyze the current social, political, and economic well-being of the country you have chosen. How has globalization helped or hindered the nation's growth and the overall quality of life of the citizens? You may want to look at the Web site www.hrw.org/en/africa or www.amnestyusa.org for more information and insight.

Today, the racial/ethnic makeup of the United States is still mostly white. However, the percentages of Hispanics/Latinos and Asian Americans are rapidly increasing. Table 8.1 indicates the racial demographics of the United States based on 2005 Census figures. A "biracial baby boom" over the three decades since the Supreme Court struck down laws against inter-racial marriage in 1967 has added to the diversity. Between 1970 and 2005, the racial intermarriage rate grew from less than 1% to 7.5% of all mar-riages (Lee and Edmonston 2005). In 1970, only 0.4% of married whites were in interracial marriages. Today, 3% of married whites are married to someone who is nonwhite. Similarly, the black interracial-marriage rate has grown from 1% to 7%. At the present time, 16% of married Asian Americans in the United States are married to a non-Asian, and approximately 25% of Hispanics/Latinos marry a non–Hispanic-Latino (usually a white person). In 2000, when people were allowed to choose more than one race on the U.S. Census for the first time, 2.4% of the population did so. An additional 5.5% said they were some "other" race than those listed on the Census (Lee and Edmonston 2005).

Some sociologists who research racial issues maintain that the racial classification system in the United States is changing. George Yancey (2003b) and others maintain that Asians and Hispanics/Latinos will eventually "become White." Other scholars, such as Eduardo Bonilla-Silva (Bonilla-Silva and Embrick 2005), say that the United States is beginning to establish a three-tiered racial hierarchy with *"Whites* ('traditional' whites, new 'white' immigrants; and, in the near future, assimilated Latinos, some multiracials [light-skinned ones], and individual members of other groups [some Asian Americans, etc.]" at the top (p. 33). Next will come a middle group composed of *"honorary Whites"* (most light-skinned Latino Americans, "Japanese Americans, Korean Americans, Asian Indians, Chinese Americans, the bulk of multiracials . . . and most Middle Eastern Americans" (p. 34). The bottom group, the *"collective Black,"* will consist of black Americans, dark-skinned Latino Americans, Vietnamese Americans, Cambodian Americans, Laotian Americans, and maybe Filipino Americans.[6] No matter what the *future* racial hierarchy will look like, racial inequity continues to exist in the present-day United States.

Table 8.1   U.S. Racial Demographics

Race	Percentage
White (not Hispanic-Latino)	66
Hispanic-Latino	15
Black	14
Asian	5.1
American Indian or Alaska Native	<1%

NOTE: Based on 2008 Census figures (U.S. Bureau of the Census 2008b). By 2050, it is projected that whites will be 46%, Hispanics 30%, blacks 15%, and Asians 9.2% of the U.S. population.

Exercise 8.2	Affirmative Action, Diversity, and Productivity

1. In two or three paragraphs, describe your opinion about affirmative action programs and how your socialization process influenced your opinion.

2. After carrying out Step 1, read "In Professor's Model, Diversity = Productivity" at www.nytimes.com/2008/01/08/science/08conv.html.

3. Describe the key points you learned from the article and how they impacted your understanding of and opinion about affirmative action programs.

W. E. B. Du Bois, one of the founders of sociology and an ardent advocate for the rights of black Americans, wrote in 1903 (1989) that "the problem of the twentieth century is the problem of the color-line" (p. 35). Unfortunately, the "color-line" (though it is shifting) is still very much a problem today. In fact, some current scholars maintain that "racism is an integral, permanent, and indestructible component of this society" (Bell 1992:ix). Certainly, race remains a social construction with very real consequences. Although civil rights laws and affirmative action programs abolished *de jure* (by law) discrimination and provided some opportunities for well-educated minorities to rise in socioeconomic status, *de facto* (by practice) racial discrimination persists.

Black and Hispanic Americans still lag behind most other racial groups of Americans in terms of income, wealth, education, and employment. According to the U.S. Bureau of the Census (2008a), the median household income for white Americans in 2007 was $54,920, but it was $33,916 for black and $38,679 for Hispanic Americans. Wealth, which requires time to accumulate, reveals even starker disparities between whites and black and Hispanic Americans. The respective wealth of both Hispanics and blacks is only one-tenth that of whites (U.S. Bureau of the Census 2005). While 53% of Asian Americans and 33% of white Americans are college graduates, only 20% of black and 13% of Hispanic Americans have college degrees (U.S. Bureau of the Census 2009). In April 2009, the unemployment rate was 8% for white Americans, 11.3% for Hispanic-Latino Americans, and 15% for black Americans (Bureau of Labor Statistics 2009).

Is this news to you? If you are white, it may well be. The research of many sociologists reveals that "many Whites are under the false impression that the socioeconomic playing field *is* now level" (Gallagher 2005).[7] This ignorance, reflecting a gap between what white Americans *think* is real and what the data show, is partially due to the way race has been depicted in the mass media since the mid-1990s.

The media has a powerful effect on how whites perceive racial minorities, particularly black Americans, because media outlets are the only places where most whites see and "get to know" people of color.[8] Very few whites live in racially integrated neighborhoods (National Commission on Fair Housing and Equal Opportunity 2008). So they tend to formulate their opinions about the socioeconomic status of persons of color (and everything else about racial minorities) from what they see in the media or hear from other secondary sources.

Unfortunately, the media sends a conflicting message. On the one hand, we hear rappers and some sports figures glorifying the lives of "gangbangers," connecting blackness with street life and violence (Oliver 2006). On the other hand, we also receive messages from the media that race-based disparities no longer exist. In magazines, movies, television, and so forth, U.S. society is often portrayed as if race no longer matters. Interracial couples and integrated friendship groups are depicted in advertisements for everything from restaurants to sneakers; popular television shows like *Grey's Anatomy* and *Lost* have interracial casts that never speak about race; and rarely do news programs or public officials devote time to exposing and analyzing the great racial disparities that continue to persist in the United States today.

Therefore, few white Americans realize that they benefit from *white privilege*. The concept of white privilege refers to the fact that almost every aspect of life (e.g., finding a mate, buying a car, securing a mortgage, shopping for clothes, attaining employment, driving) is easier for white Americans than for Americans of color. This privilege can be "invisible" to white Americans if they have never faced racial discrimination themselves and are disconnected from those who do experience race-based discrimination on a regular basis.[9]

The Color-Blind Ideology

Barack Obama's 2008 speech on race during the Democratic presidential primary will be long remembered because he addressed and contextualized the race-based resentments of both black and white Americans in a straightforward (and eloquent) manner. His doing so was unprecedented and downright remarkable for a public figure seeking the highest political office in the United States. When Obama won the presidency a few short months later, many commentators declared that his election signaled that we are now in a "post-racial" era. However, that is not the case. His election did not change the fact that racial inequality still exists in the United States. Although the election of an African American president certainly marks a moment of great progress, the points Obama made during his March 2008 speech on race were still true in November of 2008 and still ring true today.

Many Americans do not want to hear about the realities of racial inequality. Echoing the media portrayal of race described above, a popular view among many Americans today—particularly white Americans—is that race no longer matters. Promoters of the *color-blind ideology* maintain that we should all act as though we are "color-blind" when it comes to race. Many even go so far as to say that people who talk about and notice racial differences are actually causing racial friction that would otherwise not exist. However, as President Obama pointed out, this is far from true. Racial tensions have existed in the United States for centuries and continue to the present day. Trying to avoid noticing them will not alleviate them.

Exercise 8.3   Survey on Race in the United States

Conduct a survey of the members of one of your classes. On the survey, ask respondents to respond to the following statements and questions:

(Provide them with the following options for statements 1 to 3, and ask them to circle one to indicate their level of agreement: Strongly Agree, Somewhat Agree, Not Sure, Somewhat Disagree, Strongly Disagree.)

1. The socioeconomic status of whites and people from other races in the United States is relatively equal.

2. Racism is often exaggerated by members of minority groups.

3. People of all races have relatively equal chances to become successful in the United States today.

4. What, if any, college courses have you taken that deal with racial and ethnic relations?

5. What is your race/ethnicity?

Compare the answers of respondents of (a) different racial/ethnic groups and (b) those who have and those who have not taken any courses that deal with racial and ethnic relations. Analyze your results.

Partly in response to the influence of the color-blind ideology, most people feel uncomfortable noticing racial differences or talking about race, particularly with members of another race (those most likely to provide us with a different perspective). One of the authors of this book found through her research (Korgen 2002) that even blacks and whites who are close friends tend to avoid talking about racial issues. This avoidance is problematic for anyone interested in promoting racial justice. If we want to end racial discrimination, we have to acknowledge that races are treated differently.

Before we can effectively fight racial discrimination, we must uncover and confront it. We must also make the "invisible privileges" (Rothenberg 2004) of whiteness visible. To do so, we need to notice and keep track of how different racial groups are treated. For example, if we did not do so, we would not know that, in New York City, whites have a greater chance of being hired than Hispanics and fully twice the likelihood of equally qualified blacks (Schultz and Barnes 2005). Without keeping racial data, we also would not have benefited from the recent field experiment in Milwaukee, Wisconsin, which revealed that black Americans with clean records have no greater chance of being hired than white Americans just released from prison (Pager 2007), nor would we know that governmental responses to emergencies differ, based on the race of the citizens affected (Bullard 2008). These and an overwhelming number of other studies illustrate conclusively that race *does* matter, and that we cannot be color-blind when it comes to creating and implementing policy in the United States.

The color-blind perspective on race also runs counter to the discipline of sociology. It does more than impact the efforts of racial justice organizations and policy makers working toward better equality of opportunity and outcome. It also undermines two of the most powerful goals of sociology: to observe how society really works and to give voice to the marginalized and minority groups within it.

Racism Is a Global Issue

Racism is not just an American problem. The concepts of race and ethnicity have been used to separate and distinguish groups of people from all over the globe. Wherever you go in the world, you will find, to varying degrees, some racial and ethnic tension. Western Europe provides a good example of past and present racial tensions. Historically, the peoples of Western Europe have suffered many wars among their nations that were, at least in part, due to racism and *ethnocentrism* (the belief that one's ethnic or racial group is superior to all others). In fact, the leaders of Nazi Germany deemed the Aryan race to be the ideal race and Jewish people to comprise a race that must be eradicated. They succeeded in killing 6 million Jews in history's largest genocide, and made Western Europe a place where few Jewish people remain.

Over the past two decades, Western Europe has become more racially and ethnically diverse due to the arrival of increasing numbers of Asian, Middle Eastern, and African immigrants searching for work. With this diversity have come new types of racial and ethnic tension. When plenty of jobs exist and immigrants are needed to fill the ones that citizens of those nations do not want, immigrants tend to be more welcome. However, when jobs become tight and citizens feel that they must compete with others for them, immigrants can become easy targets. The different races and religions of many of the immigrants in European nations have helped spark anger toward, and sometimes violence against, nonwhite and non-Christian immigrants. This racism and ethnocentrism is evidenced in soccer stadiums across Europe. Today, "almost every country in Europe has racist signs, chants and even violence at soccer stadiums, particularly from rightist groups that single out blacks, Jews, Muslims or other ethnic groups" (Vecsey 2003). Indeed, racism has been described as the "scourge" of soccer stadiums in Europe (Pugmire 2009).

Exercise 8.4	Racism in Sports

Go to "Beautiful Game Turned Ugly: Racism in Europe's Soccer Arenas" at www.youtube.com/watch?v=W-iRLmaZf4A.

Based upon the information in the video and what you have read in this chapter, answer the following questions:

1. Were you surprised by the information in the video? Why or why not?

2. If you were the commissioner of FIFA (the international football [soccer] federation), what would you do to curb the racist behavior at the stadiums? What makes you think your efforts would succeed (or not)?

3. How might addressing racial inequality in European nations be more or less difficult than addressing it in the United States?

Exercise 8.5	Has Martin Luther King, Jr.'s Dream Been Realized?

1. Go to the Web site www.holidays.net/mlk/speech.htm.

2. Read and watch Dr. Martin Luther King, Jr.'s "I Have a Dream" speech.

3. List the points King makes about when he will be "satisfied" with the situation for black people in America.

4. Check off those goals that have now been achieved. *Provide evidence* for your decisions to check off or not check off each point. Some of these may be partially achieved, whereas others may have been fully achieved or not at all.

5. Listen to the two stories "A Victim of Racial Profiling" at www.youth radio.org/society/kpfa051001_dna.shtml and "The Legacy of the 'Little Rock Nine'" at www.npr.org/templates/story/story.php?storyId=14692397.

6. Based on all of the above, do you think Martin Luther King, Jr., would be satisfied with the status of black Americans today? Why or why not? If not, how do you suggest that we move toward a fuller realization of his dream? What specific policy recommendations would you make?

Exercise 8.6	White Privilege

Peggy McIntosh did much to bring white privilege to public recognition with her essay "White Privilege: Unpacking the Invisible Knapsack" (1989), in which she listed some of the "daily effects of White privilege" on her life.

If you are white, come up with a list of approximately 10 privileges that you (personally) receive for being white. (Do not, for example, state that you would have an easier time getting a mortgage unless you actually have a mortgage and you had an easy time getting it.) If you are a person of color, come up with a list of approximately 10 privileges that you think a white person receives for being white.

Compare your answers with those of other members of the class.

1. What are the most significant differences among the lists?

2. Who do you think had the most difficult time coming up with the 10 privileges? Who had the easiest time? Why?

| Exercise 8.7 | Your Family and Issues of Race |

Write a one- to two-page paper that answers the following questions:

1. When you were growing up, what did you hear about racial issues from your family? (e.g., were racial issues ever seriously discussed? If so, why and how often was race a topic of serious discussion? Did your family tend to bring up race only when making jokes or insulting comments about members of other races? Did they speak from a viewpoint of color-blindness and thus discourage any discussion of the real, pressing issues associated with race and racism?)

2. How do you think the racial makeup of your family influenced how race was discussed (or not discussed) in your family?

3. How do your answers to the first two questions relate to what you have learned in this chapter? How does the information in this chapter help you, if at all, to reevaluate your views on race, immigration, and racism?

| Exercise 8.8 | "A More Perfect Union" |

Go to www.youtube.com/watch?v=pWe7wTVbLUU and watch Barack Obama deliver his "A More Perfect Union" speech.

Write a two- to three-page paper that describes (a) the major points Obama makes in the speech, (b) how they relate to what you learned in this chapter (making sure to address how this speech challenges the color-blind ideology), and (c) your reaction to the speech. (If you heard the speech when it was first given on March 18, 2008, compare your reaction to it then and your reaction to it now, after reading this chapter.)

SOCIOLOGIST IN ACTION: GEORGE YANCEY

Dr. Martin Luther King, Jr., once said that Sunday morning is "the most segregated time of the week." George Yancey is committed to the day when this statement will no longer be the case. He works with a $500,000 Lilly grant and with Dr. Michael Emerson and Dr. Karen Chai to conduct the first national attempt to map out and understand multiracial churches. From the work with this grant, he has written *One Body, One Spirit* (2003a), a book that is marketed toward Christians and that dispenses practical advice as to how they can racially diversify their congregations. In this way, Yancey is able to translate his academic research into a written format that nonacademics can use.

In addition to writing for this audience, Yancey has also consulted with churches that are seeking to become more racially diverse. Using quantitative and qualitative methodology, he is able to assess social and cultural patterns within the churches that may unintentionally set up barriers against potential worshippers from other races. Yancey also is working with Mosaix (http://mosaix.info), an organization that is committed to building a network of multiracial congregations. Within the framework of this emerging network, Yancey can also disseminate results of his research as well as aid others who are supportive of developing racially diverse congregations.

Racially diverse congregations will not be possible unless some of the misunderstandings and stereotypes that have developed between Christians of different races are resolved. To this end, Yancey has written to the Christian audience about dealing with racial issues. For example, he and his wife, Sherelyn, have edited a work about interracial families for Christian audiences in a book entitled *Just Don't Marry One* (Yancey and Yancey 2003). His writings in such works are a mixture of sociological thought and Christian theology. Thus, they are designed to reach a nonacademic group by speaking in the language of Yancey's intended audience.

Discussion Questions

1. Close your eyes and picture an American citizen. What does the person you pictured look like? Why do you think you imagined the race/ethnicity of the person in the way that you did? (It might be interesting to ask people who are not in this course the same question after you have answered for yourself. If you only ask them to "describe" the person, note whether they mention race.)

2. Do you have a good friend who is of a different race from yourself? If so, how did you meet? Do you ever talk seriously about racial issues? Why or why not? If you do not have a good friend of another race, why do you think that is?

3. How can sociology be used to (a) recognize, (b) publicize, and (c) combat racial discrimination? Be specific and clearly explain your answers.

4. Why do you think so many people want to believe that "race doesn't matter anymore"? What do you think would happen if we no longer kept track of different racial groups in our society? What might be the beneficial effects of not doing so? What might be the negative consequences?

5. What do you think your parents would say if you told them you were going to marry someone of a different race? Why? Would it depend on *what* race? Why?

6. What are some ways that racial discrimination takes place in our public school systems without anyone *intentionally* doing anything to harm a particular racial group? What are some ways unintended racial discrimination occurs on your own campus?

7. Which groups of prospective students (other than racial groups) do you think have an easier time gaining admittance and paying for a college education than other prospective students? Why do you think people have a harder time with race-based affirmative action programs, rather than the preferential treatment given to other (non–race-based) groups?

8. Do you think multiracial Americans should be given a separate "multiracial" box to check on the U.S. Census? What do you think would be some outcomes of the establishment of such a category?

9. What is the difference between *prejudice* and *discrimination*? How can you detect prejudice if there is no evidence of discrimination?

10. What do you think Marx would say is the root cause of racial discrimination? Do you agree? Why or why not?

11. How might community organizing groups make people of all races/ethnicities realize their common self-interests? Can you think of an issue that would unite students of all races/ethnicities at your school? What is it? What could you do to organize all racial groups on campus around that issue?

Suggestions for Specific Actions

1. Conduct interviews with top administrators at your school to find out (a) what they think is the obligation of an institution of higher education regarding combating racism in society and (b) what specific things your school is doing to combat racism. If you think the school should be doing more, organize a group of like-minded students, faculty, and staff to create more antiracism efforts on campus.

2. Go to the NAACP Web site at www.naacp.org/home/index.htm. Look over the volunteer opportunities listed there and find one you are interested in pursuing. Find the number of your local NAACP chapter (by calling 877-NAACP-98) and offer your services.

   Or join or volunteer with another race/ethnicity-based organization (e.g., MANA at www.hermana.org/homfrm.htm, League of United Latin American Citizens at http://lulac.org, the Conference on Asian Pacific American Leadership [CAPAL] at www.capal.org/ee/pages, or the American Indian Movement at www.aimovement.org).

Please go to this book's Web site at www.pineforge.com/korgen3e to find further civic engagement opportunities, resources, peer-reviewed articles, and updated Web links related to this chapter.

Endnotes

1. Although we have noted that ethnicity and race are two distinct concepts, we group them together in several places in this chapter. We typically do so when we are including Hispanics/Latinos in the discussion because they are an *ethnic* group that tends to be viewed—both by its own members and by other Americans—as a distinct *racial* group.

2. The quotas were based on the U.S. population back in 1890, when the numbers of darker-skinned Europeans (such as Italians) were lower than they were in 1924.

3. To enter and settle in the United States legally, immigrants must prove either that they have close family members living legally in the United States (who would initially house or support them) or that they have a certain occupational skill that is in short supply. However, the waiting list even among those eligible to receive a visa is very long because the demand to enter the United States far exceeds the quota allowed.

4. In the middle decades of the 1800s, Irish Americans were commonly portrayed in newspaper and magazine cartoons as apes.

5. Thanks to the Human Genome Project, we now know that physical differences vary more within than among races (Jorde and Wooding 2004).

6. Bonilla-Silva and Embrick (2005) acknowledge that some individual members of these groups may fall outside the designated tier.

7. For a full discussion of this, see p. 108 of Gallagher (2005).

8. Black Americans are more isolated than either Hispanic or Asian Americans (see Charles 2003).

9. For a great discussion of "invisible privileges," see Paula Rothenberg's (2004) *Invisible Privilege: A Memoir About Race, Class, and Gender.*

References

Bell, Derrick. 1992. *Faces at the Bottom of the Well.* New York: Basic Books.

Bonilla-Silva, Eduardo and David G. Embrick. 2005. "Black, Honorary White, White: The Future of Race in the United States." Pp. 33–48 in *Mixed Messages: Multiracial Identities in the Color-Blind Era*, edited by David Brunsma. Boulder, CO: Lynne Rienner.

Bullard, Robert D. 2008. "Differential Vulnerabilities: Environmental and Economic Inequality and Government Response to Unnatural Disasters." *Social Research*, 75(3):753–84.

Bureau of Labor Statistics, U.S. Department of Labor. 2009. "Employment Situation Summary: April 2009." Retrieved September 26, 2009 (http://www.bls.gov/news /release/archives/empsit_05082009.pdf).

Charles, Camille Z. 2003. "The Dynamics of Racial Residential Segregation." *Annual Review of Sociology* 29(1):167–207.

Du Bois, W. E. B. [1903] 1989. *The Souls of Black Folk*. New York: Penguin Books.

Gallagher, Charles. 2005. "Colorblindness: An Obstacle to Racial Justice?" Pp. 103–16 in *Mixed Messages: Multiracial Identities in the Color-Blind Era*, edited by David Brunsma. Boulder, CO: Lynne Rienner.

Gibson, Campbell J. and Emily Lennon. 1999. "Historical Census Statistics on the Foreign-Born Population of the United States: 1850 to 1990." *Working Paper No. 29*, U.S. Bureau of the Census, Population Division. Retrieved December 19, 2005 (http://www.census.gov/population/www/documentation/ twps0029/twps0029.html).

Jorde, Lynn B. and Stephen P. Wooding. 2004. "Genetic Variation, Classification, and 'Race.'" *Nature Genetics* 36:S28–S33. Retrieved December 19, 2005 (http://www .nature.com/ng/journal/v36/n11s/full/ng1435.html).

Korgen, Kathleen Odell. 2002. *Crossing the Racial Divide: Close Friendships Between Black and White Americans*. Westport, CT: Praeger.

Larsen, Luke. J. 2004. "The Foreign-Born Population in the United States: 2003." *Current Population Reports*. Retrieved September 26, 2009 (http://www.census .gov/prod/2004pubs/p20-551.pdf).

Lazarus, Emma. [1883] 2009. "The New Colossus." Academy of American Poets. Retrieved June 10, 2009 (http://www.poets.org/viewmedia.php/prmMID/16111).

Lee, Sharon M. and Barry Edmonston. 2005, June. "New Marriages, New Families: U.S. Racial and Hispanic Intermarriage." *Population Bulletin*, 60(2). Retrieved December 19, 2005 (http://www.prb.org/pdf05/60.2NewMarriages .pdf).

McIntosh, Peggy. 1989, July. "White Privilege: Unpacking the Invisible Knapsack." *Peace and Freedom*. Retrieved May 7, 2008 (http://www.kwsasc.org/resources/pdfs/anti- oppression/WHITE%20PRIVILEGE.pdf).

National Commission on Fair Housing and Equal Opportunity. 2008, December. "The Future of Fair Housing." Retrieved February 26, 2009 (http://civilrights.org/pub lications/reports/fairhousing).

Oliver, William. 2006. "'The Streets': An Alternative Black Male Socialization Institution." *Journal of Black Studies* 36(6):918–37.

Pager, Devah. 2007. *MARKED: Race, Crime, and Finding Work in an Era of Mass Incarceration*. Chicago: University of Chicago Press.

Passel, Jeffrey and D'Vera Cohn. 2008, February 11. "Immigration to Play Lead Role in Future U.S. Growth." Pew Research Center. Retrieved February 19, 2008 (http://pewresearch.org/pubs/729/united-states-population-projections).

Pew Hispanic Center. 2008, January 23. "Statistical Portrait of the Foreign-Born Population in the United States, 2006." *Reports and Factsheets*. Retrieved February 19, 2008 (http://pewhispanic.org/factsheets/factsheet.php?FactsheetID=36).

Pugmire, Jerome. 2009, February 2. "Little Done to Stop Racism in European Soccer." *USA Today*. Retrieved September 26, 2009 (http://www.usatoday.com/sports/soccer/2009-02-07-1089560368_x.htm).

Rodriguez, Clara E. 2000. *Changing Race: Latinos, the Census, and the History of Ethnicity in the United States*. New York: New York University Press.

Rosenfeld, Michael J. 2007. *Age of Independence: Interracial Unions, Same-Sex Unions, and the Changing American Family*. Cambridge, MA: Harvard University Press.

Rothenberg, Paula. 2004. *Invisible Privilege: A Memoir About Race, Class, and Gender*. Lawrence: University Press of Kansas.

Schultz, Steven and Steven Barnes. 2005. "Many New York Employers Discriminate Against Minorities, Ex-Offenders." *News@Princeton*. April 1. Retrieved December 19, 2005 (http://www.princeton.edu/main/news/archive/S11/23/70K64/index.xml?section=newsreleases).

U.S. Bureau of the Census. 2005, August 30. "Income Stable, Poverty Rate Increases, Percentages of Americans Without Health Insurance Unchanged." Retrieved July 24, 2006 (http://www.census.gov/Press-Release/www/releases/archives/income_wealth/005647.html).

——. 2007. "United States Population and Housing Narrative Profile: 2007" Retrieved May 28, 2009 (http://factfinder.census.gov/servlet/NPTable?_bm=y&-qr_name=ACS_2007_1YR_G00_NP01&-geo_id=01000US&-gc_url=null&-ds_name=&-_lang=en).

——. 2008a, August 26. "Household Income Rises, Poverty Rate Unchanged, Number of Uninsured Down." Retrieved May 28, 2009 (http://www.census.gov/Press-Release/www/releases/archives/income_wealth/012528.html).

——. 2008b, August 14. "An Older and More Diverse Nation by Midcentury." Retrieved May 28, 2009 (http://www.census.gov/Press-Release/www/releases/archives/population/012496.html?KeepThis=true&TB_iframe=true&height=540.9&width=800).

——. 2009, April 27. "Census Bureau Releases Data Showing Relationship Between Education and Earnings." Retrieved May 7, 2009 (http://www.census.gov/Press-Release/www/releases/archives/education/013618.html).

Vecsey, George. 2003, February 2. "SOCCER; England Battles the Racism Infesting Soccer." *The New York Times*, Section 8, p. 1. Retrieved September 26, 2009 (http://www.nytimes.com/2003/02/02/sports/soccer-england-battles-the-racism-infesting-soccer.html?fta=y).

Yancey, George. 2003a. *One Body, One Spirit*. Downers Grove, IL: InterVarsity Press.

——. 2003b. *Who Is White? Latinos, Asians, and the New Black/Nonblack Divide*. Boulder, CO: Lynne Rienner.

Yancey, George and Sherelyn Yancey, ed. 2003. *Just Don't Marry One: Interracial Dating, Marriage, and Parenting*. Valley Forge, PA: Judson Press.

9

Sex, Gender, and Power

Imagine you have just found out that you are going to be a parent. What are your hopes and dreams for your child? What games will you play with your little one? Can you picture yourself as the coach of one of your child's sports teams? Can you imagine you and your child baking cookies together? Now, think about some of your child's characteristics. Is your child going to be tough? Sensitive? A leader? A follower? More than likely, these questions are difficult for you to answer without first picturing whether your child will be a boy or a girl.

Although the physical characteristics and genetic makeup of girls and boys play a major role in the adults they will become, so do the gender roles assigned to them. All parents see their children through glasses tinted by gender socialization. Through gender socialization, we learn to apply dissimilar social roles to boys and girls. The result is that we treat boys and girls differently and they, in turn, learn to act in "masculine" or "feminine" ways. In this chapter, we examine how gender is socially constructed, how gender construction relates to the distribution of power in society, the status of women as a minority group in the United States (minority or majority status is based on power), and how we might address the inequality of power between men and women.

The Social Construction of Gender

A person's sex is determined by the physical characteristics that distinguish males and females,[1] whereas gender is determined by the social roles assigned to males and females in society. As such, gender is socially constructed. Sex

140

differences remain constant (almost always[2]), while gender differs over time and from society to society. For example, in the mid-1900s, there were more male than female doctors in the United States, but women dominated the medical field in the Soviet Union. Today, voting and driving a vehicle are both perceived as inappropriate (and, in fact, illegal) behaviors for women in Saudi Arabia, whereas they seem natural and appropriate for women in much of the rest of the world.

Here in the United States, until recently it was seen as inappropriate for girls to play ice hockey because it was thought to be too physical a game for them and was considered unfeminine. However, over the past 15 years, as women's roles and the idea of femininity have been reconstructed, the number of girls and women who have registered with USA Hockey has jumped from 10,000 in 1992–1993 to 59,500 in 2008–2009 (USA Hockey 2009) (see www.usa hockey.com//Template_Usahockey.aspx?NAV=PL_07&ID=176314).

| Exercise 9.1 | Gender, Relationships, and Socialization |

1. Make a list of the 10 characteristics you are most looking for in a boyfriend or girlfriend.

2. On a separate piece of paper, make a list of the 10 characteristics that you think a man or woman is most looking for in you.

3. Have your professor collect these and tally up the results, following the instructions we have provided on our Web site (www.pineforge.com/korgen3e).

4. Analyze the results. What are men most looking for? What are women most looking for? What are the differences between these? What are the causes of these differences? What are the social effects of these differences—that is, how do they affect the gender roles and the social power of men and women?

5. Further analysis: What did women think that potential partners were looking for in them? What did men think that potential partners were looking for in them? Compare these results to those found in the responses to question 4.

6. Were women or men more accurate in guessing what their potential partners were looking for? Why? How does gender socialization help to explain this?

7. How does gender socialization promote heterosexuality at the expense of other sexual orientations?

Although people's personalities, talents, and outlooks on life are based on a combination of genetic (nature) and social (nurture) factors, sociologists focus on the social factors. In the case of gender and sexuality, we study the social roles applied to men and women through gender socialization. While doing so, it is important to remember that gender socialization intersects with how we deal with race, ethnicity, age, sexual orientation, and so forth. So, when we discuss how gender socialization impacts men and women, also keep in mind that racism, ethnocentrism, ageism, and homophobia exist alongside socialized gender roles and sexism. Many people face multiple forms of discrimination.

Exercise 9.2	Discrimination and You

1. Make a list of five times when you have been discriminated against in your life. At least three of these should be based on some biological fact that you can't change about yourself (your race, height, sex, age, sexuality, hair color, body type, etc.). Try, if you can, to list multiple biological facts for which you have been discriminated against.

2. Make a list of five times that you have been prejudiced against or discriminated against someone (or a group of people). Make sure that at least three of the five were based on biological facts that the person (or group of people) couldn't change.

3. Write a two- to three-page essay that discusses (a) your own experiences being discriminated against, including how it felt and how it made you act/react; (b) why you were prejudiced or discriminated against others; (c) how a person can face multiple points of discrimination; and (d) what you might be able to do, in your own life, to be less prejudiced and less likely to discriminate against other groups of people.

Gender-based discrimination impacts the life chances (opportunities each individual has to improve his or her quality of life) of girls and boys even before they are born. Even in utero, parents treat children differently on the basis of their sex. The process of gender socialization begins from the moment parents learn the sex of their child. For example, mothers who speak to their unborn children tend to do so more sharply and forcefully when they know the baby is a boy (Smith 2005). Choices of baby shower gifts and the color of the baby's room and clothes are also often based on the gender roles we assign to males and females. Even how we hold, handle, and care for babies varies according to the assigned gender roles. Although it is often impossible for strangers to tell the sex of babies if they have a diaper on, those who are perceived to be girls are typically treated much more gently than those who are perceived to be boys (MacDonald and Parke 1986).

| Exercise 9.3 | Gender Differences in Personal Ads |

1. Write an advertisement for the "Personals" section of a hypothetical newspaper. In your ad, describe yourself (in at least 40 words) and what you are looking for in a partner (in at least 40 words).

2. Get in groups of four (preferably two women and two men) and read your ads to each other. What do these ads tell you about gender and the way we are socialized to maintain and conform to gender roles?

| Exercise 9.4 | Media Images of Women and Men |

Women, read the following statement by Lynne Grefe, CEO of the National Eating Disorders Association (NEDA), and answer the questions below it.

> In 1965, the average fashion model weighed just eight percent less than the average American woman. . . . The average fashion model today is 5'11" and weighs 117 pounds, which makes her thinner than 98 percent of women. Three-quarters of the female characters in TV situation comedies are underweight. Yet the average woman stands 5'4," weighs 140 pounds and wears between a size 12 [and] 16. We know that continued exposure to unrealistic images is linked to depression, loss of self-esteem and the development of unhealthy eating habits in women and girls. Genetics may load the gun, but society pulls the trigger. (NEDA 2009)

1. Do you think the media regularly exposes you to unrealistic images of women? Why or why not?

2. Do you ever find yourself trying to mold your body into one of those unrealistic images? Why or why not?

3. What do you think you and other people can do to (a) counter the effects of and (b) diminish the prevalence of such unrealistic portrayals of women in the media?

Men, read "If being a man means having body hair and sweating, why are the sexy guys in ads immune to both?" at seedmagazine.com/content/article/the_media_assault_on_male_body_image and answer the following questions:

1. Do you think the media regularly exposes you to unrealistic images of men, such as those described in the article? Why or why not?

(Continued)

(Continued)

2. What is your reaction to the findings described in the article? Does your answer relate to the amount of media you tend to consume? Why or why not?

3. What do you think you and other people can do to (a) counter the effects of and (b) diminish the prevalence of such unrealistic portrayals of men in the media?

Exercise 9.5   A (Gendered) Tour Through a Toy Store

Go to a major (chain) toy store and try to find a toy (not a piece of sports equipment) that is not marketed specifically toward a boy or a girl. Be sure to take note of the following:

1. What is the layout of the store? Are there distinct boys' and girls' sections?

2. What types of toys are marketed toward girls? What types of toys are marketed toward boys?

3. What types of words and descriptions are used on the toys to market them toward girls or boys?

4. Are there many toys that do not indicate on the packaging (e.g., have pictures of either all girls or all boys on it) the sex of the child for which they are deemed appropriate?

5. How did you find the toy you selected? Was it easy or difficult to find? Where was it located? Based upon your experience in the toy store, write a two- to three-page paper that analyzes how toys are a means of gender socialization. What values do they teach boys and girls? For what social roles are these toys teaching and training boys and girls?

Sometimes gender socialization can have life-or-death consequences for babies. For example, in some Asian nations, more boy than girl babies are carried to term and born. As James Mahon (2005) notes, limits on how many children couples are allowed to have and the culturally based preference for sons in China have resulted in "sex-selective" abortions of girls to such an extent that there are now far more boys than girls in China. A similar situation exists in India. Today, in both nations, there are 700–900 female births for every 1,000 male births (Sheth 2006). One societal consequence of this female infanticide is that there is now a shortage of women for men to marry in these nations (Hsu 2008).

As males and females move from birth to childhood to adulthood, they learn that they are expected to conform to the gender roles society has assigned to them. This process involves learning what toys to play with, how to speak (what tone, how often, to whom, etc.), how to present oneself in public, what sports to play (if any), what jobs or professions to consider, and so on. This gender socialization impacts how men and women view the world, as well as each other. For example, the political issues people deem most important tend to vary by gender. There is much evidence that women today, as a group, have different political opinions from men. There has been a "gender gap" in every U.S. presidential election since 1980. The gender gap refers to the percentage difference in men's and women's choice for president. For example, in 2008, a total of 56% of women but only 49% of men voted to elect Barack Obama to the office of U.S. president (Center for American Women and Politics [CAWP] 2009a).

Gender Socialization and Sex Roles

Gender socialization also includes learning sex roles (how to act in dating situations and sexually). As they grow older, boys and girls learn different lessons about with whom it is appropriate for them to act in a sexual manner, when it is permissible to have sex, and how they should have sexual relations. Although some societies are more open than others, the majority of people in almost all modern societies view heterosexual behavior (sex between men and women) as more appropriate and socially desirable than homosexual or bisexual behavior. This, of course, has negative ramifications for those who, despite gender socialization, are sexually attracted to certain people of the same sex or members of both sexes.

However, there are also many indications that norms around sexual orientation are beginning to shift and that same-sex romantic relationships are becoming increasingly accepted. Legal support for same-sex marriage is growing across the globe. The Netherlands, Belgium, Canada, Spain, South Africa, and Norway now recognize same-sex marriage.

Many think it is just a matter of time before same-sex marriage becomes legal throughout the United States, as increasing numbers of young people favor its legalization. Today, the majority (57%, in an April 2009 poll) of people in the United States under age 40 support gay marriage (Nagourney 2009). Same-sex marriages are now legal in the states of Massachusetts, Iowa, Vermont, New Hampshire, and Connecticut. However, these unions are not yet recognized by the federal government. Therefore, legally married same-sex couples are still not granted the federal benefits that heterosexual married couples have such as joint filing of federal taxes, health insurance for spouses of federal employees, social security benefits for surviving spouses, and so on. The battle to end discrimination regarding same- sex marriage is far from over.

Exercise 9.6   The Storm

The following videos provide good illustrations of the ongoing struggle over cultural norms about same-sex relationships: "A Gathering Storm" at http://www.youtube.com/watch?v=Wp76ly2_NolΕe and the parody of it, "A Gaythering Storm," at www.funnyordie.com/videos/6eddb255b2/a-gaythering-storm.

Watch the videos and answer the following questions:

1. Did you find yourself agreeing with the message of "A Gathering Storm"? What about your gender socialization led you to feel this way?

2. How did you react to "A Gaythering Storm"? What about your gender socialization led you to feel this way?

3. Fifty years from now, how do you think that most Americans will view each of these videos? Why? Does your response provide evidence that gender roles are social constructions? Why or why not?

Gender Roles and Power

Gender roles basically confine members of both sexes to certain types of behavior and limit their freedom to act without fear of social disapproval. Those who vary from their gender-based roles face negative sanctions. For example, husbands who choose to stay at home and take care of their children while their wives work outside the home are often looked upon as not "true" men. The neighbor of one of the authors has been called a "girly-man" because he is taking time off from full-time employment to be at home with his young children while his wife works.[3] However, his wife faced no such negative sanctions when she stayed home with their children for the preceding 3 years!

All in all, though, despite the negative ramifications men face when they do not conform to their gender-based roles, the behaviors we assign to masculine and feminine roles still provide men with more social, political, and economic power than women. In general, although the norms for gender roles are constantly evolving, boys are trained to be tough, competitive, and self-promoting,[4] whereas girls are socialized to be sensitive, cooperative, caring, and self-deprecating. These respective gender roles clearly give men an advantage in both the private and public arenas (Commuri and Gentry 2005).

Even in societies where there is *de jure* (legal) equality for women, gender socialization can promote *de facto* (in fact) inequality between the sexes. For example, in the United States, there are more women than men. However, women have less power than men and are, therefore, considered by sociologists and others who study power to be a minority group. Below, we outline some of the social, political, and economic inequalities between men and women in the United States. As you will see, these different aspects of power relations are interrelated, and they feed off one another.

Social Inequalities

Through gender socialization, both sexes are more likely to view men than women as experts and in possession of the tools of legitimate power. The different ways men and women communicate, with men more likely to interrupt and speak over others, influence power dynamics between the sexes (Tannen 2001). Men also tend to be seen as more competent, which reinforces the notion that men have more leadership abilities and should be paid attention to more than women (Carli 1999). This disparity can often be seen when men and women enter a public event, meeting, or place of business together. Almost invariably, the man will be greeted and attended to first.

The tasks that men and women are socialized to do in their own households also benefit men over women. As the number of dual-income households has increased, women are still expected to come home from work and shoulder the majority of the burden for domestic chores, including cooking, cleaning, and especially child care. Arlie Hochschild (2003) has famously called this social phenomenon "the second shift."

Today, working women who are married spend less time on housework than women used to in earlier decades, when they tended not to work outside of the home (University of Michigan Institute for Social Research [ISR] 2007). However, married men have not made up the difference in housework (Achen and Stafford 2005). Men still spend less than a third of the amount of time women do on household chores (University of Michigan ISR 2007). Aside from suggesting that homes may be less clean and neat than they once were, these figures make clear that women still bear the brunt of the "second shift." Moreover, girls and boys are still being socialized to repeat these gender patterns. Today, girls spend more time doing chores than playing (7.5 vs. 6 hours a week), while boys spend more time playing than doing chores (10 vs. 5 hours a week). Also, boys are approximately 15% more likely than girls to receive an allowance for doing chores (University of Michigan ISR 2007). Does this sound fair to you?

The effect of money on power in relationships is influenced by gender socialization and not evenly distributed between men and women. Family financial decisions are largely controlled by men when men earn more money than their female partners. Men also tend to have higher amounts of personal spending money than women in the same household, whereas women are more likely to deprive themselves when family finances are limited (Commuri and Gentry 2005). Though the power of women increases as their income rises, even wives who earn more than their partners "feel hesitant to pull the purse strings" (Pahl 2000) and violate the gender roles in which men are the head of the household. This hesitancy to make use of financial power at home is consistent with gendered roles that women assume in other areas, including in the political realm.

Political Inequalities

Although the first wave of the women's movement led to the 1920 passage of the Nineteenth Amendment that gave women the right to vote, women are still far from attaining equal representation in politics. Today, more women vote than men. However, as of 2009, women comprise only 7 out of 50 state governors, and they make up 73 out of 435 representatives and 17 out of 100 senators in the U.S. Congress (CAWP 2009b). Globally, only 26 out of 196 current heads of state or government are female ("Female Heads of State and Government" 2009).[5]

Women who run for political office (or any position of power) must, in some ways, resocialize themselves. They have to learn to be self-promoters rather than self-deprecators, to be tough as well as sensitive, and to speak up rather than defer to others. At the same time, they must trust that voters will be more impressed with their leadership credentials than turned off by their stepping out of the traditional "feminine" gender role. As anyone who followed the Democratic presidential primary race in 2008 knows, this juggling act proved difficult for Hillary Clinton (as it would for any woman running for president). For example, while many Americans were thrilled to vote for a woman for president, others frowned on Hillary Clinton's stepping outside the gender norm. Many will long remember when she was taunted while campaigning by a man who screamed at her to "iron my shirt" (Associated Press 2008). When asked to explain his actions, the heckler said, "I just don't think a woman should be president" (Joyner 2008).

While the United States has not yet elected a female president or even a female vice president, women have achieved greater political gains lower down on the political ladder. For example, in 2009, 24.3% of state legislators were women, representing, according to the Center for American Women and Politics (2009b), a quintuple increase since 1971. Although the gain in the percentage of female state legislators has slowed in recent years, the increase in female representation that has occurred at the local and state levels is very important, because many officials in higher office start their political careers in these types of political positions. Still, women remain disproportionately underrepresented even at the local level, considering that women currently comprise 51% of the total U.S. population (Spraggins 2005).

Exercise 9.7   Gender, Politics, and Political Power

Go to the Web site for The White House Project at www.thewhitehouse project.org. Browse through the information on the site and read some of the research it contains on women and politics.

1. What did you learn about women and the political realm? Does the information you've uncovered surprise you at all? Why or why not?

2. Have you ever thought about running for political office? Why or why not?

3. (Option 1) If you have thought of running, do you think your gender would affect the likelihood of your attaining the political office you sought? Based on information found on The White House Project Web site, discuss how you think your gender would (a) affect how you would be portrayed by the media, (b) how the public would perceive you, and (c) your chances of winning.

(Option 2) If you haven't thought of running, do you think gender socialization has affected this decision? Why or why not? Pretend now that you are interested in running and answer the questions posed in Option 1.

(Continued)

(Continued)

4. Imagine you are the campaign manager for a female candidate running for president. How would you advise her? What should she stress in her campaign speeches? How should she speak? How should she dress? What issues would you suggest she take on, and what issues would you advise her to stay away from?

5. How might your advice be different if the candidate were a man? What concerns might you have that you wouldn't have if the candidate were a woman? What might you *not* have to worry about if the candidate were a man, instead of a woman?

6. What do your answers to question 5 tell you about the importance of gender roles in the public imagination? What do they tell you about the social construction of these roles? What do they tell you about the connections between gender and power?

Exercise 9.8   Leadership Qualities

This exercise will require three short surveys to be administered in sequence to three different pools of respondents. (The easiest method would be to administer the survey to three of your classes, making sure no student responds to more than one of the surveys.)

1. Create a short form with one question and space for about 10 answers. Ask the respondents to write down their sex (but not their names) on the top of the page. The question on the form should read, "What personal qualities make one a natural leader?" Ask the respondents to write a list of about 10 qualities that make one a natural leader. Collect answers from a class that has at least 20 students.

2. Compile a list of all of the answers given by the respondents. Then order them from the most commonly offered responses to the least common. Finally, select the top 10 responses in terms of frequency.

3. Create a form with a four-column table, and list the 10 top personal qualities from the first survey under the heading "Personal Attributes." Label the other columns "Masculine," "Feminine," and "Equally Masculine & Feminine," as shown below.

Personal Attributes	Masculine	Feminine	Equally Masc. & Fem.
Attribute 1			
Attribute 2			

4. Ask members of a different class (with at least 20 students) to rate each attribute as fitting best into one of the three categories. Ask the respondents to write down their sex (but not their names) at the top of the page. Collect the forms when they are finished.

5. Summarize how many of the popular leadership qualities are associated with masculine identity and how many are associated with feminine identity.

6. Survey a different class (with at least 20 students) using a new form listing all of the attributes that asks respondents to indicate their sex and to evaluate each attribute on a scale from least to most desirable as follows:

For each of the following personal attributes, please circle the number that indicates how desirable you find it as a feature of a woman's personality:

Personal Attributes	Most Undesirable	Neutral	Most Desirable
Attribute 1	1 2 3 4	5 6	7 8 9 10
Attribute 2	1 2 3 4	5 6	7 8 9 10

7. Collect the forms and average the ratings. Overall, how desirable did the respondents find leadership qualities to be in women?

8. Modify the form in Step 6 to measure how desirable those characteristics are in men. Compare results.

9. Compare the responses of male and female respondents, and write a two- to three-page paper summarizing and sociologically analyzing your results. What do you believe are the causes and effects of the trends you have identified in your data?

Economic Inequalities

Women have made tremendous progress in the economic sphere over the past five decades. The civil rights movement and the second wave of the women's movement brought about passage of the Equal Pay Act in 1963, the Civil Rights Act in 1964, Title IX's prohibition of sex discrimination in schools (and in funding for school sports), acknowledgment of sexual harassment as a social issue, and the inclusion of women in affirmative action programs. These legislative acts, inflation, and the decline in the number of jobs paying enough so that one earner could support a family all contributed to the percentage of females 16 and over working full-time, rising from 41% in 1971 to 61.6% in 2007 (compared to 74.1% of men in the workforce in 2007) (Bureau of Labor Statistics 2005, 2008). However, in 2008, women held only 15.7% of corporate officer positions and just 6.2% of top earner positions at Fortune 500 companies (Catalyst 2008/2009).

While there are fewer women than men on the top of the economic ladder, women make up a disproportionate percentage of those clinging to the bottom of the ladder. Women who are heads of households, and their children, are particularly likely to reside in poverty. In 2007, an estimated 28.3% of female-headed households lived in poverty, compared to 13.6% of male-headed households (DeNavas-Walt, Proctor, and Smith 2008). Many children bear the brunt of this *feminization of poverty*. While 8.5% of children residing in married-couple families are in poverty, five times that number (43%) of those living with just a female head of house (with no husband present) are in poverty (DeNavas-Walt et al. 2008).

Although more and more women of all races and economic classes are giving birth outside of marriage, female heads of households are disproportionately poor women (and disproportionately poor women of color). While 22% of white children live with just one parent, 30% of Hispanic and 62% of black children live in single-parent households (U.S. Bureau of the Census 2009). To put it bluntly, it is more difficult for poor women—particularly poor women of color—to find "marriageable" partners (men who are not in prison, who have a job, etc.) than for middle-class and wealthy women (Edin and Kefalas 2005). As noted in earlier chapters, the unemployment rates for black and Hispanic Americans are dramatically higher than for white Americans, and whereas 1 in 106 white men (18 and older) are incarcerated, 1 in 36 Hispanic men and 1 in 15 black men are in jail or prison (Pew Public Safety Performance Project 2008).

Exercise 9.9	Marriage and Babies: Which Comes First?

1. Why does it generally make economic sense to wait to have a baby until after marriage/legal partnership?

2. Under what circumstances would it not necessarily make economic sense to wait to have a baby until after marriage/legal partnership?

Answer either 3a or 3b.

3a. For you, personally, does it make economic sense to wait to have a baby until after marriage/legal partnership? Why or why not?

3b. How do you think people's decision to have children (a) with or (b) without first becoming married/legally partnered impacts society?

4. How do you think (1) your sex, (2) your race/ethnicity, (3) your religious background, (4) your age, and (5) your social class influenced your answers to question 3a or 3b?

Gender Socialization and the Wage Gap

Despite all of the progress that the women's movement has made, women today still make only 78 cents for every dollar made by men (DeNavas-Walt et al. 2008) and still face a "glass ceiling" when trying to advance into higher levels of management for a variety of reasons, including the following:

• Gender socialization influences (a) what subjects girls study and are encouraged to study in school (e.g., girls are still heavily underrepresented among math and science majors in college); (b) what career paths they are directed toward and choose; and (c) their ability to think of themselves, present themselves, and be perceived by others as capable professionals and leaders.

• Only women can become pregnant and give birth to children. If women want to have children, they must take at least some time off from work to give birth, recover from childbirth, and care for their newborn. Women end up doing most of the child care and housework even when working outside the home (Hochschild 2003). This impacts their ability to spend extra hours at their paid job and advance in their career. Ironically, this factor further fuels the stereotype that women are less capable than men and are less hardworking, when, in fact, they are juggling more and working longer hours than men (when house/child care and professional work are combined).

• Sex discrimination and sexual harassment still exist and work to hamper the economic progress of women. For example, among the myriad sex discrimination and sexual harassment cases it handled in the past few years, the U.S. Equal Employment Opportunity Commission (EEOC) forced Morgan Stanley to pay $54 million to compensate female workers for the company's sex discrimination against them; the Dial Corporation to provide $10 million in damages to 90 female workers who suffered sexual harassment at the company's Montgomery, Illinois, production facility; Federal Express to pay $3,241,400 to a female driver who experienced both sex discrimination and sexual harassment on the job (U.S. EEOC 2004); the Tavern on the Green to establish a $2.2 million fund for 75 employees who faced sexual, racial, and national origin harassment (U.S. EEOC 2008); and the Big Vanilla Athletic Club to pay $161,000 for sexually harassing female employees and then firing them when they complained (U.S. EEOC 2009).

Clearly, challenges still exist for women in the social, political, and economic spheres. However, progress toward equality has been made through effective, organized efforts. Our culture and gender roles are continually changing and adjusting to the social and structural forces at work in our society. Legislation like the Nineteenth Amendment, the Equal Pay Act of 1963, and the Civil Rights Act of 1964 that prohibited employment discrimination on the basis of sex (as well as race, color, religion, and national origin) did much to change the actions and, gradually, gender socialization of Americans. Sociological tools have been, and will continue to be, effective means for uncovering and addressing gender inequality in society. The Sociologist in Action section below, highlighting the work of Mary Gatta, is a good example of how sociology can be effectively used in this endeavor.

SOCIOLOGIST IN ACTION: MARY GATTA

Gender, race, class, age, and educational levels, among other variables, alter the effectiveness of public policies. Yet public officials and policy makers are not often trained to understand the effects of such variables. Dr. Mary Gatta, Director of Workforce Policy and Research at the Center for Women and Work, Rutgers University, works collaboratively with policy officials to help craft social policy and programs that take into account the effects of these variables on marginalized groups. Specifically, Gatta works with policy officials to create and implement workforce development programs that provide access to education and skills training for single, working-poor mothers in ways that attend to their work and family needs. She is helping to craft programs that are flexible so that women can receive their education without compromising their family or work responsibilities.

Using a sociological framework, Gatta examines how workforce development policies are formulated and implemented in order to understand why so many such policies have not succeeded in helping poor working women. Using her sociological eye, Gatta can see that working-poor women are caught in a system in which they are not only unable to support themselves, but also unable to acquire human capital resources to attain self-sufficiency via the traditional mechanisms of education and skills training. She understands that this is the dual challenge that working-poor women face: How do they economically survive, day by day, and then how do they attain the skills that will enable them to be more marketable in the future? Women, and in particular single, working-poor mothers, face a system of structural barriers—child care, elder care, irregular work hours, transportation inequities—that makes it hard for them to gain education in traditional classroom settings.

To address these issues, Gatta is overseeing a new and rapidly expanding system of training single working mothers via the Internet. Her work enables single mothers to obtain better jobs and become more active participants in U.S. society by providing them with flexible educational alternatives.

The Internet is available around the clock, so women can fit education into their lives, as opposed to fitting their lives into educational structures. In addition, these programs provide computers for the women and their children, helping to bridge the digital divide.

Gatta's background in sociology helps her to educate policy makers on gendered effects of policy. Her book *Not Just Getting By: The New Era of Flexible Workforce Development* (2005), which she wrote in collaboration with Kevin McCabe, a former Commissioner of Labor for New Jersey, is an excellent example of her ability to use sociology for the public good. Gatta's use of her sociological training in her work with policy makers helps them to do their job more effectively and ensures that gender is taken into account at the policy table.

Exercise 9.10   Promoting Gender Equality in the World

"Strong evidence from around the world confirms that gender equality accelerates overall economic growth, strengthens democratic governance, and reduces poverty and insecurity" (Kemal Dervis [2005], United Nations Development Programme Administrator).

Read through the information on the following Web sites:

The United Nations Development Programme's (UNDP) Women's Empowerment Web site at www.undp.org/women

The United Nations Development Fund for Women (UNIFEM) Web site at www.unifem.org

Oxfam America's Web site at www.oxfamamerica.org (In the search box, put in the word *women.*)

(Continued)

(Continued)

Write a four-page paper that

1. Explains how "gender equality accelerates overall economic growth, strengthens democratic governance, and reduces poverty and insecurity."

2. Gives two examples of UN or Oxfam America programs that are promoting gender equality.

3. Discusses how the success or failure of such efforts will affect women across the globe (as members of the same minority group).

Extra Credit: Write a one- to two-page paper that uses your sociological imagination in developing the plan for a program that would promote gender equality worldwide (or in a specific country). Be creative, strategic, and specific.

Discussion Questions

1. Think about the division of labor along gender lines in the household in which you grew up. Who did what? Why was it like that? Would you want to maintain or change this in your own adult household? Why? If you are cohabitating now (with a spouse, partner, or roommates), discuss how you divide the labor in your current household, and if it is similar to the way household chores were distributed in your family of origin (and why or why not).

2. What does "equal rights" mean to you? How much equality is there between men and women in U.S. society?

3. Gender-role socialization begins at birth, or before. Friends and relatives want to know the sex of the expected child so that they can purchase gender-appropriate blankets, pillows, bibs, and clothes (blue or pink). The socialization continues and becomes more intense as children get older. Is it possible to raise boys and girls the same way? Is it desirable? What are some of the obvious ways in which children are taught gender roles? Can we change those to reduce gender-based discrimination? Should we? If so, how? Be specific in outlining some proactive ways to create gender equity through changing gender roles and expectations.

4. How are gender roles related to sex roles? What do they teach us about how to act sexually and with whom to have sex?

5. Why should women in the United States care about the status of women in Bangladesh or Ethiopia or other distant nations? Is there any responsibility for the U.S. women's movement to participate in the global women's movement? Why or why not? If so, what are some of the ways that U.S. women can contribute?

6. Why should men be interested in promoting equal rights and opportunities for women? What are appropriate ways for men to help women gain greater social, political, and economic power?

7. Would you feel (a) more comfortable and (b) more secure with a female or a male president? Why? How do you think gender socialization influenced your answer? How do you think courses that made you aware of gender socialization influenced your answer? If you answered that you would feel more secure with a man as president, what would need to happen to change your mind?

8. What do you think would be the most effective way to diminish social inequality between the sexes in the United States? Political inequality? Economic inequality?

9. If you were to conduct a study about sex discrimination, how would you go about doing so? What theoretical perspective would best help you make sense of your findings?

10. Describe how women of color are "doubly oppressed" and lesbian women of color are "triply oppressed" in our society. Does your friendship circle include people of various (a) genders, (b) sexual orientations, and (c) races? Why or why not?

Suggestions for Specific Actions

1. Interested in promoting economic equality for women? Go to the Web site for 9 to 5, National Organization of Working Women, at www.9to5.org. Read about the efforts 9 to 5 is making to fight for the issues of working women. If you want to become part of one of the 9 to 5 campaigns, follow the steps on their "Get Involved" and "Action Alert" pages.

2. Help women's collectives in a developing country by supporting an alternative income program that will allow them to gain economic and social power in their societies. Learn about some collectives in India by reading the article "Banding Together, Indian Women Change Their Villages," by Mark Sappenfield, at www.csmonitor.com/2007/0510/p01s04-wosc.html. Then, go to www.freethe children.com/whatwedo/international/index.php and help raise the money to adopt a village! (Make sure to click on "Alternative Income" to learn more about this specific program as well.)

3. Go to the Human Rights Watch Web site at http://hrw.org, learn about their campaigns to stop human rights violations against women, and participate in one!

   Please go to this book's Web site at www.pineforge.com/korgen3e to find further civic engagement opportunities, resources, and peer-reviewed articles related to this chapter.

Endnotes

1. A very small percentage of the population is born with both male and female sexual characteristics (known as intersexuality). Almost always in these cases, an operation is performed shortly after birth to make the child's sex organs primarily male or female (usually female).

2. Sex change operations, although very painful and expensive, are possible. However, few people choose to go through them, and even fewer have the means and opportunity to have such operations.

3. His comments about making conversations with the other parents (all mothers!) waiting to pick up their children from school are quite amusing. While he can hold his own when the conversations turn to laundry, he says he would much rather be discussing football. Just because people have the power to defy some gender role expectations does not mean that gender socialization has not affected them at all.

4. And boys are taught to distance themselves from "girlish" behavior. The saying "you throw like a girl" is one of the many ways boys are taught to be anything but "like a girl."

5. See the Center for American Women and Politics (CAWP) at www.cawp.rutgers .edu/index.php for more information about women in the political realm.

References

Achen, Alexander C. and Frank Stafford. 2005, September. "Data Quality of Housework Hours in the Panel Study of Income Dynamics: Who Really Does the Dishes?" Institute for Social Research. Retrieved May 9, 2006 (http://psidonline .isr.umich.edu/Publications/Papers/achenproxyreports04.pdf).

Associated Press. 2008, April 4. "Clinton Responds to Seemingly Sexist Shouts." Retrieved September 27, 2009 (http://www.usatoday.com/news/politics/elec tion2008/2008-01-07-clinton-iron-emotion_N.htm).

Bureau of Labor Statistics, U.S. Department of Labor. 2005. "Women in the Labor Force: A Databook Updated and Available on the Internet." May 13. Retrieved January 10, 2005 (http://www.bls.gov/bls/databooknews2005.pdf).

——. 2008. "Table 1. Work Experience of the Population During the Year by Sex and Extent of Employment, 2006–07." December 10. Retrieved June 4, 2009 (http:// www.bls.gov/news.release/work.t01.htm).

Carli, Linda L. 1999, Spring. "Gender, Interpersonal Power, and Social Influence." *Journal of Social Issues* 55:81–100.

Catalyst. 2008, December (updated January 12, 2009). "2008 Catalyst Census of Women Corporate Officers and Top Earners of the Fortune 500." Retrieved June 4, 2009 (http://www.catalyst.org/publication/283/2008-catalyst-census-of-women-corporate-officers-and-top-earners-of-the-fortune-500).

Center for American Women and Politics (CAWP). 2009a. "Fact Sheet: The Gender Gap." Retrieved March 5, 2009 (http://www.cawp.rutgers.edu/fast_facts/voters/documents/GGPresVote.pdf).

——. 2009b. "Fast Facts: Facts on Women Officeholders, Candidates and Voters." Retrieved March 5, 2009 (http://www.cawp.rutgers.edu/fast_facts/index.php).

Commuri, Suraj and James W. Gentry. 2005, September. "Resource Allocation in Households With Women as Chief Wage Earners." *Journal of Consumer Research* 32:185–95.

DeNavas-Walt, Carmen, Bernadette D. Proctor, and Jessica Smith. 2008, August. "Income, Poverty, and Health Insurance Coverage in the United States: 2007." U.S. Census Bureau. Retrieved September 26, 2009 (http://www.census.gov/prod/2008pubs/p60-235.pdf).

Dervis, Kemal. 2005, September 6. "Statement to the Executive Board of UNDP/UNFPA." Retrieved June 18, 2009 (http://cmsappstg.undp.org/go/newsroom/2005/september/board-undp-unfpa-20050906.en?categoryID=349463&lang=en).

Edin, Kathryn and Maria Kefalas. 2005. *Promises I Can Keep: Why Poor Women Put Motherhood Before Marriage*. Berkeley: University of California Press.

"Female Heads of State and Government Currently in Office." 2009. Guide2womenleaders.com. Retrieved June 17, 2009 (http://www.guide2womenleaders.com/Current-Women-Leaders.htm).

Gatta, Mary (with Kevin McCabe). 2005. *Not Just Getting By: The New Era of Flexible Workforce Development*. Lanham, MD: Lexington Books.

Hochschild, Arlie Russell (with Anne Machung). 2003. *The Second Shift*. New York: Penguin Books.

Hsu, Jeremy. 2008, August 14. "There Are More Boys Than Girls in China and India." *ScientificAmerican.com*. Retrieved June 4, 2009 (http://www.scientificamerican.com/article.cfm?id=there-are-more-boys-than-girls).

Joyner, James. 2008, January 8. "Hillary Clinton 'Iron My Shirt' Stunt." *Outside the Beltway*. Retrieved June 8, 2009 (http://www.outsidethebeltway.com/archives/hillary_clinton_iron_my_shirt_stunt).

MacDonald, Kevin and Ross D. Parke. 1986. "Parent–Child Physical Play: The Effects of Sex and Age of Children and Parents." *Sex Roles* 15:367–78.

Mahon, James. 2005. "Weber's Protestant Ethic and the Chinese Preference for Sons: An Application of Western Sociology to Eastern Religion." *Max Weber Studies* 5(1):59–80.

Nagourney, Adam. 2009, April 28. "Signs G.O.P. Is Rethinking Stance on Gay Marriage." *New York Times*. Retrieved on April 28, 2009 (http://www.nytimes.com/2009/04/29/us/politics/28web-nagourney.html?hp).

National Eating Disorders Association (NEDA). 2009, February 26. "National Eating Disorders Association Unveils Powerful & Provocative Ad Campaign." Retrieved June 5, 2009 (http://www.nationaleatingdisorders.org/in-the-news/news-releases.php).

Pahl, Jan. 2000. "Couples and Their Money: Patterns of Accounting and Accountability in the Domestic Economy." *Accounting, Auditing & Accountability Journal* 13(4):502–17.

Pew Public Safety Performance Project. 2008, February 28. "One in 100: Behind Bars in America 2008." Retrieved March 19, 2008 (http://www.pewtrusts.org/our_work_report_detail.aspx?id=35900).

Sheth, Shirish. S. 2006. "Missing Female Births in India." *The Lancet* 367:185–86. Retrieved May 9, 2008 (http://www.thelancet.com/journals/lancet/article/PIIS0140673606679312/fulltext).

Smith, Kara. 2005, Spring. "Prebirth Gender Talk: A Case Study in Prenatal Socialization." *Women and Language* 28(1):49–53.

Spraggins, Renee E. 2005. *"We the People: Women and Men in the United States." Census 2000 Special Reports.* Retrieved June 18, 2009 (http://www.census.gov/prod/2005pubs/censr-20.pdf).

Tannen, Deborah. 2001. *You Just Don't Understand: Women and Men in Conversation.* New York: HarperCollins.

University of Michigan Institute for Social Research. 2007, January. "Time, Money and Who Does the Laundry." *Research Update* 4. Retrieved January 15, 2008 (http://www.isr.umich.edu/home/news/research-update/2007-01.pdf).

USA Hockey. 2009. "Girls/Women's Hockey." Retrieved June 4, 2009 (http://www.usahockey.com//Template_Usahockey.aspx?NAV=PL_07&ID=176314).

U.S. Bureau of the Census. 2009. "As Baby Boomers Age, Fewer Families Have Children Under 18 at Home." Retrieved September 27, 2009 (http://www.census.gov/Press-Release/www/releases/archives/families_households/013378.html).

U.S. Equal Employment Opportunity Commission. 2004. "Office of General Counsel FY 2004 Annual Report—Summary of Accomplishments." Retrieved January 10, 2006 (http://www.eeoc.gov/litigation/04annrpt/index.html#IID1).

——. 2008. "Fiscal Year 2008 Performance and Accountability Report." Retrieved June 8, 2009 (http://www.eeoc.gov/abouteeoc/plan/par/2008/index.html).

——. 2009, February 6. "Big Vanilla Athletic Club to Pay $161,000 to Settle EEOC Lawsuit for Sexual Harassment." EEOC Press Release. Retrieved September 26, 2009 (http://www.eeoc.gov/press/2-26-09.html).

10

Social Institutions

Family and Economy

What do social institutions have to do with your life? A lot! The makeup of your family, the laws you must follow, your professional career, your schooling, and even whether or not you believe in a higher power (and, if so, what kind of higher power) are all based on the social institutions in your society. You begin your life among family and learn about the world through educational institutions (schools) and religious institutions (including rituals surrounding birth, marriage, and death). Much of your education is about preparing for life within structured economic institutions (the labor market).[1] All the while, your public life, and even your private one, is moved and shaped by the workings of political institutions. If the institutions change, so do you. Imagine how different your life would be if the United States did not uphold just one element of the Bill of Rights: the freedom, based on the First Amendment, to not experience unreasonable monitoring of personal phone and email conversations.[2]

How do we know an institution when we see one? In everyday language, physical places, like a jail, are sometimes referred to as institutions. But in sociology, *social institutions* are patterns of behavior governed by rules that are maintained through repetition, tradition, and legal support. Members of every society create and maintain social institutions to control human behavior and go about meeting their basic needs. How do we know what is a basic need for a society? Create your own imaginary society and think about what you need to do for it to survive. Keep in mind that you can eat what you like at home, but we all share the problem of where the garbage will go when you are done.

Imagine you and your fellow students are stranded on a distant planet that looks and feels like Earth but has no other human inhabitants. What is the first thing you would do? Almost certainly, you would (a) figure out what you need to do to survive and (b) start assigning people to those tasks you determine need doing. The first thing you would probably need to do is ensure some semblance of order for these undertakings. So, the first institution you would set up is some sort of *government*. (We're assuming that there are a lot of other students with you, not just a few classmates.) Second, you would have to start producing some food, finding water, and arranging for some system to distribute these goods. Whether you all share equally or distribute the goods according to some complex system of entitlements, you would be creating a system that includes ownership and "exchange value." In other words, you would be creating an *economic* institution, an institution that organizes how a society generates, allocates, and uses wares and services. Because the needs of your group on this imaginary world would be different from the needs of the society in which you actually live, you would not need the same institutions in the same way. But here is the interesting part about ideas and practices that become *institutionalized:* It is hard to imagine them differently. For that reason, you would have a very hard time creating a government or an economy that did not strongly resemble the one you know now (or at least one that you have read or heard about). And, yet, when you stop and think about it, there are innumerable ways in which societies *could* choose to organize their governments and economies.

Although not everyone believes in a higher power or practices a religion, every known society has had some form of religious institution (just ask an anthropologist). Would you and your companions adopt a unified system of belief to help you make sense of your new situation? If you were not rescued quickly, you might start trying to establish, in an organized way, a connection between yourselves and a higher power. Organizing a new religion or reestablishing an old one (from Earth) might help you come to terms with your situation; feel that someone (or something) was watching over you; and enable you to believe that, eventually (if only when you die), you would be going to a better place, seeing old loved ones, and so forth. If you remained in the distant world for more than a very short period of time, you would also have to set up rules about who could have sex with whom (to avoid nasty fights, and to protect physically vulnerable members of the population), and (eventually) who should take care of the offspring of such unions (and how). In doing so, you would be establishing the institution of the *family*.

Finally, if you remained stuck on that planet, you would have to ensure that new members born into your society could learn your culture and the skills necessary to help your society survive. You would have to establish a social institution responsible for educating the members of your society. Once you had done so, you would have established the fifth basic institution found in almost every society, an *educational system*.

As you have probably already noticed, these institutions are all related to one another. A functionalist would maintain that they are also all *interdependent*. Just as a living organism begins to die if a single one of its major organs (like the heart) starts to fail, functionalists maintain that if one institution is not working properly in a society, all the others (and the aggregate society) will suffer as well. For example, if our education system is not carrying out its function properly, young adults will not be prepared to get good jobs and therefore will not be able to support a family, pay taxes, financially support their religious organizations, or buy goods. Eventually, the faulty educational system would harm the family, economic, religious, and political institutions.

Unlike functionalists, conflict theorists examine the manner in which different interests in society work against one another. Karl Marx, for example, famously demonstrated that the worker class and the owner class were necessarily in conflict over just about everything that went on in society, from the organization of work to the proper use of police and courts to the workings of a free press. But conflict also occurs among social institutions. For example, some religious institutions believe they should have control over governmental and educational institutions, and throughout the history of the United States, there has been a see-saw power relationship between the economic and governmental institutions.

Marx maintained that there was one institution that influences and largely directs all the other institutions. According to Marx (1859/1970), as the type of economic system changes, so does the makeup of the other institutions. The government, the schools, the family, and religion are all tools for those who own the means of production. Marxism, therefore, begins with the assumption of *economic determinism*—that is, that the economic institutions shape the rest. Some political theorists, like Niccolo Machiavelli (1469–1527), are *political determinists*. (Machiavelli, who is most remembered for his classic text, *The Prince* [1909/2001], defined war as an extension of politics, merely another means by which leaders seek to extend their influence.) There are also those for whom religious institutions, or even social institutions (like systems of racial privilege), form the determining institution, with the rest following. Although all the major institutions are tied to one another in some way, in this chapter we will focus on the social institutions of the family and the economy.

The Family

Marx (1859/1970) maintained that relations among family members and even the average size of families are influenced by changes in the economic system. For example, under an agrarian economic system, in which work is centered on the family, the size of families is large so that they can produce many workers to till the land and produce crops. As societies become industrialized and work shifts to factories and other centralized locations, families become smaller. The move from farm to city means that families can no longer feed themselves through producing more food in the fields. More children would mean more mouths have to be fed through low-wage work in factories.

According to Karl Marx's writing partner, Friedrich Engels (1884/1942), families maintain the economic system of capitalism and the existing class structure. Legal marriages were created so that men would be able to know clearly who their heirs were so that they could bequeath their wealth to their male offspring. A marriage contract transferred a kind of ownership of the bride from her father, whose name she bore, to the husband, whose name she adopted. The traditional patriarchal family structure also worked to perpetuate the capitalist economic system because it allowed men to devote themselves to making money while the wives took care of them, their children, and their home (for no pay). This system also contributed to the maintenance of gender inequality.

Exercise 10.1   Functions of the Economy

Imagine you live in a society in which the economic institution is not working properly (e.g., there is high unemployment or high inflation). According to the functionalist theoretical perspective, how might the decline in the economic institution affect the other institutions in society? Specifically, how would it affect the (a) family, (b) educational, (c) religious, and (d) governmental institutions?

Now, imagine that you live in a society in which the economic institution is strong and thriving. According to the functionalist theoretical perspective, how might the thriving economic institution affect the other institutions in society? Specifically, how would it affect the (a) family, (b) educational, (c) religious, and (d) governmental institutions?

Whereas conflict theorists use a macro-level approach to see connections between families and economic systems, symbolic interactionists use a micro-level analysis to focus on how institutions influence the roles men and women play and the status they assume in the family. As you learned in Chapter 9, even today, and even in the most egalitarian nations in the world, gender socialization within families contributes to inequality between men and women.

A sociological study (Nyman 1999) that examined power dynamics among two-income couples in Sweden indicated that socialization can trump earning power even in one of the most gender-egalitarian societies in the world. Gender-based socialization is prevalent even in Sweden. Growing up, Swedish girls are more likely than Swedish boys to be taught that they should think of others before themselves. This gender-based socialization led to the women in the study tending to feel more responsible for taking care of such household needs as buying food and clothes for the children. They often used their own money to buy goods for the household. Even though the men and women each had the same amount of money to spend, the women ended up having less money to use for themselves and, therefore, less power to determine how the couple's joint income should be spent. As the author described the situation, the women in the study seemed to subordinate their own needs to those of other family members, yet did not see their behavior as a sacrifice. Instead, it seemed to be something that they did without reflecting over the reasons or consequences.

Therefore, even though both husbands and wives in Sweden are likely to say they should share their income equally, the "women seemed to experience less influence over economic decision making and less access to personal spending money" (Nyman 1999:789). However, even though gender inequality remains in many societies around the world, the institution of the family is changing. Across the globe, the marriage rate is falling and the cohabitation rate is rising. For example, whereas the divorce rate in the United States is falling (5.1 in 2006 from 7.9 in 1980, for every 1,000 people between 15 and 64 years of age) (U.S. Bureau of the Census 2009), the percentage of babies born to unwed parents has increased steadily since the late 1990s. According to the Centers for Disease Control and Prevention (CDC), 39.7% of all babies in the United States are now born to unmarried women (cited in Ventura 2009). As Stephanie Coontz, the author of *Marriage, a History: From Obedience to Intimacy, or How Love Conquered Marriage* (2005b), states, "From Turkey to South Africa to Brazil, countries are having to codify the legal rights and obligations of single individuals and unmarried couples raising children" (Coontz 2005a). The pattern is clear: Fewer children are being raised by married parents.

Other changes to the institution of the family are now taking place. Same-sex couples and working mothers are becoming increasingly common and influencing the shape of families in the United States and across the globe. For example, as noted in Chapter 9, a growing number of U.S. states and nations across the globe recognize marriages or civil unions between same-sex adults. Also, most mothers now work outside the home (as well as in it). Today, 72% of American mothers between the ages of 15 and 44 work outside the home. The percentage of employed mothers with infants has also increased dramatically over the past 20 years (31% in 1976 to 55% in 2005, according to the U.S. Bureau of the Census [2005]). Even children raised by two married parents tend to have working mothers. In 2007, a total of 63% of children with married parents had both parents in the workforce (U.S. Bureau of the Census 2008).

It's important to note that working both outside and inside the home is not a new phenomenon for women, particularly for women of color (Coontz 1992). However, the fact that so many women of all races and social classes are now doing so is a relatively new social phenomenon. Today, the options families have, such as keeping one potential breadwinner at home, hiring a caregiver for their children, sending their children to day care facilities, and so forth, all relate to the economic position of the family. With both day care fees and household expenses, such as medical insurance, rising rapidly, parents with limited education and job skills face almost impossible choices when trying to both support their families financially and supervise and care for their children.

Family life can be even more expensive and stressful for parents who are part of the "sandwich generation," meaning they have both dependent children and elderly parents who need care. While grandparents can provide great assistance to their adult children, they can also need assistance from them. As life expectancies rise and the baby boomers age, their adult children are often faced with figuring out how to assist their parents while raising their own children. Limits on prescription and health care coverage can leave many elderly people unable to pay for their medical needs or to afford nursing assistance when they need care. Adult children, often with children of their own, must frequently face tough family and economic choices. The situation is even bleaker if they are among the almost 20% of adults between the ages of 18 and 64 who are uninsured (CDC 2009). If that is the case, it is likely that they cannot even afford to take care of themselves!

Exercise 10.2	The Changing American Family

There are multiple structural and cultural causes for the changes in the institution of the family that are noted above. There is also ongoing debate as to whether these changes are more positive or negative for society. Write a one- to two-page essay that examines these changes in the family from either (a) a conflict perspective or (b) a functionalist perspective. (If need be, refer back to the descriptions of these perspectives in Chapter 2.)

When writing your essay, be sure to

1. Provide an overview of how society operates according to the theoretical perspective you have chosen, and then apply that perspective to the changes in the social institution of the family.

2. Discuss whether someone coming from the theoretical perspective you chose would approve or disapprove of the changes in the family (and why or why not).

Exercise 10.3   When the Family Breaks Down

What happens when the family breaks down? What does our society do to strengthen families and make sure children are protected? Listen to "'Hope's Boy,' a Memoir of Childhood in Foster Care" at www.npr.org/templates/story/story.php?storyId=68349288 and then answer the following questions:

1. What is the position in the economic institution of most people who experienced foster care? Do they tend to be economically successful?

2. Use Cooley's concept of the looking-glass self (Chapter 5) and/or the theories covered in the deviance chapter (Chapter 6) to make sense of why foster children tend not to succeed.

3. Using the theories you discussed and the information in the story you listened to, what policy recommendations would you make to improve the foster care system in the United States?

4. Detail three suggestions for how you and other students could create bridges between your campus and the local foster care system.

The Economic System

Economies organize how a society creates, distributes, and uses its goods and services. Today, we live in a global economy in which the economic system of capitalism dominates. As Max Weber described it, the rational capitalism that arose in the West and that has spawned globalization requires paid (not slave) labor, the free movement of goods, and sound legal and financial institutions. It also requires a bureaucratic system that hinges on educated administrators, accurate record keeping, and the technology to allow for long-distance communication and transportation (Collins 1980). Goods and services are created and sold, for profit, across national borders at an increasingly rapid pace.

Inequality among nations is related to what each contributes to and takes from the global economy. "Global North" nations (most postindustrial nations like the United States, Western European nations, and Japan) primarily contribute service work in the knowledge economy, with high-skilled workers (Garrett 2004). In contrast, "global South" nations (e.g., most Latin American, African, Middle Eastern, and Asian nations) tend to produce raw materials or provide cheap labor to produce goods consumed in global North nations. While some global South nations like India and China are becoming increasingly competitive (in 1998, there were 3.4 million college students in China, while in 2008 there were just over 20 million. [Mong 2009]), most global South nations are far from equal competitors to nations in the global North. In addition, corporations based in global North nations often control the resources of global South nations, and this makes it difficult for the poorer nations to build the infrastructure needed to create stronger economies. To participate in the knowledge economy, nations need strong educational, banking, and legal systems, like those found predominantly in global North countries.

The nations with those assets have benefited the most from the globalization process and used their economic advantage to increase their power in determining global governance and the future of the global economy. Other sectors of the world have not benefited as much from globalization. The World Trade Organization (WTO), which oversees the terms of global trade; the International Monetary Fund (IMF), which manages global financial markets; and the World Bank, which provides loans for economic development, are primarily controlled by global North nations and influenced by the concerns of global corporations. For the most part, these organizations have had a net effect of increasing the power and wealth of global North nations while decreasing the power, wealth, and quality of life in global South nations. For example, the United Nations' 2005 "Report on the World Social Situation: The Inequality Predicament" notes that

> the cumulative result of [global North–encouraged] structural reform in Latin America over the past two decades has been a rise in inequality. . . . [Moreover], protectionist practices and agricultural subsidies in developed countries have led to a drop in agricultural productivity and, in turn, agricultural income. At present, the Latin American and Caribbean region imposes an 8.5 percent duty on non-agricultural imports from industrialized countries, but its own agricultural imports are subject to a 20.4 percent duty in industrialized countries, perpetuating rural poverty. (n.p.)

Developing nations have also been hardest hit by the current worldwide recession. Although the global response to the fiscal crisis in 2008 and 2009 was unprecedented, in mid-2009 the United Nations declared that "greater efforts are needed, including through better policy coordination and larger financial transfers to developing countries [so that] . . . developing countries [can] . . . protect their vulnerable populations and align the response with long-run sustainable development goals" (n.p.).

Exercise 10.4   The World Trade Organization (WTO)

1. Go to the WTO History Project Web site at http://depts.washington.edu/wtohist.

2. Under "Resources," click on "Top 10 Documents."

3. Read at least two of each of the "Documents Not Produced by the WTO" and the "Documents Produced by the WTO."

4. Write a paper that answers *either* questions a, b, and c *or* questions d and e below.

   a. What groups or organizations are represented in each document?
   b. As a sociologist, which documents do you think are most convincing? Explain why.
   c. Did you know very much about the WTO before reading this chapter and these documents? If yes, what gave you that knowledge? If not, why do you think you didn't know much about the WTO?
   d. How would a conflict theorist describe the function of the WTO?
   e. How would a functionalist theorist describe the function of the WTO?

Exercise 10.5   Critiquing Modern Globalization

1. Go to the Global Exchange Web site and read the following Fact Sheets: www.globalexchange.org/campaigns/wbimf/faq.html and www.globalexchange.org/campaigns/wbimf/facts.html.

2. Write a one- to two-page essay outlining the major arguments being presented against the current manner of globalization.

| Exercise 10.6 | From Free Trade to Fair Trade |

1. Read "Economic Alternatives" at www.globalexchange.org/campaigns/alternatives and "Are Workers Waking Up?" at www.globalexchange.org/campaigns/econ101/laborday.html.

2. Write a two- to three-page essay in which you (a) outline the suggestions made by the authors to move toward a different form of globalization, (b) discuss why you agree or disagree with the authors, and (c) offer further/different suggestions of your own and outline how they might be carried out.

Growing levels of economic inequality can also be seen *within* global North nations. In the United States, inequalities have steadily increased over the past 20 years. Between 2001 and 2008, low- and moderate-income earners have seen no improvement or a drop in their incomes, adjusting for inflation, whereas the wealthiest 20% have seen their income increase substantially (Bernstein, McNichol, and Nicholas 2008). A June 2005 article in the *New York Times* entitled "Richest Are Leaving Even the Rich Far Behind" pointed out that, in recent years, the richest Americans "have pulled far ahead of the rest of the population . . . [and] have even left behind people making hundreds of thousands of dollars a year" (Johnston 2005). The next year, 2006, the average income of the 400 wealthiest Americans was $263 million, a 23% increase from 2005. "That same year, [those] very wealthy paid, on average, an effective tax rate of 17 percent—the lowest in 15 years" (National Public Radio [NPR] 2009:n.p.).

One of the most drastic outcomes of these trends in wealth and poverty is that there are currently more than 32 million Americans living in or at risk of hunger, including more than 12 million children (which is nearly 17% of all American children!) (Food Research and Action Center [FRAC] 2008). Many of the hungry are the working poor. The following quote from "Betsy," a middle-aged mother in Jonathan White's *Hungry to Be Heard: Voices From a Malnourished America* (forthcoming), illustrates this fact:

Right now I'm holding down two different jobs, one that's pretty much full-time and then another one that gives me about 20 hours or so a week and this is six days a week that I'm working now. And I work hard, too. . . . I work real hard, and I'm tired from it as well. . . . But no matter [how hard I work] when it gets time to pay the bills we simply can't get by on what I'm making. . . . Minimum wage at one place and a little better at the other doesn't help me enough in terms of feeding my children, paying the bills, and providing as I need to for them. (n.p.)

At the low end of the global economic spectrum, there are men, women, and children who find themselves forced to try to make a living on farms that cannot compete with global agribusinesses (as seen in the United Nations' 2005 "Report on the World Social Situation" described above), or through minimum-wage jobs or labor in "sweatshop" factories that offer low wages, hard and often unsafe work, and no benefits. As the quote above illustrates, the result is often hunger and deprivation for the workers and their families.

Exercise 10.7   Poor? Pay Up!

Read "Poor? Pay Up!" at www.washingtonpost.com/wp-dyn/content/article/2009/05/17/AR2009051702053.html and answer the following questions:

1. Can you relate to the lives of the people described in this article? Why or why not?

2. Why do you think so many middle- and upper-class people are unaware of the extra time and money it takes poor people, like those described in this article, to pay bills, buy good food, live in an apartment, and so forth? Dig beneath the surface in your analysis.

3. Using your sociological eye, what social patterns do you detect in the stories you read?

4. Outline a plan that would enable you to fulfill the second core commitment of sociology (social activism) to try to change those social patterns.

Although sweatshops are most common in global South nations because of lack of unions and inadequately enforced (or nonexistent) labor laws, there are also pockets of sweatshops in global North nations, including many right here in the United States. Recognizing the existence of sweatshops in its own city and throughout the world (and under pressure from The Global Exchange and other anti-sweatshop groups), the city government of San Francisco recently declared a campaign against sweatshops worldwide. An editorial in the *San Francisco Chronicle* described the campaign and the problem of sweatshops this way:

> By launching a campaign to eliminate worldwide sweatshop-labor abuse, San Francisco Mayor Gavin Newsom and Supervisor Tom Ammiano made a powerful statement denouncing a global travesty. From China to Mexico, garment workers—many of whom are young children—work up to 15 hours a day with no bathroom or eating breaks and make as little as 13 cents an hour.
>
> But tucked away in San Francisco's South of Market and in pockets of the Mission District, those who are looking can find similar conditions right here at home. These workers are mostly middle-age and older immigrant women, who have little education and speak no English. They work up to 12 hours a day with few or no breaks and get paid by "piece rates," meaning, per garment. On average, this adds up to $1 or $2 an hour. ("Sweatshop Crackdown" 2005, n.p.)

The city of San Francisco is far from being the only governmental voice against sweatshops. As more and more organized citizens demand that their elected leaders do something to curb the abuse of workers, anti-sweatshop legislation becomes increasingly common. The states of California, Illinois, Maine, New Jersey, New York, and Pennsylvania have all passed legislation that sets no-sweat standards for the procurement of state clothing such as uniforms, and 36 cities are now sweatfree[3] (see www.sweatfree.org/sweat freecities and www.sweatfree.org/sweatfreestates).

College students have been some of the most powerful opponents of sweatshops. On campuses across the nation, undergraduates have been striving to make sure that the apparel sold on their campus is made in sweat-free factories. As noted earlier in the book, 186 colleges and universities (such as The College of the Holy Cross, Bridgewater State College, Beloit College, Indiana University, California State University San Bernardino, and Miami University) have joined the Worker Rights Consortium (WRC) "to combat sweatshops and protect the rights of workers who sew apparel and make other products sold in the United States" (WRC 2009).[4]

SOCIOLOGIST IN ACTION:
LUCY ANNE HURSTON

In the paragraphs that follow, Professor Lucy Anne Hurston describes how her life experiences led her to become a public sociologist and a professor who empowers her students to use their sociological training to recognize, understand, and confront economic injustice.

I am Lucy Anne Hurston, a sociologist—what I consider to be the best job in the world. I build activists and they, in turn, change the world. I was born in Brooklyn, New York (Bedford Stuyvesant) and later raised in Bristol, Connecticut, at a wonderful time. It seemed the whole world was in flux. There was a tremendous amount of change occurring all around me; it was the sixties. Barricades and obstacles to all types of freedoms were being torn down or at least questioned and challenged. At the same time, other forces struggled to maintain the status quo; many were unwilling to relinquish their unequal access to power.

Starting college at age 31 also contributed to my having a "different" way of employing my sociological imagination and my motivation to use it. My being the niece of Zora Neale Hurston (the phenomenal and renowned cultural anthropologist from the Harlem Renaissance) also molded how I learned to view and interrogate the world around me.

Feeling comfortable with being "different" means that when I became a professor, I was almost fearless in my teaching methodologies and in what I was willing to try with my students in an attempt to steep them in sociology. It is quite empowering for students to feel they have had their hands on an actual social problem and done something about it. My students are able to experience this through coursework connected to Foodshare (an organization dedicated to end hunger and alleviate poverty), Hartford Area Habitat for Humanity, and our campus projects.

One very successful campus project enabled the students to immerse themselves in the world of poverty. We built and lived in our very own Cardboard City on our campus for 24 hours. Before creating Cardboard City, the students conducted a great deal of research on poverty and learned about its causes and repercussions. The project was, in part, a fundraiser for our campus chapter of Habitat for Humanity. The students decided to involve local businesses and solicited and sold them ad space on the sides of their abodes. Over 30 local businesses were tapped, and all rose to the occasion. Many of the students went to their families and employers for support, as well, and all contributed in some fashion. Drawing in others from outside the college community was a way for the students to inform and educate others about the issue at hand.

The local businesses were more than happy to involve themselves with the college community, and some even visited our city during the event. This overall effort garnered $1,283. To entice people to approach and enter the city, our campus radio station, ICE, broadcast live from the city for several hours and campus bands performed. The students decided that they would solicit change from the local traffic within the perimeter of the city. They decorated and placed a large water cooler jug on a table

(Continued)

(Continued)

in a highly visible spot from where they distributed Hartford Habitat for Humanity information and fact sheets. Students also took turns wandering the grounds with the jug in tow. From these efforts, an additional $542 was collected. The funds were donated to the Hartford Area Habitat office to underwrite some of the expenses for their annual trip to New Orleans, where they continue to work in the aftermath of Katrina and the levee failures. In this way, through their donation and awareness-raising, the students had a direct effect on both local and national issues of poverty, homelessness, and economic injustice.

Cardboard City was also an exercise in living in a stratified situation of poverty. So, it was a physically stratified layout and, of course, I made all the decisions. "That's not fair!" I heard, but then I justified it to them: The person in charge, the person with the most power, the person who could make all the decisions was the one with the most education (yup, me): the bourgeoisie. The students bought into this easily. I created a layer of decision makers just below my level (the petite bourgeoisie)—student coordinators—and they made a flurry of rules. The rest of the students (the proletariat) bought into that, too.

When it was actually construction day for our city, there were more rules: I had the first pick of where to build and who could live near me. I had the best spot, of course, and hand-picked my neighbors. My community was called "Sugar Hill," and only those closest in status to me could be on this level, even ground which was shielded from too much sun or wind (my coordinators lived there). We also had the better building materials. My home, of course, had a full wood framework for the interior and was larger than any other home in the city. It was furnished with folding chairs, art work, live plants, floor mats and padding, and lots of fun electronics (DVD player, iPod, extension cords) . . . oh and another new rule: No one could have anything I had. And the students went along with this. There was one rebel who tried to use a mini DVD player in her box after 2:00 AM when she thought we were all asleep. . . . I confiscated it and she let me!

All the other students were divided up between two other areas of the city: aptly named the ghetto and the slum. They could choose between the two but both developments were far inferior to Sugar Hill and so were their building supplies. Rather than resist or fully rebel, they squabbled among themselves. They did not collaborate or combine forces; no revolution ensued nor did any solidarity movement. Oh, more new rules: No doors were allowed on slum or ghetto homes. Yes, they actually started believing it: They lived in a ghetto or a slum. We found that "those" areas had more trash than Sugar Hill, and when one of those shabby homes fell apart, the residents of the ghetto and the slum stole cardboard from one of their neighbors for repairs. The students adapted to their environment, rather than trying to overthrow their ruler (me), who created such an unjust society. They remained in their subservient positions even when it was time to break down the city and remove the trash.

It was an exciting and engaging 24 hours, and the discussions in the classroom around this activity carried on through the balance of the semester. I saw, through their submitted work, their ability to make a sophisticated connection between textbook, community, and class activity. Through the use of their newly developed sociological imagination, they attained a better understanding of the ways in which people respond to one another and the invisibility of the poor. This exercise emphasized the blurred boundaries between an arbitrarily created social class system and the unequal distribution of power. Ultimately, the students learned that social change comes from redefining or reconstructing social reality.

Exercise 10.8	**Students Creating Change: The Anti-Sweatshop Movement**

Go to the United Students Against Sweatshops (USAS) Web site at www.studentsagainstsweatshops.org.

Write a two-page paper that describes (a) one campaign on which USAS is currently working, (b) whether or not you could see yourself joining that campaign, and (c) why you could or could not see yourself participating in the campaign.

Exercise 10.9	**Work, Unemployment, and Our Changing Economy**

Go to the Web site for the U.S. Department of Labor's Mass Layoff Statistics page at www.bls.gov/mls/home.htm#overview%20htm and click on "Mass Layoffs (Monthly)," then click on "Mass Layoffs Summary." Read the most recent summary and answer the following questions:

1. What were the top three reasons (in order) for the most recent mass layoffs?

2. Which metropolitan area was most affected by recent mass layoffs?

3. How does the most recent quarterly report on mass layoffs compare to those of the previous 4 years?

(Continued)

(Continued)

Now go to www.google.com. Search for "Unemployment Insurance and [name of your state]" and answer the following questions:

1. What percentage of their salary do unemployed people receive in unemployment insurance (assuming they met the eligibility requirements for maximum unemployment insurance coverage in your state)?

2. For how long can they collect unemployment insurance?

3. How well do you think they can support themselves or a family on unemployment insurance? Elaborate.

Exercise 10.10   Immigration and Citizenship

Select two nations outside the United States (one in the Western hemisphere and one in the Eastern hemisphere), and go to the U.S. Citizenship and Immigration Services homepage at www.uscis.gov/portal/site/uscis.

In an approximately two-page paper, use the information on the Web site to figure out how you might successfully emigrate from each respective nation to the United States. Be sure to include the factors that would ease your path to American citizenship (being a highly skilled worker, having a family member here, etc.).

Conclude your paper by describing what you learned from the exercise and how it impacted your perspective on the immigration process. (If you did not learn anything new, explain why you did not.)

SOCIOLOGIST IN ACTION: ALAN ASHBAUGH

In the following paragraphs, recent college graduate Alan Ashbaugh describes how he uses the sociological tools he gained as a sociology major at Colby College in Maine in working to bring about social justice locally, nationally, and globally.

Studying sociology greatly influenced the course of my life, giving me the tools to examine the social world, the skills and inspiration to affect positive change, and the direction to use my sociological training meaningfully and effectively.

In my sociology classes at Colby College, Waterville, Maine, I learned about the nature of society; the harsh and complex realities of social issues; and, most importantly, that change toward a more just world is possible. A sociological truth that I will always remember is that society is not a static, unstoppable force, as it is so often referred to in popular media, but it is instead a constantly emerging and shifting combination of individuals making decisions and taking action. Thus, the world is already changing; we need only to guide it in the right direction by taking effective social action.

Of the many issues we explored in my introductory sociology course, the one that stood out for me is the vast economic inequality in my own community and internationally, as well as the social classes that create and perpetuate these inequalities. A subsequent sociology course on globalization broadened my sociological perspective to focus on the global issues of poverty, inequality, and justice, and the impact of each individual's actions on people worldwide. Examining these issues led me to a more vivid understanding of the social world; [a stronger grasp of] issues in my local and international communities; and a better sense of my place in Colby, Waterville, and society as a whole. This newfound understanding inspired me to get involved on and off campus, using my sociological training to move toward change. I became a founding leader of the Colby South End Coalition, which addresses the social and economic divide between Colby and its hometown of Waterville by encouraging volunteerism, dialogue, and a coming together of the two communities. I also took on the role as head of Colby Habitat for Humanity, which tackled economic inequality locally by connecting low-income families with decent, affordable housing. Moving beyond Waterville in scope, for the 2004 presidential election I helped to organize the Voter Coalition to "get out the vote," and I traveled to Chile to investigate the social promise of the emerging concept of *corporate social responsibility*.

Graduating from Colby in May of 2005, I did not have a set career path. I only knew that I loved raising awareness of social issues and bringing students together to take action, and that I wanted to continue to be socially active beyond college. My senior year, I had the good fortune of learning about a job opportunity at an organization called Free the Children through an inspiring, socially involved professor in my Sociology department. Free the Children was founded in 1995 by a 12-year-old boy named Craig Kielburger, who was so appalled at the practice of child labor he had read about in the newspaper that he gathered a group of his friends and classmates to raise awareness and take action to effect change—exactly what I was passionate about. In the past 10 years, Free the Children has grown to become the largest network of children helping children through education, having built over 400 schools, educating more than 35,000 children

(Continued)

(Continued)

every day, having sent more than $9 million worth of medical supplies, and having implemented alternative income projects benefiting more than 20,000 people in developing countries. Free the Children's mission and the work they do matched my own personal goals and beliefs, so I applied for the position just prior to graduation and was hired! Today, as an International Youth Coordinator at Free the Children, I provide youth with the tools to make a difference in the world, such as information on social issues, effective fundraising and awareness-raising techniques, and the public speaking skills to powerfully communicate their passion to their peers. I use my sociological training each day in my work at Free the Children in examining the social issues that we are working to address, discovering the best ways to encourage and enable young people to effect positive change, and "become agents of change for their peers around the world." The image of society I formed from my sociology classes of a constantly emerging collection of individual actions, in conjunction with the social issues we studied, help me to remember every day the power that each individual has to make a huge difference and the tremendous importance of doing so.

SOURCE: Courtesy of Alan Ashbaugh.

Discussion Questions

1. What role do you think economic globalization plays in legal and illegal immigration to the United States?

2. How do you think the changes in our economic institution (e.g. inflation, fewer jobs that pay a "family" wage, the growing need for a college education) are impacting the social institution of the family?

3. Why is it in the interest of global North workers to organize with global South workers for higher wages?

4. What families might be most vulnerable to negative impacts of the current (as of this writing) global recession? Why? Do you feel your family has been (or might be) impacted by the recession? If not, why not? If yes, why and in what ways?

5. Which theoretical perspective, conflict theory or functionalism, would you choose to best make sense of how the economic institution operates in U.S. society? Why?

6. Imagine that the institution of the family suddenly disappeared. How might U.S. society be different without this primary institution? Do you think U.S. society could survive without it? Why or why not?

7. If you marry or begin a domestic partnership, do you think you will share domestic chores equally with your spouse? Why or why not? Be sure to discuss

how your gender socialization, your family of origin, and your place in the economic institution impact your answer.

Suggestions for Specific Actions

1. Research the family-related personnel policies at your college. Do you think they provide adequate benefits for employees who must care for a sick family member? If not, come up with a reasonable suggestion for policy reform, and work with your student government leaders to present your ideas (and advocate for them) to the administration.

2. Research the policies that your college has for providing benefits to partners of LGBTI (Lesbian, Gay, Bisexual, Transgender, or Intersexed) employees. Are they the same as for the partners of heterosexual employees? If not, why not? How do your findings, in either case, reflect the values of your college (*your* institution!) and of the greater society? If you find inequalities and believe they need to be changed, what steps could you take to ensure that the partners of all employees receive equal benefits?[5]

3a. Review the information on the U.S. Immigration and Customs Enforcement's Students and Exchange Visitors Web page at www.ice.gov/sevis/students.

3b. Interview the administrator on your campus who is in charge of international students. Ask him or her how your school assists international students through the process of becoming students on your campus.

3c. Interview five international students at your school. Ask them about the steps they went through to become students there. Be sure to note any differences in their experiences and why these differences may have occurred (the year of their matriculation, the nation from which they came, their economic status, etc.).

3d. Use this information to create a resource for international students that could be put on your school Web site (if approved by your college or university administration).

4. Go to Free the Children's Web site at www.freethechildren.com. After browsing through it, read the information provided on child labor (http://we.freethechildren .com/learn-facts?issue=child-labour). One of the most powerful ways to fight against child labor is to ensure that children have schools to attend and the resources (funds for school fees, books, uniforms, etc.) to afford to go. Now that you know about child labor and how important education is, you can start a campaign to raise money to build schools in regions known for child labor. Check out the resources at www.freethechildren.com/whatwedo/international/aav/education and begin a school-building campaign at your college.

Please go to this book's Web site at www.pineforge.com/korgen3e to find further civic engagement opportunities, resources, peer-reviewed articles, and updated Web links related to this chapter.

Endnotes

1. Of course, some students leave high school and join the military institution. Many do this in hopes of receiving the training and experience they need to succeed economically once they leave the military.

2. As this book was being written, Americans were debating the extent of the First Amendment–based freedom from unreasonable monitoring of personal phone and email conversations.

3. For example, the city of Bangor, Maine, passed legislation stating, "All clothes available on local store shelves should be made according to established international standards of ethical production" (see www.newrules.org/gov/cleancloth.html).

4. For more information about the campaign, go to the WRC Web site at http://workersrights.org.

5. It is also important to note that being offered "domestic partner benefits" such as health insurance does not mean that equality has now been achieved. The U.S. federal government does not currently recognize same-sex partnerships, so the Internal Revenue Service requires the employed partner to pay tax on any benefits received for the non-employed partner. As of this writing, a bill to change this law has been written but is stuck in committee and has not been put to a vote. So, equal benefits are a start but not a solution to this issue of inequality.

References

Bernstein, Jared, Elizabeth McNichol, and Andrew Nicholas. 2008, April. "Pulling Apart: A State-by-State Analysis of Income Trends." Washington, DC: Center on Budget and Policy Priorities and Economic Policy Institute.

Centers for Disease Control and Prevention. 2009, April 9. "Uninsured Americans: Newly Released Health Insurance Statistics." Retrieved June 10, 2009 (http://www.cdc.gov/Features/Uninsured).

Collins, Randall. 1980. "Weber's Last Theory of Capitalism: A Systematization." *American Sociological Review* 45:925–942.

Coontz, Stephanie. 1992. *The Way We Never Were: American Families and the Nostalgia Trap.* New York: Basic Books.

——. 2005a, May 1. "For Better, for Worse: Marriage Means Something Different Now." *The Washington Post.* Retrieved January 2, 2006 (http://www.washingtonpost.com/wp-dyn/content/article/2005/04/30/AR2005043000108_pf.html).

——. 2005b. *Marriage, a History: From Obedience to Intimacy, or How Love Conquered Marriage.* New York: Viking.

Engels, Friedrich. [1884] 1942. *The Origin of the Family, Private Property, and the State.* Translated by Frederick Lewis Morgan. New York: International Publishers.

Food Research and Action Center. (FRAC). 2008. "Hunger in the U.S.: Hunger and Food Insecurity in the United States." Retrieved September 29, 2009 (http://www.frac.org/html/hunger_in_the_us/hunger_index.html).

Garrett, Geoffrey. 2004, June. "Trade Blocs and Social Integration." Presentation at the Trade Blocs, Neoliberalism, and the Quality of Life in Latin America Conference, Los Angeles. Retrieved June 10, 2005 (http://www.isop.ucla.edu/lac/article.asp?parentid=12060).

Johnston, David Cay. 2005, June 5. "Richest Are Leaving Even the Rich Far Behind." *New York Times,* p. A1.

Machiavelli, Niccolo. [1909] 2001. *The Prince,* Vol. 36, Part 1. Translated by N. H. Thomson. New York: Collier.

Marx, Karl. [1859] 1970. *A Contribution to the Critique of Political Economy.* Translated by Maurice Dobbs. New York: International Publishers.

Mong, Adrienne. 2009, May 18. "China's Graduates Face Grim Job Prospects." MSNBC.com. Retrieved June 12, 2009 (http://worldblog.msnbc.msn.com/archive/2009/05/18/1935896.aspx).

National Public Radio. 2009, January 30. "In '06, Rich Earned More, Paid Less Tax." *All Things Considered.* Retrieved June 9, 2009 (http://www.npr.org/templates/story/story.php?storyId=100073978).

Nyman, Charlotte. 1999, November 1. "Gender Equality in 'the Most Equal Country in the World'? Money and Marriage in Sweden." *Sociological Review,* 47(4):766–93.

"Sweatshop Crackdown." 2005, June 30. *San Francisco Chronicle,* p. B8. Retrieved November 28, 2005 (http://www.sfgate.com/cgi-bin/article.cgi?file=/chronicle/archive/2005/06/30/EDGOODGAUA1.DTL).

United Nations. 2005. "Report on the World Social Situation: The Inequality Predicament." Retrieved September 29, 2009 (http://www.ilo.org/public/english/region/ampro/centerfor/news/inf_05.htm).

———. 2009. "World Economic Situation and Prospects 2009: Update as of Mid-2009." Retrieved June 10, 2009 (http://www.un.org/esa/policy/wess/wesp2009files/wesp09update.pdf).

United Students Against Sweatshops. 2009. "USC Signs Onto the DSP!" Retrieved June 9, 2009 (http://www.studentsagainstsweatshops.org/index.php?option=com_content&task=view&id=228&Itemid=2).

U.S. Bureau of the Census. 2005. "Mother's Day: May 8, 2005." *Facts for Features.* Retrieved October 7, 2005 (http://www.census.gov/Press-Release/www/releases/archives/facts_for_features_special_editions/004109.html).

———. 2008, July 28. "50 Million Children Lived With Married Parents in 2007." Retrieved June 8, 2009 (http://www.census.gov/Press-Release/www/releases/archives/marital_status_living_arrangements/012437.html).

———. 2009. "Table 1292. Marriage and Divorce Rates by Country: 1980 to 2006." Statistical Abstract of the United States: 2009. Retrieved June 12, 2009 (http://www.census.gov/compendia/statab/tables/09s1292.pdf).

Ventura, Stephanie J. 2009, May 18. "Changing Patterns of Nonmarital Childbearing in the United States." *NCHS Data Brief* No. 18. Retrieved June 8, 2009 (http://www.cdc.gov/nchs/data/databriefs/db18.htm).

White, Jonathan M. Forthcoming. *Hungry to Be Heard: Voices from a Malnourished America.* Oxford, UK: Oxford University Press.

11

Social Institutions, Continued

Education, Government, and Religion

Should students in U.S. public schools be required to "pledge allegiance to the flag of the United States of America and to the Republic for which it stands, one nation under God, indivisible, with liberty and justice for all"? This question reveals the connection among educational, political, and religious institutions in the United States. How is God connected to our nation? Which God? Whose God? Are you less of an American if you don't believe in God? And why is this question yielding a political fight *now*?[1] These queries have been debated by politicians, religious leaders, and educators across the United States. In this chapter, we examine the institutions of education, government, and religion and their relationships to one another and to the other primary institutions in U.S. society.

Educational Institutions

Educational institutions teach young members of society the basic and (in some cases) advanced skills needed to function effectively in our society. In turn, educated citizens enable societies to run smoothly and to become more technologically advanced, more productive, and more prosperous. The educational level of a nation's population is directly related to its level of income equality and overall economic health.[2] As other key institutions in society change, the functions of the educational system must adjust accordingly. For example, as economies change, so do the skills needed by citizens and those taught in the educational systems. As institutions become increasingly complex and bureaucratized, they need an increasingly well-educated workforce. As Max Weber pointed out, "trained expertness is increasingly indispensable for modern bureaucracies" (quoted in Gerth and Mills 1970:240).

You are undoubtedly aware of the fact that nowadays most new jobs that pay well require at least an undergraduate college education. This is very different from a half-century ago, when it was possible (at least for white men) to earn a good salary by working in a factory with a strong union. No college degree was required or expected for such positions, and only a small percentage of the population completed college.

In the United States, educational institutions are also connected in a variety of ways to the institution of government. As a recent report published by the National Academy of Sciences, National Academy of Engineering, and Institute of Medicine points out, "Only by providing leading-edge human capital and knowledge capital can America continue to maintain a high standard of living—including providing national security—for its citizens" (Augustine 2007:1). In order to provide such a workforce, our educational system must be effective and properly funded.

State and local governments supply most of the funding for public schools. Today, states provide 47% of the funding, local communities 44%, and the federal government 9% (U.S. Bureau of the Census 2008) (though the federal support for schools may climb from 9% to 19% under President Obama's stimulus plan). In most states, primary and secondary public schools receive funding based largely on local property taxes. Both the state and federal government create educational goals. In recent years, the federal government has played a larger role in regulating the function and operation of public schools. For example, the federally mandated No Child Left Behind Act of 2001 established test-focused goals and timetables that public schools must adhere to in order to receive federal funding.

Most of what occurs within our schools is determined or administered by local governments. School boards, whose members are locally elected or appointed, oversee the operation of schools and create goals at the local level that are consistent with state and federal laws. Although they do have greater freedom in determining curriculum, even private schools are bound to abide by U.S. laws, such as those that protect against discrimination. In short, government fingerprints can be found at all levels of the institution of education, in school curricula, school buildings, and teaching approaches.

All three of the institutions examined in this chapter—education, government, and religion—are evident when we look at the No Child Left Behind Act[3] and the school boards that are working to put this legislation into action. For example, one aspect of this federal law allows religious organizations to receive federal education grants to run after-school programs for students in the public education system. The merits of forming or sustaining other connections between religious organizations and public schools are fought over, in many areas of the country, among local school board members and their supporters.

One of the most heated school board battles has centered on whether to teach "intelligent design" or evolution in science classes. Proponents of the faith-based idea of intelligent design—the notion that some intelligent, supernatural force was responsible for the creation of the world—have tried to influence the composition of school boards in their efforts to have this belief represented in the public school curriculum. Elected members of the State Board of Education in Kansas, for example, recently changed that state's science curriculum to include the Christian notion of intelligent design in science classes alongside the teaching of evolution, whereas residents of Dover, Pennsylvania, voted to oust all eight of their local school board members after the board proposed to do the same thing there.[4] Over the past few years, state and school officials in at least 14 states have been debating the issue (Ralston 2009). Today, polls indicate that just 39% of Americans believe in evolution (Newport 2009a).

Exercise 11.1   How Are Your Local Schools Funded?

Find the official Web page of your local school board by going to an Internet search engine (e.g., Google.com, Yahoo.com, etc.) and searching for the name of your town or city and the phrase "school board." Write a one- to two-page paper that answers the following questions:

1. How are your local schools funded?

2. Has funding increased or decreased over the past few years (and why)?

3. How do people become school board members? Are they elected? Are they appointed (and if so, by whom)?

4. Are the school board members nonpartisan, or are they affiliated with a political party? If they are politically affiliated, how many are Democrats? How many are Republicans? Any independents or other party affiliations?

5. How has the school addressed the federal No Child Left Behind Act? (This information should be on the school board Web site.)

6. According to the school board Web site, what are the key challenges facing your local public schools? How does the board claim to be addressing these challenges?

7. Now, imagine you are an official member of the school board. What two key challenges do you want to focus on? These may be similar to the ones that the board has identified or they may be your own, based on the research you have done. Outline these challenges and then describe several ideas you would suggest to address them. For at least one of these suggestions for change, elaborate upon your plan and discuss in detail how your skills as a sociologist can help create this change.

Exercise 11.2   Education for All?

Read "Ten Things You Need to Know About Education for All" at www .unesco.org/en/efa-international-coordination/the-efa-movement/10-things-to-know-about-efa. Then go to www.un.org/millenniumgoals/2008highlevel/pdf/newsroom/Goal%202%20FINAL.pdf and read the information about inequality in education across the globe. Then answer the following questions:

1. Why do you think education was established as a basic right under the 1948 Universal Declaration of Human Rights?

2. Why should you care about whether or not people in other nations have access to an education?

3. What do you think that you, working with others, can do to promote the goal of universal education by 2015?

Government

The U.S. Constitution sets the framework for governance in the United States. As anyone who has ever taken a U.S. government or history course (or watched *Schoolhouse Rock*) knows, the Preamble to the Constitution describes what the founders of this nation hoped to gain from establishing their government under the Constitution.

We, the people of the United States, in order to form a more perfect Union, establish justice, insure domestic tranquility, provide for the common defense, promote the general welfare, and secure the blessings of liberty to ourselves and our posterity, do ordain and establish this Constitution for the United States of America. (See a transcript of the Constitution of the United States at www.archives.gov/exhibits/charters/constitution_transcript.html)

As the Preamble indicates, the government regulates a wide range of interactions and processes in our society. Government is responsible for the smooth functioning of society. This broad mandate includes ensuring public safety, from personal safety in neighborhoods, to making sure that levees are properly built and maintained to protect citizens from flooding,[5] to overseeing public commerce (everything from an efficient transportation system to stable financial markets), to running fair and democratic elections. The government, in short, is responsible for overseeing the well-being and social welfare of the nation's citizens.

However, the majority of Americans do not actually exercise the power they have to elect their governmental representatives. Many do not even know who their elected representatives are, never mind whether or not they are actually "promot[ing] the general welfare." Just over half of all Americans who are eligible to vote exercise that right in presidential elections. Far fewer tend to vote in nonpresidential, local elections. Only 40% of eligible voters vote in nonpresidential year state elections (Pew Center on the States 2009), and even fewer tend to vote in elections when only local government representatives or initiatives are on the ballot.

Many Americans feel disconnected from the political process and turned off by the huge amounts of money spent on the campaigns they see covered on television. However, unlike national or statewide elections that involve millions of dollars and depend in great part upon who can raise the most money, local elections are more open to people who commit the resources of time and energy to cultivating local contacts and to urging people personally and in small groups to vote for them. While many state and national politicians spend much of their energy focused on potential large donors, most local political hopefuls spend their energies trying to persuade community leaders to convince their own followers to vote for them. Therefore, whereas organized money is more important in state and federal elections, in local elections organized people can propel someone into office. However, in all cases, those running for election or reelection to political posts can safely ignore people who do not involve themselves in politics and who are not likely to vote.

Exercise 11.3   How Does Your Representative Vote?

1. Go to the Web site for the U.S. House of Representatives, www.house.gov.

2. Look up your state representative by entering your zip code under "Find Your Representative" in the top left corner of the page and clicking on the "Go" button.

3. When the page opens, click on the representative's name and look at his or her Web site by clicking on the pull-down menu "Representatives' Web sites A–Z by last name" at the top of the page.

4. Find information on the positions your representative is taking on five issues.

5. Answer the following questions:

   a. Do you agree with the votes? (In other words, do they represent you?) Why or why not?

   b. Will you vote in the next (i) local, (ii) state, and (iii) national election? Why or why not?

   c. Does reading about how your representative has voted recently make you more or less interested in voting for or against him or her in the next election? Why?

   d. If you do not agree with his or her vote on one or more issues, what actions can you (as a citizen) take to express your dissatisfaction?

   e. What actions can you take toward having your representative vote more to your liking on future issues?

Religious Institutions

According to a 2008 study, 78.4% of Americans identify as Christian. The term *Christian* encompasses a plethora of religions ranging from mainstream Protestant to Evangelical Protestant to Catholic. Evangelical Protestants comprise 26.3% of the population and Catholics 23.9%. Mainline Protestants make up 18.1% of the population, and 6.9% of Americans belong to Historically Black Churches (HBCs). Smaller religious groups include Jewish (1.7%), Buddhist (.7%), Jehovah's Witness (.7%), Muslim (.6%), and Hindu (.4%). Slightly more than 16% of Americans did not affiliate themselves with a religious group (up from 8.2% in 1990) (Pew Forum on Religion & Public Life 2008).[6]

Portrayals of religious institutions differ rather dramatically among the three primary theoretical perspectives in sociology. These theories help us to understand the different roles religions play in society, how religions adapt to changes in society, and how they influence society and individuals in it. It is important to note that sociologists are interested in the interaction between religion and society rather than in the veracity of the teachings of a particular religion.

Following Durkheim's famous writings in this area, functionalists maintain that religion serves several functions for society: It unites its followers, helps establish order by providing a "correct" way of living, and gives people a sense of meaning and purpose in their lives. Of course, this particular functional analysis of religion assumes that there is only one religion in the society and does not consider societies with multiple religions, such as that in the United States.

Conflict theorists argue that religions tend to distract oppressed people and prevent them from concentrating on the inequities of their societies. Marx once described religion as "the opiate of the people" (quoted in Bottomore 1964:27). He argued that religion helps maintain the status quo by encouraging workers to ignore their sufferings here on Earth, thus acting as an "opiate" by keeping the oppressed subdued and uninterested in rising up against their oppressors. The clergy, financially supported by the owning class, counsel their followers not to protest the inequality that led to their poor conditions but rather to be docile and "good" here on Earth so that they may receive their reward for their earthly suffering and forbearance in Heaven.[7]

Symbolic interactionists point out that religions are socially constructed, created and recreated by followers through the use of symbols and rituals. They agree with functionalists that religion gives order to our lives. However, they also stress that individuals have agency (the ability to create and change institutions) and play active and consistent roles in the design and maintenance of their religion. Just as societies change and people create, adjust, and discard symbols, religious institutions change as well. For example, the change in symbols and attitudes within the Catholic Church brought about by the Second Vatican Council (1962–1965) changed the outlook of the Church and many of its rules. The language of the Mass changed from Latin to the tongue of the parishioners, the priest no longer faced away from his parishioners when saying Mass, and guitars and folk groups replaced many organs and choirs. These symbolic shifts changed how members of the Church related to one another and saw their roles within the Church. Just changing certain symbols helped foster a rise in status of the Catholic laity and created a Catholic Church that Catholics who lived 100 years ago would scarcely recognize.

The Relationships Among Educational, Governmental, and Religious Institutions

Like all other major institutions in society, educational, governmental, and religious institutions must find a way to coexist. Depending on one's theoretical perspective, the grounds of this coexistence can vary widely. For example, functionalists maintain that they can cooperate for the good of the whole society, whereas conflict theorists argue that the educational, governmental, religious, and family institutions merely carry out the desires of those who control the economic institution.

No matter the theoretical perspective, it is clear that social institutions must interact with one another in a variety of ways. However, *how* they interact with one another differs from one society to the next. For example, the influence of religion on government and educational systems varies widely from society to society. The laws of some societies are based on religious doctrines. In other societies, religions are not even officially acknowledged by the government.

The Relationship Among Religion, Government, and Education: Comparing the United States and France

Due in part to the fact that there was no one dominant religious organization at the time of the founding of the United States, the First Amendment to the U.S. Constitution contains the phrase, "Congress shall make no law respecting an establishment of religion, or prohibiting the free exercise thereof." There is an inherent tension between the two clauses in this phrase. Some people stress the separation between church and state, whereas others emphasize the First Amendment's declaration that government cannot prohibit the exercise of religion.

Although there is no officially state-sponsored religion in the United States, there are obvious examples of the influence of religion on U.S. government. From the words "In God We Trust" on our money to the routine inclusion of religious imagery in speeches by our presidents, the imagery prevalent throughout the United States is Christian. France, on the other hand, has a constitution that does not even mention religious differences among its people. The French people are free to practice whatever religion they would like, but they must do so in a private manner. In the United States, religious organizations are given tax-exempt status and are frequently recognized and honored by political leaders, whereas the French government's only official relationship with religious organizations is to make sure they do not infringe upon the liberty of others. Unlike in the United States, where some advocate bringing back compulsory prayer in schools and where there is an ongoing debate about requiring students to say a pledge that includes the word *God* in it, France expressly forbids religion in its public schools. In keeping with French laws that prohibit public displays of religion, not only are students forbidden to pray publicly, they also may not wear religious garb (such as head coverings) in school, even if their religion mandates that they wear such things in public.

Although U.S. law prohibits the government from endorsing or sanctioning one religion over another, it does not in any way prevent citizens from invoking religious grounds as a basis for their voting or other political participation, even to the point of forming national social movements to change the law. For example,

> In the 1830s, temperance and antislavery [movements] mobilized hundreds of thousands of Americans in a wave of confessional protests. In these protests, men and women gathered together to bear witness against what they deemed as the sins of drinking and slavery to pledge fellowship with reform societies, and to demand that religious and civil institutions repent. They were met with fierce resistance, and much of it was violent. (Young 2002:661)

However, the goals of both of the movements mentioned above were eventually adopted as law. What is significant here is that Christian activists, believing that drinking or slavery was morally wrong, led movements to change the laws concerning drinking and slavery, but not to change the laws concerning the role of religion in society.

In the United States, public schools are educational institutions, mandated by law, funded and regulated by government, and answerable to all citizens. Is it possible to have religious practices within a public school system without violating the laws mandating the separation of church and state? Consider the case described in Exercise 11.4 below.

Of course, not all those who say they are members of a religion actually attend religious services. As noted in Chapter 5, an estimated 42% of Americans attend religious gatherings regularly (once a week or more), compared to 20% of Western Europeans and 14% of Eastern Europeans (Newport 2009b). On the other hand, it is possible to believe in a god or universal spirit to whom you feel connected without attending religious services. For example, while only about 4 out of 10 Americans attend weekly religious services (Newport 2009b) and just over 16% are not affiliated with a religious organization (Pew Forum on Religion & Public Life 2009), 78% say they believe in God, and an additional 15% say they believe in a universal spirit (though not a god) (Newport 2008).

Exercise 11.4	School Sports and Prayer

The Bill of Rights Institute's Web site (www.billofrightsinstitute.org) lists the landmark Supreme Court cases that deal with the tension between the separation of church and state and freedom-to-worship clauses in the First Amendment. *Santa Fe Independent School District v. Doe* (2000) is one of the more recent decisions. For this case, Justice Stevens wrote what follows below for the majority opinion of the Court (three justices dissented).[8]

Prior to 1995, a student elected as Santa Fe High School's student council chaplain delivered a prayer over the public address system before each home varsity football game. Respondents, Mormon and Catholic students or alumni and their mothers, filed a suit challenging this practice and others under the Establishment Clause of the First Amendment.

While the suit was pending, the petitioner school district (referred to as "District" below) adopted a different policy, which authorizes two student elections, the first to determine whether "invocations" should be delivered at games, and the second to select the spokesperson to deliver them. After the students held elections authorizing such prayers and selecting a spokesperson, the district court entered an order modifying the policy to permit only nonsectarian, nonproselytizing prayer. The fifth circuit court held that, even as modified by the district court, the football prayer policy was invalid.

Held: The District's policy permitting student-led, student-initiated prayer at football games violates the Establishment Clause. Pp. 9–26.

(a) The Court's analysis is guided by the principles endorsed in *Lee v. Weisman,* 505 U.S. 577. There, in concluding that a prayer delivered by a rabbi at a graduation ceremony violated the Establishment Clause, the Court held that, at a minimum, the Constitution guarantees that government may not coerce anyone to support or participate in religion or its exercise, or otherwise act in a way that establishes a state religion or religious faith, or tends to do so, *id.,* at 587. The District argues unpersuasively that these principles are inapplicable because the policy's messages are private student speech, not public speech. The delivery of a message such as the invocation here—on school property, at school-sponsored events, over the school's public address system, by a speaker representing the student body, under the supervision of school faculty, and pursuant to a school policy that explicitly and implicitly encourages public prayer—is not properly characterized as "private" speech.

(Continued)

(Continued)

1. Do you agree with this opinion? Why or why not?

2. What might a symbolic interactionist say about the use of symbols by those carrying out these prayers? What do these symbols convey to the students and other fans attending the games? In particular, what do they imply about the appropriateness of public praying at football games?

3. What might a conflict theorist say about the Court's decision?

Exercise 11.5	The Role of Religion in the Lives of Individuals

Survey 10 people about their religion. In the survey, include questions about (a) their religious affiliation (if they have one), (b) how often they go to religious services, and (c) if they think their belief in God or a Higher Power guides their actions during an average day.

Then interview them, asking them to provide examples to illustrate their answers. Compare the results of your surveys and interviews. Were the findings consistent? Why or why not?

The 2005 Riots in France

The riots in France in October and November of 2005 provide an example of how the relationships among educational, governmental, and religious institutions can go awry. The rioters experienced both racial and religious discrimination in a society that officially recognizes neither racial nor religious differences. Most of the rioters were poor teenagers of North African and Arab descent whose parents immigrated to France a generation ago when jobs were plentiful. As job availability decreased, however, the unemployment rate in the neighborhoods where people rioted hovered around 40% (compared to the national rate of 10% throughout France) (Cesari 2005).

The rioters and their families had also faced discrimination in housing and in the French criminal justice system. Finishing or dropping out of school without the skills needed to attain a job and facing racial/ethnic discrimination in the workforce, their employment prospects were dim (Bell 2005). Although it appears that most of those who rioted had *parents* who are practicing Muslims, they did not riot because of religious beliefs. In fact, they were largely alienated from religious as well as from governmental and educational institutions in France (Cesari 2005). Whereas a Marxist might argue that they were able to rise up because they were not hindered by the "opiate" of religion, a functionalist would point out that, as nonpracticing Muslims, they did not have the influence of religious organizations to help them establish a sense of purpose in their lives. Symbolic interactionists might also note that the rioters were not part of an organization (either religious or secular) constructed to advocate for them effectively and make sure that their demands were addressed by the French government.

Exercise 11.6   Responding to the 2005 French Riots

Since the 2005 riots, some French citizens have questioned the government's practice of ignoring racial and religious differences among French citizens and advocated for the establishment of racial and religious statistical categories so that the government can discern patterns of discrimination.

Listen to "Diverse Marseille Spared in French Riots" at www.npr.org/templates/player/mediaPlayer.html?action=1&t=1&islist=false&id=5044219&m=5044222 and read "Should France Count Its Minority Population?" at www.time.com/time/world/article/0,8599,1887106,00.html.

Write a two- to three-page paper that answers the following questions:

1. What did you learn about the reasons for the 2005 riots in France and the French attitude toward race and religion? How do these differ from American attitudes?

2. What are three reforms that the French government could enact to prevent riots like those in 2005 from breaking out again in France?

3. What strategies would you use to try to convince the French public to support these reform measures? How would your tactics to garner support for these reforms take French attitudes toward race and religion into consideration?

Exercise 11.7	Secularism, Religion, and Democracy in Turkey

Turkey is now fiercely debating the place of religion in its society. Turkey's secularism, originally inspired by and based upon the same ideas behind France's secularism, is now being challenged. Listen to "Turkey Moves to Lift Headscarf Ban" at www.npr.org/templates/story/story.php?storyId=18847867 and answer the following questions:

1. Why do you think many women in Turkey want to wear headscarves?

2. Do you agree with the female interviewee who believes that headscarves are "a male-driven patriarchal symbol" or that they are an expression of freedom of religion and democracy?

3. How do you think your own religious, political, and social upbringing influenced your answer to question 2?

Now read "Issues for Muslim Women in Europe Evolve" at www.npr.org/templates/story/story.php?storyId=18226044.

4. What information from this piece made you realize that headscarves are a contested symbol with different meanings for various political, economic, and social groups?

SOCIOLOGISTS IN ACTION: DAVID BRUNSMA AND KERRY ROCKQUEMORE

Are school uniforms an easy fix for problems in U.S. public schools? Many people have proposed that uniforms would reduce status competition among school kids, including violent competition. Proponents of school uniforms maintain that they help to create a sense of belonging and communal feeling among students while also fostering a greater sense of discipline.

Although this hypothesis appears reasonable, there was no actual data until sociologists David Brunsma and Kerry Rockquemore (1998) conducted a sociological study to determine the effects of school uniforms on substance abuse, behavioral problems, attendance, and academic achievement among tenth graders. Using data from a 1994 follow-up study on the National Educational

Longitudinal Study of 1988, Brunsma and Rockquemore revealed that school uniforms had no direct effect on substance abuse, behavioral problems, or attendance, and a slight *negative* effect on academic achievement. When improvements were seen, they were related to other factors (funded attempts to change course content, improve teaching, etc.).

In the words of Brunsma and Rockquemore (1998),

> Instituting a uniform policy can be viewed as analogous to cleaning and brightly painting a deteriorating building in that on the one hand it grabs our immediate attention; on the other hand, it is only a coat of paint. That type of change attracts attention to schools and implies the presence of serious problems that necessitate drastic change. It seems possible that such attention renews an interest on the parts of parents and communities and provides possibilities for supporting additional types of organizational change. . . .

> [However], the nature and magnitude of the support behind the mandatory uniform policies . . . seem to illustrate the quick fix nature of school reform policies in the 1990s. A policy that is simplistic, readily understandable, cost free (to taxpayers), and appealing to common sense is one that is politically pleasing and, hence, finds much support. When challenged with broader reforms, those policies with results not immediately identifiable and those that are costly and demand energy and a willingness to change on the part of school faculty and parents are unacceptable. (p. 63)

Through this research, Brunsma and Rockquemore shed light on arguments and strategies for school reform that had up to then been driven by political agendas (pressure for quick fixes without spending money) and anecdotal and incomplete evidence. The results of their work provide clear evidence that governments and families must invest more than the cost of school uniforms in attempts to improve the public school system.[9]

Discussion Questions

1. Before you read this chapter, did you know the names of your U.S. senators and representative? Did you know their party affiliations? Why or why not? Why is it important to know who they are and how they vote?

2. What do you think the purpose of *public* schools should be? Do you think your education fulfilled that purpose? Why or why not? Did you go to public schools to get your primary and secondary education? Why or why not?

3. Do you think religious symbols should be allowed in public schools? Why or why not?

4. Do you ever wonder why the word *God* is used so often by public officials in their public statements? Discuss why you think this happens.

5. Do you think students in U.S. public schools should be required to "pledge allegiance to the flag of the United States of America and to the Republic for which it stands, one nation under God, indivisible, with liberty and justice for all"? Why or why not?

6. Do you think that the French government needs to officially recognize the religious, racial, and ethnic diversity within France? If yes, why? (And how might the government go about doing so?) If not, why not?

7. How might you go about studying the influence of religion at your school? What methodology would you use to collect your data? What theory would you use to make sense of your data?

8. What role do you think the federal government should play in improving the public education system in the United States? Why? If you think funding for schools should be increased, from where do you think the money should come? Why?

9. Describe the relationship between the economic, family, and educational institutions in your own life. What do you think would happen to you if you did not have access to a college education? How would that lack of access impact your economic position and your ability to support a family?

Suggestions for Specific Actions

1. Go to the Web site www.house.gov. Find one issue up for debate in the House of Representatives that interests you. Research the issue and write a letter to your representative to encourage him or her to vote your way.

2. Attend two different types of religious services in your local community. Observe and compare what kinds of people are in positions of authority (their gender, race, and age). Think about how these different religious groups might influence society if they were the "official" national religions.

3. Research a religious organization that is working on a social justice issue. Write a two-page essay outlining the scope of the issue, why the organization is addressing it, and how they are carrying out their campaign (what methods they are using). Include at least one paragraph analyzing the power that religious groups can have in organizing citizens toward a more just society and an additional paragraph that discusses the possible negative consequences of religiously

motivated social justice. Finally, determine how you can help with their campaign, and follow through with at least one action to do so.

Here are some possible campaigns that might interest you: Bread for the World's campaign to end hunger (www.bread.org), Interfaith Worker Justice's campaign against wage theft (www.iwj.org/template/index.cfm), MAZON's fight to combat hunger (www.mazon.org), American Friends Service Committee's work on debt relief for poor African nations (http://afsc.org/AfricaLifeOverDebt), Catholic Relief Services' efforts to fight AIDS in Africa (http://crs.org), and Evangelicals for Darfur (www.savedarfur.org/pages/evangelicals_for_darfur). These are just a few examples; feel free to come up with your own as well.

Please go to this book's Web site at www.pineforge.com/korgen3e to find further civic engagement opportunities, resources, peer-reviewed articles, and updated Web links related to this chapter.

Endnotes

1. The pledge, originally written in 1892, was amended in 1923, 1924, and 1954. The phrase "under God" was the most recent addition, added during the Cold War in part to distinguish the United States from the USSR, which had outlawed religious practice.

2. See Gary Becker's article, "Human Capital and Poverty," at the Acton Institute Web site, www.acton.org/publicat/randl/article.php?id=258.

3. See the federal government's No Child Left Behind Act Web site at www.ed.gov/nclb/landing.jhtml.

4. A U.S. district court ruled in 2005 that the school board's decision to mandate the teaching of intelligent design violated the constitutional separation between church and state (see Associated Press 2005).

5. The government's failure to fulfill this responsibility during and after Hurricane Katrina in 2005 was (and continues to be) painfully displayed. Hundreds of Americans lost their lives and millions more lost their homes, livelihoods, and neighborhoods, due to the breach that occurred in the levees protecting New Orleans.

6. The remaining percentage either refused to answer, didn't know, or indicated that they were affiliated with other religions. According to George Gallup, Jr. (1996), "a representative global village of 1000 would include: 300 Christians (183 Catholics, 84 Protestants, 33 Orthodox), 175 Muslims, 128 Hindus, 55 Buddhists, 47 Animists, 210 without any professed religion, and 85 from miscellaneous religious groups" (n.p.).

7. It is important to note that Marx was not exposed to religions that actively promoted social justice, as many have done in the past century. In fact, in recent years, some religious leaders (such as Liberation Theologians) have been accused of being Marxists!

8. To see the Supreme Court's full opinion for this case, go to the Legal Information Institute Supreme Court Collection, found at http://straylight.law.cornell .edu/supct/html/99-62.ZS.html.

9. To learn more about the issue of school uniforms, read Brunsma's *The School Uniform Movement and What It Tells Us About American Education: A Symbolic Crusade* (2004).

References

Associated Press. 2005, December 20. "Judge Rules Against Intelligent Design." *MSNBC*. Retrieved March 14, 2006 (http://www.msnbc.msn.com/id/10545387).

Augustine, Norman R. 2007. *Is American Falling Off the Flat Earth?* The National Academies Press. Retrieved September 30, 2009 (http://www.nap.edu/catalog.php? record_id=12021).

Bell, Susan. 2005, November 9. "French Curfew Will Keep Rioters Off Streets." *The Scotsman*. Retrieved May 9, 2008 (http://thescotsman.scotsman.com/world/ French-curfew-will-keep-rioters.2676638.jp).

Bottomore, Thomas, trans. and ed. 1964. *Karl Marx: Early Writings*. New York: McGraw-Hill.

Brunsma, David. 2004. *The School Uniform Movement and What It Tells Us About American Education: A Symbolic Crusade*. Lanham, MD: Scarecrow Press.

Brunsma, David L. and Kerry A. Rockquemore. 1998, September/October. "Effects of Student Uniforms on Attendance, Behavior Problems, Substance Use, and Academic Achievement." *Journal of Educational Research* 92(1):53–63.

Cesari, Jocelyne. 2005, November 30. "Ethnicity, Islam, and *les banlieues*: Confusing the Issues." Social Science Research Council Web site, Riots in France. Retrieved March 14, 2006 (http://riotsfrance.ssrc.org/Cesari).

Gallup, George, Jr. 1996. Foreign Policy Research Institute [FPRI] Wire: "Religion and Civic Virtue at Home and Abroad." *The Templeton Lecture on Religion and World Affairs* 4(1). Retrieved September 30, 2009 (http://www.fpri.org/fpriwire/ 0401.199606.gallup.religioncivicvirtue.html).

Newport, Frank. 2008, July 28. "Belief in God Far Lower in Western U.S." Gallup.com. Retrieved June 11, 2009 (http://www.gallup.com/poll/109108/ Belief-God-Far-Lower-Western-US.aspx).

——. 2009a, February 11. "On Darwin's Birthday, Only 4 in 10 Believe in Evolution." Gallup.com. Retrieved June 11, 2009 (http://www.gallup.com/poll/114544/Darwin-Birthday-Believe-Evolution.aspx).

——. 2009b, March 23. "Despite Recession, No Uptick in Americans' Religiosity." Gallup.com. Retrieved June 3, 2009 (http://www.gallup.com/poll/117040/Despite-Recession-No-Uptick-Americans-Religiosity.aspx).

Pew Center on the States. 2009. "Demand for Democracy." Retrieved September 30, 2009 (http://www.pewcenteronthestates.org/trends_detail.aspx?id=31674).

Pew Forum on Religion & Public Life. 2008. "U.S. Religious Landscape Survey."
    Retrieved June 11, 2009 (http://religions.pewforum.org/reports).

——. 2009, April 19. "Faith in Flux: Changes in Religious Affiliation in the U.S."
    Accessed on May 21, 2009 (http://pewforum.org/docs/?DocID=409).

Ralston, Michelle. 2009, February 4. "Fighting Over Darwin, State by State." The
    Pew Forum on Religion & Public Life. Retrieved June 11, 2009 (http://pewforum
    .org/docs/?DocID=399).

Santa Fe Independent School District v. Doe. 2000. Certiorari to the United States Court
    of Appeals for the Fifth Circuit, No. 99–62. Argued March 29, 2000—Decided June
    19, 2000. Retrieved May 9, 2008 (http://straylight.law.cornell.edu/supct/html/99-62
    .ZS.html).

U.S. Bureau of the Census. 2008, April 1. "Public Schools Spent $9,138 Per Student
    in 2006." Retrieved June 10, 2009 (http://www.census.gov/Press-Release/www/
    releases/archives/education/011747.html).

Weber, Max. 1970. From Max Weber. Edited by H. H. Gerth and C. Wright Mills.
    Oxford, UK: Routledge.

Young, Michael P. 2002. "Confessional Protest: The Religious Birth of U.S. National
    Social Movements." American Sociological Review 67(5):660–88.

12

The Engaged
Sociologist in Action

Congratulations! After reading this book and completing exercises in the earlier chapters, you have no doubt developed a sociological eye and can make use of the sociological imagination. Now there's no turning back. With a toolbox packed full with *sociological* tools, you cannot help but perceive social patterns that affect all of us but are often unnoticed by those without your sociological training. The best news is that you have also acquired the means to be an effective agent of social change!

Through this sociology class (and perhaps through other means, as well), you have developed the skills you need to become an informed and effective citizen who can help shape our society. But, as any good superhero knows, with great power comes responsibility. Your sociological training allows you to understand how society works. It is your obligation now to use that knowledge to influence society in ways that will make it better. And just as a carpenter must not only purchase tools but also learn how to use them properly, so must a sociologist in action learn how to use his or her tools. So, now it is time for you to practice using your sociological tools to research and address social issues by completing one of the projects we outline below.

THE BASIC STEPS OF SOCIAL SCIENCE RESEARCH

No matter what topic you choose to research, you will need to remember and to follow the basic steps of all social science research:

1. Choose a research topic.

2. Find out what other researchers have discovered about that topic.

3. Choose a methodology (how you will collect your data).

4. Collect and analyze your data.

5. Relate your findings to those of other researchers.

6. Do something with your findings!

Select one of the projects below. Then, use the detailed research directions that follow to plan and carry out your chosen project.

Project 12.1 Civic Engagement and Higher Education

In recent years, many educators and leaders in society have talked and written about the obligation of colleges and universities to educate citizens.[1] However, it is still not clear (a) how many *students* think civic engagement should be a part of a college education and (b) how many students are actually civically engaged. Your task will be to seek answers to these questions about students on your campus and to devise ways to encourage them to play an active role in shaping society.

Project 12.2 Social Responsibility on Campus

Is your college or university a "socially responsible" institution? In this project, you will (a) use different indicators of social responsibility to measure how socially responsible your school is and (b) use your findings in an effort to make your school more socially responsible.

Some of the questions to consider are the following: Does everyone on campus have equal access to education and other resources? Are campus faculty and staff paid and treated fairly? Do athletes wear, or does your campus store sell, apparel made in sweatshops? Does your university recycle everything that it can? Has your university invested in any corporations that are cited for human rights violations? Are female and male professors compensated equally? Would students know if your school was not acting in socially responsible ways? If students did know, would they organize to create change?

Project 12.3 Connecting the Campus to the Community

What are the needs of the community around your college? Are they being met? Does your college or university actively seek input from local leaders on how it might help the community in which it resides? Do student groups and clubs connect the student body with the local community? Is there a chasm (social or status) between the college community and the larger community? Do students have prejudices toward the local community, or does the local community have prejudices toward students? Does your college contribute to the economic well-being of the greater community? This project will examine the social and economic environment of the community of which your school is a part and determine to what extent your school is working to improve the vitality of that community.

Step 1: Research Preparation

A. What You (Think You) Know

Before you start your research, it is important to take stock of what you *think* you know about the topic and *why* you think you know it. This will help focus your thinking and make you aware of some of the potential biases you may have toward the issue. Write a one-page paper that (a) describes what you hypothesize (think) will be the answer to your research question and (b) supports your hypothesis with examples from your own life, previous research you have done, and your "best guess" sociological analysis (utilizing, of course, your sociological imagination and sociological eye!).

B. Reviewing the Literature

The next step is to examine previous research on your topic. Go to your school library and locate the databases of academic articles in the social sciences. We recommend Sociological Abstracts, JSTOR, or Academic Search

Premier. Conduct several searches for articles using any combination of key words or phrases such as the following:

For Project 12.1 "student activism," "student apathy," "college and activism," "civic engagement and college," "educating students," and "student attitudes"

For Project 12.2 "civic engagement and colleges," "student activism," "students and social responsibility," "colleges and social responsibility," and "student movements"

For Project 12.3 "poverty," "hunger," "homelessness," "unemployment," "town and gown," and "campus and community"

If you are having problems with your searches or the search terms are not producing the desired results, please ask a reference librarian at your school for assistance. Reference librarians are amazing resources and can be a huge help to you as you proceed.

Choose four or five recently published articles available in your library that appear relevant to your research question.

Of course, none of the articles will answer the research question completely. However, each may contribute a piece of related data or way of thinking about the question. For each article, note the following:

- Which of your major concepts (e.g., student attitudes, social responsibility, campus and community relations) is discussed?
- What did the researchers find that adds to your knowledge about the question?

Write a two-page summary of the articles you have read. Then, write a one-page paper summarizing what you have learned from the articles that influences your thinking on the question you are addressing. Have your expectations changed at all? Why or why not? If yes, revise your hypothesis.

Step 2: Obtain Your Data

You have developed a research question and conducted some background work. No doubt your thoughts about what you will find from your research have changed since you first thought about the research question. Now, it is time to obtain the data to test whether your present expectations are on target. In each of the three guided exercises below, we present a research design appropriate for one of the research projects. Be sure to continue with the project you selected when you began Step 1 (i.e., if you chose Project 12.1 in Step 1, you should continue with Project 12.1 throughout the chapter). You can work individually or in small groups, depending on your professor's preference.

Project 12.1 Civic Engagement and Higher Education Data Collection Exercise

In this exercise, you will survey at least 30 students to determine (a) how interested students at your school are in learning how to become active, effective members of society, and (b) the extent to which students on your campus are socially active.

1. Go to this book's Web site. Select "Research Tools" and download "survey for Research Project 12.1"; also download the "scoring guide" for Research Project 12.1.

2. Determine where and when to find respondents. Do not just haphazardly hand out forms to people. Rather, select a large general education class that will provide a fairly representative sample of the student body (representing students from different years, majors, races, ethnicities, sexes, etc.). Be sure to secure prior permission from the professor teaching the course before you hand out your survey at the beginning of one of the class meetings.

3. Ask the students to take a 5- to 10-minute survey. Read them the instructions and then hand out the survey. Instruct the students not to sign their names, and tell them to put the completed surveys face down in a pile in a specified place in the classroom. (That way they know you will not be able to connect them with their individual responses.)

4. Follow the instructions in the scoring guide in order to analyze the results. You may want to try grouping your data with those of other students who are also carrying out this project. (This will enable you to have a larger sample on which to base your findings.) Write a three- to four-page paper that presents and analyzes your results and relates them to the previous research you found on the topic.

Project 12.2 Social Responsibility on Campus Data Collection Exercise

In this exercise, you will interview at least 10 students about how socially responsible they believe your school is. You will ask them questions that address both specific indicators of social responsibility and their overall impression of the social responsibility of the school.

1. Go to this book's Web site. Select "Research Tools" and download the interview guidelines, coding guide, and the informed consent statement for Research Project 12.2.

2. Determine where and when to find respondents. Be sure to interview students who are most likely to know (and care) about your topic (e.g., leaders

in student government, club officers, members of student activist groups, student representatives to the Board of Trustees, etc.).

3. Ask the students you select for permission to interview them. Give them the informed consent sheet to read and sign. Ask permission to tape-record the interview. (If they won't allow you to record, you will need to take detailed notes.)

4. Ask them the questions you devised after reading and following the instructions in the interview guidelines.

   Start with your own questions, but let the respondent guide the conversation. Do not try to force all of your respondents to answer the same questions in the same way. However, do make sure they each cover all of the questions you have prepared. The point is to get their individual perspectives and then compare them with one another. A good interviewer asks *probe questions* throughout the interview. These are very short and simple questions such as "Can you expand on that?" or "Interesting. What else might you add?" Probe questions give a cue to the person being interviewed to talk more on the subject, while not pushing the interviewee toward your own biases.

5. Follow the instructions in the coding guide to analyze the results. If possible, group your data with those of other students carrying out the same project. (This will enable you to have a larger sample on which to base your findings)

6. Write a three- to four-page paper that presents and analyzes your results and relates them to the previous research you found on the topic.

Project 12.3 Connecting the Campus to the Community Data Collection Exercise

Please note: For this project, you can collect data through *either* interviews *or* surveys.

Interviews: You will interview leaders in the local community about the relationship between your school and the community.

1. Go to this book's Web site. Select "Research Tools" and download the interview guidelines, coding guide, and the informed consent statement for Research Project 12.3.

2. Identify at least three leaders in the local community who would have reason to know the extent and nature of the connection between your school and the college (e.g., the mayor, deputies to the mayor, the city manager, city council members, directors of local nonprofit agencies).

   You can find local nonprofit organizations in your area by using World Hunger Year's (WHY) Grassroots Resources Directory (www.whyhunger.org/resources/grassroots-resources-directory.html), which includes organizations that deal with various issues related to poverty, in addition to hunger). Simply fill in the information, and the database will give you a list of organizations in your area. You can also find such organizations by using the database at http://idealist.org.

3. Ask each community leader for permission to do the interview. If he or she agrees, provide a copy of the informed consent sheet to read and sign. Ask permission to tape-record the interview. (If he or she won't allow you to record it, you will need to take detailed notes.)

4. Ask the community leaders the questions you devised after reading and following the instructions in the interview guidelines.

   Start with your own questions, but let the respondent guide the conversation. Do not try to force all of your respondents to answer the same questions in the same way. However, do make sure they each cover all of the questions you've prepared. The point is to get their individual perspectives and then compare them with one another. A good interviewer asks *probe questions* throughout the interview. These are very short and simple questions such as "Can you expand on that?" or "Interesting. What else might you add?" Probe questions give a cue to the person being interviewed to talk more on the subject, while not pushing the interviewee toward your own biases.

5. Follow the instructions in the coding guide to analyze the results. If possible, group your data with those of other students carrying out interviews for this project. (This will enable you to have a larger sample on which to base your findings.)

6. Compare your findings with those of your classmates who collected survey data for this project.

7. Write a three- to four-page paper that presents and analyzes your results (and, if possible, the results of your classmates' interviews), relates them to the previous research you found on the topic, and compares them to the findings of your classmates who conducted surveys on this topic.

Surveys: You will survey at least 30 students in order to measure the (a) attitudes of students toward the local community and (b) the degree of interaction between students and the community.

1. Go to this book's Web site. Select "Research Tools" and download "survey for Research Project 12.3"; also download the "scoring guide" for Research Project 12.3.

2. Determine where and when to find respondents. Do not just hand out forms to people haphazardly. Select a large general education class that will provide

a fairly representative sample of the student body. Be sure to secure prior permission from the professor teaching the course before handing out your survey at the beginning of one of the class meetings.

3. Ask the students to take a 5- to 10-minute survey. Read them the instructions and then hand out the survey. Instruct the students not to sign their names and tell them to put the completed surveys face down in a pile in a specified place in the classroom. (That way they know you won't be able to connect them with their individual responses.)

4. Follow the instructions in the scoring guide to analyze the results. If possible, group your data with those of other students carrying out the survey for this project. (This will enable you to have a larger sample on which to base your findings.)

5. Compare your findings with those of your classmates who conducted interviews for Research Project 12.3.

6. Write a three- to four-page paper that presents and analyzes your results (and, if possible, the results of your classmates' interviews), relates them to the previous research you found on the topic, and compares them to the findings of your classmates who conducted interviews on this topic.

Step 3: Do Something About It

Now that you have personally investigated an important social issue, you are in a strong position to address it. The following exercises will help you to use your sociological knowledge to make a difference in the lives of people in your community.

Project 12.1 Civic Engagement and Higher Education: Civic Engagement Exercise

From your research, you have some data that indicate how many students think civic engagement should be a part of a college education and how many students are socially active. For this exercise, you will prepare a *talking points* document designed to change the minds of those students who do not think civic engagement should be a part of a college education. You will then organize a campus panel with other students at which you will present your talking points.

A talking points document is a brief summary of relevant issues to help you put things into perspective, to establish a context for your concerns, and to focus on what is most important in your argument. It is also a fact sheet that provides evidence to support your position.

1. Drawing on your knowledge of the topic (through your background reading), list the five most important reasons why students should want civic engagement to be a part of their college education.

2. Using information from your survey data, this book, or published research on the topic, identify the specific reasons why students might *not* want civic engagement to be a part of a college education, and then counter their arguments (e.g., if you think that students will say they don't have time to be socially active, mention the fact that many schools have included civic engagement activities within courses. If students don't understand how they can benefit from becoming socially active, describe to them the connection between social activism and social power.).

3. Write a one-page summary of the talking points that is designed to help you communicate your five points to a group of students.

4. Try it out. Bring your talking points to a few friends or relatives and ask them if they will let you briefly discuss why you think civic engagement should be part of the college experience. Think about their responses, criticisms, and suggestions, and then change your document in ways that will strengthen it.

5. Prepare a 5-minute presentation based on what you have learned.

   Consider the reasons why rational and thoughtful people might not want civic engagement as part of a college education, and think carefully about what you might say that will address and possibly overcome their hesitations. You can find a great guide to help you with putting together and delivering your speech at www.unicef.org/voy/takeaction/takeaction_379.html.

6. Work with other students who carried out this project to organize and participate in a student panel presentation for the campus community about the connection between civic engagement and higher education.

Project 12.2 Social Responsibility on Campus: Civic Engagement Exercise

Based on your preparation work, you should have a fairly good idea about what social issues students believe your college or university should be addressing on campus (e.g., sweatshops, right to a living wage, health care benefits, sex discrimination, racism).

1. Write a two-page summary of the issue that most concerns you.

   Include in it a simple description of (a) what the social issue is, (b) who (which group or groups) is suffering as a result of it, (c) who has the power or authority to change it, and (d) what makes you feel that there is a need to address the social issue in the first place.

2. Rewrite your statement in the form of a two-paragraph letter to the editor of your school paper. Begin the letter with the phrase "we the undersigned..." Work and rework this document until you feel confident that you have included your major points and that you have presented them in a clear and powerful manner.

3. Ask people around campus if they would be willing to join you in signing the letter. Provide a signature list form where they can sign their names, print their names, and optionally identify themselves (student, professor, staff, etc.). Also ask them if they wish to become more active in resolving the injustice. If they do, take down their contact information (including their phone numbers and email addresses).

4. If you find that most people do not agree with your letter, stop and rethink it. Have you represented the issue fairly? What are their objections? Are they right? If so, you might want to consider a different issue or a different approach, and start again. If you feel they are wrong, you should consider what you could do differently that might convince them to join your cause.

5. After you have collected at least 20 signatures (hopefully more!), send the letter to your school newspaper, to the president of your college, and to any other key people on campus that you have identified as having the power to affect this issue.

6. Call a meeting of the people who want to act on the issue. Discuss what to do and do it. That is, devise an action plan and strategy to take action on your issue. On the following Web sites you can find some excellent resources compiled by other student groups that will help you to write letters, organize meetings, and gain all of the tools you need to work for your issue:

   - http://studentsagainstsweatshops.org/docs/organizing.doc
   - http://www.thetaskforce.org/reports_and_research/campus_manual
   - http://www3.thestar.com/static/PDF/060217_jrjour_guide.pdf
   - http://www.campusactivism.org/uploads/FireItUp.pdf

   You may also want to consult such books as *Take More Action* by Marc and Craig Kielburger and Deepa Shankaran (2004) or *Organizing for Social Change: Midwest Academy—Manual for Activists* by Kimberley A. Bobo and colleagues (1999) for some guidelines on how to organize effectively. Michael Gecan's book *Going Public* (2004) is also an excellent overview of how to build power through organizing people.

Project 12.3 Connecting the Campus to the Community: Civic Engagement Exercise

Identify a few nonprofit groups in your area that are working on poverty-related issues. There may be an office on campus that can help you find one, such as the Community Service Office. If you are an active member of a church, mosque, synagogue, or other civic organization, find out how it is addressing poverty in the community. Call your local mayor's office and ask if there are community groups that the city or town works with on poverty-related issues such as hunger, homelessness, and housing. You should also search World Hunger Year's (WHY) Grassroots Resources Directory (www .whyhunger.org/resources/grassroots-resources-directory.html). As we note above, you can simply fill in the information, and the database will give you a list of organizations in your area.

You can also find such organizations through the Idealist Web site at http://idealist.org.

1. Visit the organization you have chosen (or visit several if you are having trouble choosing). Speak with people there, pick up their literature, and look over their Web site if they have one. Identify and summarize what their basic work is, how it is organized, and what they want from volunteers. Given your knowledge of the issue, make note of how well the group's work relates to your area of interest.

2. Get to know the group better. Attend a meeting or volunteer for an event. Speak with other volunteers about their experiences.

3. If you are excited by the work of the organization, get a group of students together to volunteer their time and talents to work with them. Tell the other potential volunteers what you know about the issue and what this group is doing. Try to get a meaningful sense of what kind of commitment other students are willing to make so that you don't promise too much, and then offer your group's services to the organization as volunteers.

   Two notes of caution should be added before you recruit too many volunteers. First, make sure that you have spoken to the people coordinating the efforts of the organization to find out what they need. They may need help with staffing, clerical work, building repairs, fund-raising, or a variety of other tasks. It is very important that they are part of your process! Second, many organizations prefer to start their volunteers off with clerical tasks, like faxing or filing. The point of this exercise is to get your hands dirty and to do something about an ongoing social problem, even if the work you are doing may seem mundane. However, make sure you have a clear sense of what the organization wants from you before you commit to doing it.

SOCIOLOGIST IN ACTION: YOU!

(Place brief biography here, and description of the class project you just completed or any other social change exercise you undertook as part of this course.) You've now joined the ranks of the other "Sociologists in Action" highlighted in this book. Like their work, your efforts can inspire others to become knowledgeable, engaged, and effective citizens. Although such sociologists may not look like superheroes, they have all managed to harness the power of sociology to make society better. Congratulations on becoming one of them. Please email us your "Sociologist in Action" piece (engagedsociologist@hotmail .com), and let us know if we can use it on our Web site or in future editions of *The Engaged Sociologist: Connecting the Classroom to the Community.*

Conclusion

You now have sociological tools, skills, and knowledge. You do not have to be a professional sociologist to use them. Just keep your eyes open to how society is working (the sociological eye), make connections between personal troubles and public issues (the sociological imagination), and always look for multiple perspectives. Ask questions and find your own answers. Question your answers and always dig deeper. Change is always happening all around us. Whether or not we choose to help direct it is up to us. We don't know what social problems or issues you will confront in your life, but we do know that you can make a difference. The anthropologist Margaret Mead once said, "Never doubt that a small group of thoughtful, committed citizens can change the world. Indeed, it's the only thing that ever has." Using your sociological tools, *you* can help change the world.

Endnote

1. The Campus Compact and American Democracy Project efforts are a direct result of this growing realization among academic and government leaders. You can find many sources and links to articles about this topic on the Web sites for these organizations (www.compact.org and http://www.aascu.org/programs/adp).

References

Bobo, Kimberley A., Jackie Kendall, and Steve Max. 1999. *Organizing for Social Change: Midwest Academy—Manual for Activists.* Santa Ana, CA: Seven Locks Press.

Gecan, Michael. 2004. *Going Public.* New York: Random House.

Kielburger, Marc, Craig Kielburger, and Deepa Shankaran. 2004. *Take More Action.* Toronto, Ont., Canada: Thomson/Nelson.

Index

About the Authors

Kathleen Odell Korgen, PhD, is Professor of Sociology at William Paterson University in Wayne, New Jersey. Her primary areas of specialization are race relations, racial identity, and public sociology.

Professor Korgen's work on public sociology includes coediting (with Jonathan White and Shelley White) *Sociologists in Action* (forthcoming). She has written or edited the following books on race relations and racial identity: *Multiracial Americans and Social Class* (forthcoming), *Crossing the Racial Divide: Close Friendships Between Black and White Americans* (2002), and *From Black to Biracial: Transforming Racial Identity Among Americans* (1999).

Raised in Massachusetts, Professor Korgen now lives in Montclair, New Jersey, with her husband, Jeff; daughters Julie and Jessica; and mother Patricia.

Jonathan M. White, PhD, is Associate Professor of Sociology at Bridgewater State College in Massachusetts. His primary areas of specialization are inequality, poverty, globalization, human rights, and public sociology. Dr. White has received numerous teaching and humanitarian awards. He is the Founding Director of Sports for Hunger, the Hunger Resource Center, and the Halloween for Hunger and Pass-the-Fast campaigns. He serves on the board of directors for Free the Children, Peace Through Youth, Me to We, and the Graduation Pledge Alliance. Dr. White has authored several articles in the fields of inequality and globalization. He is currently writing a book entitled *Hungry to Be Heard: Voices From a Malnourished America,* and coediting *Sociologists in Action* (with Shelley White and Kathleen Odell Korgen).

Dr. White lives in Waltham, Massachusetts, with his wife, Shelley, and is the very proud uncle of his 13 nieces and nephews, Jarred, Kyle, Tyler, Arielle, Cameron, Brianna, Mikayla, Joshua, Jack, Logan, Tyler, Joey, and Brookelyn.

Supporting researchers for more than 40 years

Research methods have always been at the core of SAGE's publishing program. Founder Sara Miller McCune published SAGE's first methods book, *Public Policy Evaluation*, in 1970. Soon after, she launched the *Quantitative Applications in the Social Sciences* series—affectionately known as the "little green books."

Always at the forefront of developing and supporting new approaches in methods, SAGE published early groundbreaking texts and journals in the fields of qualitative methods and evaluation.

Today, more than 40 years and two million little green books later, SAGE continues to push the boundaries with a growing list of more than 1,200 research methods books, journals, and reference works across the social, behavioral, and health sciences. Its imprints—Pine Forge Press, home of innovative textbooks in sociology, and Corwin, publisher of PreK–12 resources for teachers and administrators—broaden SAGE's range of offerings in methods. SAGE further extended its impact in 2008 when it acquired CQ Press and its best-selling and highly respected political science research methods list.

From qualitative, quantitative, and mixed methods to evaluation, SAGE is the essential resource for academics and practitioners looking for the latest methods by leading scholars.

For more information, visit **www.sagepub.com**.